THE TRIAL OF CHAPLAIN JENSEN

THE TRIAL OF CHAPLAIN JENSEN

BY

Chaplain Andrew Jensen
with Martin Abramson

ARBOR HOUSE
New York

 Published in the United States by Arbor House Publishing Co., New York, and simultaneously in Canada through Musson Book Co.

Library of Congress Catalog Card Number: 73-82184

ISBN: 0-87795-065-2

Manufactured in the United States of America

This book is dedicated to the large number of Americans who feel powerless and helpless when confronted by today's faceless machines of organizational power. It is hoped that this book will give you strength and encouragement.

ACKNOWLEDGMENTS

I hereby acknowledge my deep debt to those who faithfully supported me in my fight to establish my innocence. This includes all but a very few at my home base, Cecil Field, Florida, most of the people in the Jacksonville area, and literally thousands of officers and enlisted personnel in the various branches of the military service. In addition to these, there were scores of people all over the world who sent words of encouragement to my wife and me, and many of them formed prayer groups in support of us in virtually all parts of the world. I further acknowledge the attorneys who believed in me and worked faithfully in the support of justice: Jack W. Blackmon; Selected Military Counsel, LCDR C. E. Pope, JAGC, USN; Appointed Military Counsel, LCDR J. B. Durham, JAGC, USN; and my local Jacksonville attorney, Mr. Lyman Fletcher. Most of all, I wish to acknowledge the many witnesses who courageously came forward in support of the truth. Without these people this book could not have been written, or if written, it might have had a different ending.

CHAPTER 1

"There are two women here, in my outer office. They say they've been having an affair with you. They're wives of officers on the base—you know them. Mrs. Mary Ann Curran and Mrs. Lora Gudbranson. They say you've got to be exposed and they want you charged with adultery. Don't come back to this base. I'm warning you now. Commander Gudbranson is carrying a gun and threatening to kill you."

That was the way it began—a voice talking to me over the telephone. The shock at what I was hearing caused me to choke; I couldn't speak at all.

The voice belonged to Captain John W. Shute, Executive Officer at the Naval Air Station at Cecil Field, Florida, where I served as senior Protestant chaplain. "Didn't you hear what I said, Jensen?"

"Look here," I finally managed to say, "what you're saying makes no sense . . . it's crazy . . . this kind of accusation against me won't stand up . . . it's completely untrue. . . . You don't mean to say you hear something like this and you believe it, just like that? . . . I can't imagine what's come over these women but I'm sure they'd never make such charges to my face or to my wife's face. . . ."

"Jensen, these women act as if they're dead serious about pressing charges. They haven't signed formal statements yet, but if they do, there's going to be a court-martial. I'll call you back in an hour or so, to let you know if they've signed."

It was August 11, 1971. I was on leave from my base and had

come up to Philadelphia to conduct funeral services for my wife's best friend, who had died of cancer. Kathleen had come up earlier with our two sons so she could stay at the bedside of her dying friend. We had been staying at my mother-in-law's home in Philadelphia and at the home of Kathleen's sister and brother-in-law, Margaret and Frank Lamania. Frank, like me, is a Baptist minister. We had been at the Lamanias' when my mother-in-law called me to say that somebody was trying to get me from my base.

I knew they had started a manpower survey at the base just before I left. Some question must have come up about the chaplains' service. I called my assistant chaplain, Lt. Commander Hoyt Swann, and asked him if he'd been trying to contact me about the manpower survey.

He hesitated before he answered, "No, I didn't call you, Andy. But maybe you'd better call the Exec Officer. He's in charge now with the skipper away on vacation and I think he may be trying to get you."

Swann sounded odd, but I took his suggestion and called Captain Shute, prepared to give him figures on our chaplains' working schedules for the survey. That was the first I heard of the accusations Mary Ann Curran and Lora Gudbranson had made. Now I was waiting to hear again from Captain Shute to find out if Mary Ann and Lora had signed formal statements against me.

I didn't know what to do or who to turn to. Besides, what could I say about all this? I knew nothing of the facts. So, tense and anguished as I was, I just had to wait—and think.

There are "swinging ministers" in civilian life and "swinging chaplains," but I had never been in either category. My temperament, my tastes, my outlook on religion and on life are conservative, even puritanical. I do not drink, though drinking is a routine aspect of Navy life. The temptation to be a "regular fellow" at the Officers Club is always a strong one, but I never have yielded. I do not even follow the practice common among many of my colleagues of putting an arm around female members of a chapel or parish in the most innocent way. I have always shied away from any physical contact which could be misinterpreted by people eager to gossip. People seem to trust Kathleen and myself and confide in us and we in them.

In my counseling sessions with Navy personnel and their family members, I worked long and hard. These sessions might go on for hours, and along with the other religious, welfare, and recreational programs I ran, I had been putting in 14 to 16 hours a day. The chapel at Cecil Field was only two blocks from our house. People come in and out or call constantly on the phone, even in the late evening. My doctor warned me several times about the risks to my health of such a schedule. My medical history includes skin cancer and an asthmatic and allergic condition. He ordered me to get away from the base whenever I could and suggested brief retreats to resort motels as a means of maintaining my strength. As I waited for the phone call from Captain Shute at the base, the call that would tell whether I would be branded an adulterer by these two women, I had no idea that my occasional medically prescribed stays at nearby motels would have any bearing whatsoever on what was about to happen to me.

Around the base I was known, even by my best friends, as Chaplain Square or Square Andy. Those are terms I in no way resent. The fact is that I am deeply committed to the tenets of my religious denomination, the American (Northern) Baptist Convention, and to the words of the Holy Scriptures regarding drinking of alcoholic beverages, the sanctity of the family and of marriage, and the proscriptions against premarital and extramarital sexual activities. That doesn't mean I do not understand the demands of the flesh but simply that I believe they must be withstood and that abstinence and continence, however much they may clash with so-called modern ideas, are fundamental virtues. The "square" nicknames that have been applied to me seem to be no more than recognition by others of the depth of my convictions. I don't apologize for those convictions. Still, I recognize that temptations of the flesh afflict every human being, whatever his or her calling may be, specifically including members of the clergy. Adhering to these convictions is not easy at any time and especially not in the present age of new moral permissiveness or freedom. Nevertheless, I have tried to adhere to them without regard to what others may think and with the awareness that that makes me something of an "oddball" these days.

Two sex cases involving chaplains had surfaced at the base during the past year and had entangled me in a peripheral way. Shortly after I was assigned to Cecil Field in February, 1970, a parishioner complained to me that one of my assistant Protestant chaplains was having a romance with the wife of a petty officer. Rumors and complaints mounted, and it became necessary for me to investigate. The facts were verified. I arranged for a quiet transfer of this chaplain. My handling of the matter was criticized by the investigating officer of the Naval Investigative Service (N.I.S.) and by the Navy's Chief of Chaplains in Washington, who wanted me to bring formal charges that would have resulted in the chaplain's discharge.

The other case involved a Roman Catholic chaplain. Despite his vows of celibacy, he had fallen in love with the widow of a Navy officer. He subsequently married her and left the priesthood and the Navy.

I felt that when a person makes a commitment to follow the rules of a religious order, he should abide by them to the point of self-sacrifice. But I understand human desires and feelings, and I resisted suggestions that I condemn him.

In both these cases, rumor and gossip had been rampant before action finally was taken. But as far as I had any indication at all, nobody had ever made any derogatory remarks about my behavior in the year and a half I had been at the base. Not a word to link me to my accusers or to anyone else. Cecil Field, near Jacksonville, was small by Navy standards, with five attack squadrons and a complement of 5,000. The officers lived in houses close together on a long tree-lined street. This created a close-knit, open atmosphere with much socializing. If there had been any talk about me and Mary Ann Curran or Lora Gudbranson, my wife or I would surely have heard something about it. But there was never a word.

We both knew Mary Ann and Lora. In fact, they had—in the recent past—been our friends as well as our neighbors. Mary Ann was a striking and well-endowed blonde, about 24, married to a Navy pilot. The Currans lived off-base, in an apartment near the field. She was active in our chapel community and was a registered nurse who had taken care of Kathleen and our children on occasion. She had stayed overnight in our home several times when her husband was away, because she had a strange fear of being alone.

She and her husband, Joe, had first come to me for counseling in the spring of 1970 because their marriage was falling apart. After a while, Mary Ann continued to come alone. She confided to me that when her husband was stationed in Beeville, Texas, she had had an affair with another man. She seemed to need this involvement with other men, and she wanted me to help her understand herself and sort out her feelings. She was a troubled person whose beauty masked undercurrents of deep hostility and resentment. She retained an abiding hatred for her father, she had told me, because of the way he had humiliated her mother by flaunting his many sexual liaisons. She had been brought up as a Catholic, but she was considering converting to her husband's Protestant faith.

Despite her own adulterous conduct, she was critical of the morality of others, including our commanding officer, who dated with a woman who was not his wife. She was upset that the C.O. allowed so-called go-go girls at stag parties at the Officers Club. And she had said that it was my duty to investigate the matter and reprimand the Captain.

When Mary Ann started working at a nursing home, she began an affair with a married doctor. Mary Ann and her husband separated for a few months but both gave me permission to act as intermediary in trying to effect a reconciliation. I was pleased when they got back together and seemed grateful for my efforts. Then Mary Ann told me she had resumed her affair with the doctor and also indicated that she was seeing bachelor fliers and salesmen who came to the nursing home. She also told me that she found herself concerned about lesbian tendencies.

This was evidence to me that she needed more help than I could give her. I had had some experience and training in marital counseling, and was a member of the California Marriage Counselors Association. I had also been taking a special course in pastoral counseling at the Methodist Hospital in Jacksonville. But Mary Ann's state of mind now seemed to require treatment beyond my scope. I recommended that she see a psychiatrist and assured her she could get a competent one through a special Navy program conducted through the Naval Hospital.

She reacted to this recommendation with anger. "Why are you sending me to a psychiatrist? If I find out you've been talking about me, I'll get you!"

Shortly before I left for my leave in Philadelphia, her manner became increasingly hostile. She compared me with her father, denounced me for "sitting in judgment" on her, and made several references to me as "good old Chaplain Jensen." But by the time I took my leave, I had the impression that she was consulting a psychiatrist.

Lora Gudbranson, 39 and some 15 years older than Mary Ann, was more intellectual than Mary Ann, but she too had what seemed to me a consuming interest in sex. She and her husband, the senior supply officer at the base, lived across the street in a three-bedroom stucco house just like ours. They had a daughter of 14 and a son of 12, who played with our 10-year-old son Drew. Lora was an attractive woman, with short light-brown hair. Her clothes were smartly if somewhat severely tailored.

An ardent member of the Environmental Council in Jacksonville, Lora also became active in our chapel soon after I came to Cecil Field. I appreciated her work on behalf of the chapel but I also noticed that her domineering manner seemed to antagonize some of the enlisted men and their wives. Though she never came to me for counseling, Lora would engage me in discussions and complain about her husband's lack of intellectual capacity and rapport with her. She also said that her husband drank a good deal and they'd had quarrels, something which was already well known to some neighbors.

Lora began bringing books to me, hers usually devoted to sexual matters. She also brought up the subject of free love, which she said she favored. Her attitude toward Christianity was curious. While working for the church, she nevertheless said she considered Christianity and indeed all religion a "gigantic hoax."

She came to my office often, even when she wasn't expected. She dropped in at our house frequently, and finally I suggested to Kathleen that it might be well for me to start ducking her and discouraging her. Kathleen advised me to do it in a diplomatic fashion.

One day, in the office, Lora suddenly took my arm and propositioned me. I tried to treat her advance as a joke so as not to embarrass her, or myself. At about this time I was informed by other parishioners that Lora was involved in an arrangement. Wife-swapping apparently had become a new pastime around some Navy bases, though I regarded it as a degradation that I should do all in my power to stop. I wanted, though, to do it only in the "Navy way" —that is, with quiet persuasion, keeping it, so to speak, "in the family."

Apparently Lora learned of what I had been told because she demanded to know if I knew about her and her "husband-swapping." I tried not to give a direct answer because I did not want to tell her what others had said to me in confidence and because I was not her counselor. She warned me that if I talked, I would be in "great trouble."

Though I have had training and experience in psychology and counseling, I cannot claim to have a great deal of skill in the diagnosis of mental illness. But as a minister, I know that false accusations of sexual misconduct made by members of congregations are recurring problems in all denominations. Ministers and priests and rabbis must confront such charges from time to time. Some lonely neurotics tend to see their clergymen as the causes of their own feelings of guilt over real or imagined transgressions, perhaps because our vocation stands for morality and the distinctions between right and wrong. This is probably especially true when counseling and confession are a significant part of the pastor's relation to his flock. However much understanding and sympathy we may offer a troubled person, we can't approve what is to us sinful behavior. Adultery may be a symptom of sickness, it may be an abberation, it may stem from real emotional and physical need, but my religious training and my convictions make it a sin, a violation of a commandment of God.

In most instances where ministers are accused of sinning with members of their congregations, these matters are dealt with privately by religious superiors or congregation trustees. Where there are no causes for action, these cases are usually settled tactfully and discreetly. They involve, after all, religious matters concerning delicate feelings and valued reputations. In the rare instances where such charges are proved true, ministers are allowed to resign without publicity or are tried and punished according to the tenets of the denomination.

The accusations that were being made against me by Mary Ann and Lora were somewhat different, because the complaints were being made to the Navy, not to my denomination's superiors, which would have been the appropriate procedure. Though I had dealt with both these women in what I had considered a proper professional and moral manner, they had apparently chosen to bring charges against me in such a way that if they were successful, my calling, my family, and my own life would be seriously and publicly damaged if not destroyed.

As I sat there waiting for the call from Captain Shute about whether they would sign formal complaints, I realized that I might be facing the fight of my life. And since they apparently felt no compunction about revealing the most intimate aspects of their private lives, if they did bring formal charges they would give me no choice but to use that same information to protect my religious obligation, my family, and my own life. I hoped anyone who would criticize me for revealing matters offered in a private counseling session or by friends and neighbors in confidence would keep in mind the terrible dilemma I might be about to face.

A chaplain in the military or naval service can not, of course, be transferred or drummed out easily. He is not a hired hand of a congregation but an officer in the service and employment of the government. But the chilling words "court-martial" raised the possibility of penalties and disgrace far more serious than would attend the unpublicized banishment of a civilian minister.

When the telephone finally rang, I picked it up with mingled feelings of hope and foreboding. The voice was harsh, and the news was bad. The conversation, in substance, went like this:

"They've signed the formal statements, all right," the Exec told me. "They say they saw you at motels and places like that and one of them has love notes she says she got from you. You'd better resign from the service as soon as possible. Otherwise, there'll be a court-martial, just as I warned you before, and a lot of innocent people will get hurt."

"But I'm innocent of all this. I never had any physical involvement with these women and yet you seem to be accepting what they say without question and don't even want to listen to my side of it," I said.

"If you don't want to resign, you'll have your chance to tell your side when the N.I.S. goes to work (the Naval Investigative Service's investigation would be required for hearings that would precede any summoning of a court-martial). But don't come down here for the time being. Gudbranson's still talking about wanting to kill you and you won't be safe. Don't even come into the Jacksonville area unless you call me first. I'll extend your leave for the time being."

I was so agitated now that I found it hard to express myself clearly. Later on, I would argue that appropriate warnings should have been issued against a man threatening to kill, rather than against the intended victim. But at the moment I didn't think of that. What I did demand to know was how and why charges came to be filed against me while I was on leave, why nobody seemed interested in defending my rights, and why no consideration was apparently being given to a service record that had been completely clean for sixteen years, that included four tours in the Vietnam theater of war, and had permitted me to advance to the rank of commander and senior chaplain.

"Well, I didn't start this or plot this, if that's what you're thinking," was the rejoinder. "I understand it was Gudbranson who first demanded the formal charges. But some of the chaplains have known about this and they agreed it should be handled through the command rather than through the chaplain service. And Chaplain Danielson knew about it. In fact, he was one of the first who called me on it."

So my assistant, Swann, knew about it and had not even bothered to tell me. And Danielson (Captain John Danielson, senior chaplain at the Jacksonville Naval Air Station, and staff advisor to Admiral L. W. Geis) had known about it too. I tried calling Danielson at Jacksonville and Swann at his home and the chapel, without success. I left an urgent message for Danielson to call me back. Swann's wife told me he had been very busy around the base all that day but that he would be available later.

When I called again, at night, Mrs. Swann told me her husband was just getting ready for bed. When he came to the phone he said he'd been busy praying for me. "Why didn't you tell me all about this the minute you heard?" I said. "Didn't you try to reason with those women? You must know I'm no adulterous swinger and that I couldn't have done what they're saying."

"I didn't know anything about it until the Exec called me," Swann said, contradicting what the Exec had told me. (I later learned that Swann had witnessed the sworn statements by the two women, again contradicting his claim that he knew nothing of what was going on.) "And when he told me, it was in confidence and I couldn't reveal anything to you until you'd been notified by the command. But now that you know what you're up against, I think you'd better take the easy way out and resign."

"I'm not resigning," I said. "I'm not admitting guilt. Why should I?"

"Well, if you don't want to resign, you'd better get a very good lawyer. Incidentally, you'd better stay away from here for a while. Gudbranson's threatening to kill you."

Now there were two people advising me to resign and warning me away from a would-be killer. When I finally got through to Chaplain Danielson—who consented to talk to me only when I told an employee at the Officers' Quarters to bring him to the phone to answer an urgent call—there were three. "Innocent people will get hurt if it goes to court-martial," he warned, adding that the officer who was threatening me was a very determined man.

"How did you learn what these women were saying and why wasn't I informed of this by one of the chaplains?" I asked him.

"Well, it seems that Mrs. Curran went to Naval Hospital and asked to see a marriage counselor. They referred her to Chaplain Lew Allred and she confessed to him that she'd been having an affair with you. Lew filled me in on all this. You know Lew's been attending the chaplains' seminar down in Pensacola and the day the women talked of filing charges, they called him and discussed it with him. So they know about it down in Pensacola. And when it was discussed with me, I said this was a matter for the command to handle, and that the chaplains shouldn't be involved with it. That's why I didn't return your call the first time I got your message."

So now it turned out that Mary Ann had not gone to a psychiatrist after all, but had seen another chaplain. And it seemed that these men of God, who had taken vows committing them to justice and tolerance and charity had secretly encouraged the notion of bringing charges against a colleague, and not through ecclesiastical channels but in a formal military procedure. Worse yet, the chief of the Navy's Chaplain Service, Admiral Francis Garrett, himself a Methodist minister, was in Pensacola and apparently had been apprised of all this and had done nothing to stop it.

Why had these two women made such charges against me, and why was the Navy bureaucracy supporting them so quickly and without even asking for a word from me? These were two questions that would plague me all through the ordeal I was about to face, and probably throughout the rest of my life.

I had some knowledge of the kind of people Mary Ann and Lora were, and it occurred to me at the outset that I somehow had apparently become a focal point of their own guilt about sex and of their anger toward others in their lives. That their feelings should have reached such an intensity that they had got together in this conspiracy may have had other roots as well. Mary Ann had admitted homosexual tendencies that must have disturbed her even more than she had conceded. Lora was a dominant personality with aggressive traits and had argued to me that any behavior between consenting adults, including homosexuality, should be acceptable. Perhaps there was some deeper relationship between these two that neither had admitted to me. Or, if not an overt act, at least some special affinity that caused them both to focus their fears and their guilt on me. That seemed the most plausible explanation for them taking action that they knew would not only cause me and my family terrible harm but would brand them as adulterers as well. Still, I reminded myself that in the literal sense I had no more to go on than what they had actually told me.

As for the action of the command against me, there were several possible explanations. I suspect that there were many who resented what they considered my self-righteous attitude toward drinking and promiscuity. There were probably some who worried that my unconcealed opposition to wife-swapping and other such practices might lead to their exposure as participants. There were some who stood to gain materially from my leaving the Navy, other chaplains who were in line for the vacancy that would be created. But beyond these plausible explanations, there was still another. The Navy—like any large governmental, corporate, or religious institution—necessarily tends to evolve into an impersonal bureaucracy in its efforts to recruit, train, command, compensate, and supply large numbers of people and their dependents. The command of a base or area is, in that respect, no different from the management of a corporation. Human feelings and considerations tend to give way to impersonal machinery whose main purpose is to get the job done without making a fuss or rocking the proverbial boat. Even if my superiors and colleagues had followed proper procedures of military justice or had taken the matter up with my religious denomination, I would have been in for a time of pain and difficulty. The route they chose made it worse. They used the machinery as a weapon against me, presumably because of their own fears, guilts, and hopes of gain. The system of military justice is at best a coldly impersonal and relentless one. As used against me, it was far beneath its best.

After I spoke to the Exec, I went to Kathleen and asked her to step out of the house with me. She immediately understood that something was very wrong. When I broke it to her, she began to shake as if in a fit, and then burst into tears. "My God, how can this happen?"

"Kathleen, you must believe me, I never even put an arm around either of those women," I said.

"Of course I know it's a lot of made-up nonsense," she said finally. "I know *you*, Andy. I won't for a second believe you could be capable of such things. Besides, it's so crazy. I always knew where you were, we were always in touch. You couldn't have had the time, let alone the strength—oh, Andy, I confided so many things to those two. They used to tell me so many personal things about their husbands and their problems and then they'd ask me personal things and I found myself going along, telling them. I guess it just seemed natural in the spirit of the moment, confidences exchanged between friends. I told them how the doctor had told you to take time out from your duties to rest off the base, and how sometimes I couldn't get away to go with you. Once Mary Ann began talking about circumcision. She said her husband wasn't circumcized and wanted to know if you were. I was embarrassed but I told her about you. Now I'm afraid they'll claim they found out all these things when they were with you. I was naïve and foolish—but how could I have dreamed that they'd be crazy enough to make these terrible charges—"

Naturally these admissions disturbed me at the moment. They involved personal matters that I should have thought would never become public under any circumstances. I don't claim to understand every aspect of the relationship between friends and neighbors, but I knew Kathleen would never intentionally do anything to hurt me. Whatever momentary anger I had quickly passed and I began to think of other things that Captain Shute had just told me.

"Kathleen, the Exec said something about Mary Ann having love notes. I never sent her a note, or Lora, either. What can he be talking about?"

"I used to keep notes and cards that you and the children sent me in a box near my night-table. She could have taken some of them when she stayed overnight. I'll bet that's exactly what she did! But what kind of a woman can she *be*? This whole business is so unreal that I can't accept it's happening to us."

She began to shake and cry again and I tried to comfort her. We agreed we should tell her sister and brother-in-law and ask their advice.

"It could happen to any minister," Frank said immediately. "This is a problem you run into when you're counseling mixed-up women. These two must *really* be crazy. Maybe now that they've got the dirt off their consciences and realize what damage they've done, they'll pull back and the whole thing will be dropped."

Kathleen and I clung to that hope when we went to bed. I kept reproaching myself for not having had the professional skill to realize just how dangerously sick my two accusers were. And Kathleen kept reproaching herself for the confidences she'd disclosed, which she was sure would be used against me.

In the morning I decided to fly to Jacksonville that day and face the issue immediately rather than wait for a summons. I was determined not to be kept off the base by Gudbranson's threats. Before leaving, I called a judge I knew in Jacksonville and asked for informal advice about my situation. Like Frank, he was sympathetic and said that lawyers who handled cases involving women were also sometimes subjected to fantastic charges of adultery, just as ministers were. I then looked up a member of the Judge Advocate's staff at the Philadelphia Navy Yard who might give me an informal view of what kind of legal case could be made against me.

The Navy lawyer at first seemed not to believe me when I told him I'd been asked to resign or face a court-martial. He wanted to know if I'd been a rabble-rouser, a "radical" they wanted to get rid of. I told him that my background was conservative, both in politics and religion. I had voted for Goldwater in 1964. I had always supported the Navy's program and the Navy's mission. I had won decorations and commendations, and my slate was clean. I admitted I had become increasingly upset by certain aspects of the Navy life I saw on occasion—the illicit sex, the hard drinking, the racist attitudes. But I had never tried to embarrass the Navy by public campaigning. I felt I had just tried to do my job, to try to improve the ethical and moral climate of the service by working quietly from within.

"Then there would seem to be no reason for them treating you this way," he said. "Apparently the brass at your base must be terribly uptight." Still, he said he was sure that if I sat it out and resisted the pressure to resign, the whole thing might die down and be forgotten.

"They don't even have grounds for a court-martial in your case because of the ruling by the Supreme Court in the O'Callahan case," he told me. "From what you say, the misconduct they're talking about happened *off* your base, and in the O'Callahan case the ruling was that the military services have no legal jurisdiction over this kind of offense committed off-base."

Even though this legal advice was off-the-cuff, it seemed very reassuring. The assurance was to turn into a delusion. I was destined to become *the only chaplain in the history of America to be court-martialed on any charge, and the only officer in the history of the U.S. Navy to be court-martialed on charges of adultery only.*

It was hardly what I had in mind when I first planned a career of serving God as a minister in His church.

CHAPTER 2

It was a nurse who acted as midwife at my birth who first had the idea that I should become a minister. It seems I did not breathe at birth, and she became frantic that she had delivered a dead baby. She immersed me in cold water, then switched to hot, then switched alternately from hot to cold. Finally, I gasped and cried. Later she told my mother that she had prayed I would repay God for His miracle by serving in the ministry when I grew up.

This happened on January 12, 1929, on a grape ranch a few miles outside of Selma, California. Selma is close to the center of California, about fifteen miles from Fresno in the middle of the San Joaquin Valley. It was a bad year for this part of the country. People weren't worried about their destiny or the eventual vocation of one more new baby. They worried about survival. Crop prices were low, and many crops had been ruined by the coldest winter freeze in the history of the Valley. The Wall Street stock-market crash that would come in October would set off financial shock waves that would further deflate the Valley's economy.

We lived in a wooden frame house on land that my grandfather —my father's father—had bought when he moved into the Valley at the turn of the century. His family owned a good deal of land around Selma, and he began to raise grapes and raisins. As soon as he was old enough, my father joined him.

My grandfather on my mother's side was a native New Englander who sailed one year on a whaling ship, then decided to jump ship when it reached California. He made his way to Sacramento, where he met and married my grandmother. She also had an eastern background. Her family originated in Pennsylvania and came west in a covered wagon. My mother was the oldest of their six children. She was only 11 when her mother died, and she assumed a major responsibility in raising her younger brothers and sisters. She managed to act as mother to them whlie attending school herself, and somehow got through college to earn a teaching degree, almost unheard of in that area in that day and age.

My mother was teaching in a little school in Selma when she met and married my father. She retired soon after to have children. My brother Christen is ten years older than I, and my sister Mildred is six years older. I was named Andrew Frederick Jensen, Jr., after my father. Although my mother told me the story of my nurse's wish for me many times, she herself was a more important influence on my interest in church work. She taught a Sunday School class in the Baptist Church, the largest in the community, and later served as superintendent of the Sunday School. She had a good knowledge of theology and this evoked an interest on my part in learning about theology and reading a great deal about religious history.

One reason I did so much reading is that I grew up with practically no friends to play with. There were a number of cousins on my father's side who lived in the area but none of them was my age. The children on nearby farms were older than I. My school was a three-room country school three miles away. The students who attended it came from many miles around. I would ride a bike or walk to the school, although there was one year when we managed to get a car pool together.

With only three rooms in the school, the classes were much too large for the teachers to handle properly. As a result, there was a great deal of restlessness and many of the bored students would start fights and free-for-alls. I began to take violin lessons when I was in the fifth grade and found I couldn't see the music unless I stood very close to the stand, so I had to wear strong glasses, which I hated.

During the Great Depression of the thirties, farmers couldn't sell their crops, couldn't pay their mortgages or taxes, and many lost their land. Most of the ranches and farms around us were foreclosed. I would walk and hear the farmers as they aired their problems, denounced the government, and cursed the banks.

The feeling of trust and neighborliness usually associated with farm communities often vanished under the impact of economic hardship and poverty. When lending institutions wanted to foreclose on ranches or seize property in payment of debts, they never had any trouble finding local people to do the dirty work for them. Often the local person was an old friend of the farmer whose property was being repossessed. When my mother berated one of them for his "lack of Christian charity and Christian spirit," he answered, "I'm getting paid a fee for doing this and I need the dough."

I remember seeing farmers and their families thrown off the land they'd worked for twenty or thirty years and forced to leave the community with only a few belongings. It tore at your heart—and it made you grow up in a hurry. The faith these people had in the Protestant work ethic and their political faith in the Republican Party was rudely shattered. My mother was a particularly strong Republican, but when Franklin D. Roosevelt came into office she told me she was praying for his success and became an ardent Democrat.

There was little in the way of fun to relieve the gloom and hardship of the Depression years. My father took a job in a raisin-packing plant in Fresno because the ranch no longer yielded enough income to provide for the family, although he would still work the ranch for a few hours every evening. My mother and I worked it a good part of the day. The work in the hot San Joaquin sun contributed to a skin-cancer condition which was eventually to prove fatal to my mother. My own skin-cancer condition also may have had its origin in this hot, dirty work in the fields.

During the winter we rarely ventured away from home, and our only relaxation was in card games or checker games. In the summer months we played some ball and would also go to local softball and baseball games. Sometimes, on Sunday afternoons after church, we would play croquet.

To help us meet the tax bills and keep our property, my mother took a summer job in the mid-thirties at the Libby cannery in Selma. I felt humiliated for her. She was highly intelligent and a skilled teacher and I felt she shouldn't be in a cannery. But there were no teaching jobs available then and she did what she had to do.

The opening did finally come, during the World War II years when younger teachers and supervisors were called into the service or war work. Mother proved herself so competent that she was eventually assigned to teach shut-ins, as well as to instruct the most trouble-prone, difficult students. Her patience and warm Christian spirit got through to them and she became known as an authority in the field of "teaching the unteachable." She was so good, in fact, that the local superintendent of schools kept her on past the retirement age. She also continued with her Sunday School work until her illness became too severe.

My brother and sister also began doing summer work in the cannery during the Depression years, but my father would usually take off from his factory job in the summer, so he could join me in working the ranch. My dad shared my mother's warm, open nature, and sometimes people took advantage of this. Although he was only five foot five, he was very strong and could have whipped almost any man he came into contact with. Instead, he used his strength to keep peace among the grape-pickers. The hard work they did in the broiling sun often made them unruly and they'd fight at the slightest provocation.

During my early years in the grape and raisin country, most of the laborers came from three minorities: the Okies, the Chicanos, and the Japanese-Americans. The Okies, desperate to find work in the Depression years, came to California with great hopes that soon turned to despair. They couldn't afford house rentals so they lived for the most part in tent camps and were constantly being harassed by the authorities.

As times got a little better, the Chicanos—Mexican-Americans—would come up during the harvest season to pick grapes and peaches. They would start in the Imperial Valley, go to Bakersfield, through our Valley, and on to Salinas. Often they would set up tent camps near our house, and I became very friendly with them. They always had a lot of cheerful kids and they gave me my first taste of Mexican food. I greatly admired their close-knit family life, the respect they showed for the elderly, and their ability to work long hours in the blistering sun without complaint.

The Japanese-Americans were the most law-abiding and polite

residents of the Valley, but this did not prevent them from absorbing slurs about the "yellow peril." I felt sad that so few people defended Japanese-American students in my school against insults and mistreatment. After Pearl Harbor, anti-Japanese feeling became hysterical. Under emergency war powers, they were stripped of their cars, farms, and other possessions, and then herded into camps. We desecrated our own American traditions of justice in trampling on the civil rights of people who had a record of loyalty to this country.

My friendships with members of these minority groups gave me first-hand insight into the way bullies operate. The Chicanos and Nisei, being small, were natural targets for "tough guys." I became a natural target too when I stood up for my friends. And being short, quiet, and astigmatic didn't help much. I had several fights without saying anything to school authorities because I felt if I kept quiet and didn't become a "troublemaker," they would eventually leave me alone. I also didn't fight back. I soon learned this was the wrong way to respond to abuse by bullies. They zeroed in on me as an easy mark who would not counterattack, and the attacks against me increased.

One day when I was walking home from school, one of my least-favorite tormentors came after me. Something snapped. I saw a stick lying on the road, grabbed it, and whacked him hard. He ran off yelling. I was astonished the next day to be called in by the principal and reprimanded. The bully had complained to school authorities that he had only wanted to play with me and I had taken unfair advantage by attacking him with a stick. Though he was twice my size, the principal had promptly accepted his version of our fight.

This incident, and several that followed, taught me a good deal about the mentality of bullies and their protectors, and that passivity was the road to destruction when dealing with them. When the target stands up and fights back, the cowardly bully will usually break off the attack. But he will also run to somebody in authority and whine that he's being unfairly abused. Surprisingly—at least to me in the beginning—a great many people who represent authority will react like my principal did and take up for the oppressor instead of the oppressed. Many people in authority tend to have the same mentality as the bullies. Sometimes a bully working under an authority—a student under a teacher, a worker under a boss, a junior officer under a senior officer—becomes a sort of masochistic partner of his superior, paying this price for the ego boost he gets from identification—however unhealthy—with what he sees as the power source. And it has been suggested by psychiatrists that some of these relationships may have homosexual overtones. From the superior's viewpoint, I suspect an often overriding reason for blind defense of the bully is his aversion to anybody who seems to be rocking the boat, disrupting the status quo—regardless of the justice and merits of the situation.

Even though my fighting back got me a reprimand—I was a "peacemaker," rocking the boat by going up against a powerful kid—I made up my mind to stand my ground against people like him. I sent away for a book on self-defense, learned the basics of judo, and surprised some people who considered me a punching bag by landing a few sharp blows on the neck. I suspect this early experience and what was to happen years later at Cecil Field have their parallels. By not quickly, for example, subsiding under attack, I was a troublemaker, surely rocking the boat. And as with those kids and their protectors of my youth, Mary Ann and Lora and their protectors in authority were surprised and angered.

My parents were determined that all three of their children would go to college. But early in 1940, my dad's leg was crushed in an accident at the packing house. He could not work for months. It looked as if we'd have to forget about college, but he insisted on his plans for us.

My brother went to college at San Jose State, majored in journalism, and edited his college newspaper. He was drafted in 1942 but spent most of his service time in Texas and California. After the war he decided not to go into newspaper work. He first farmed my father's ranch, then became successful in real estate and insurance. He and his family live in our hometown.

My sister was a bright student and graduated from high school at sixteen. She also got her college degree at San Jose State, taught school in the San Francisco area, and married a former Navy pilot who now works for the Navy in Washington, D.C., as an engineer.

Despite my interest in religion and Bible studies, I did not decide on the ministry as a vocation until I was in college—I first majored in horticulture at California State Polytechnic College. My interest in farming dwindled when I took a series of allergy examinations to determine the cause of my asthma and bronchial attacks. The examinations showed that my respiratory problems came mainly from the fact that I was allergic to fruits, insect bites, and pollen, which obviously made farming an unhealthy occupation for me.

At about the same time I became very friendly with a group of religiously oriented students at college. We discussed theology, philosophy, and social problems in America and tried to relate the solutions to these problems to what we had learned from the Bible.

One of the courses that gave me the most trouble was surveying. The final exam was so tough I was sure I'd flunk it. During the exam the proctor left the room, and a student who'd swiped a copy of the answers passed them around. Almost everybody grabbed for them. I refused. As a result I failed both the test and the course. Several of my classmates derided my "silly honesty," while my religious friends supported me when they found out what had happened.

I suppose it was a case of rocking the boat again. I hardly felt especially virtuous or "holier than thou." For me—I guess because of family and early training and inclination—it was really a case of doing what came naturally. But I was beginning to learn that like it or not, there was such a thing as taking sides, and at various crucial times in one's life there just was no alternative to taking sides regardless of who was or how many were on the other side. I literally couldn't survive any other way. Curse or blessing, I'm not sure.

I went down to Los Angeles that summer to work in a packing house and to live with a group of students interested in religion in an old house near the U.S.C. campus. Again there were long discussions of religion, politics, and social problems. During our free time, some of us went around to local churches to volunteer our help with youth groups. My experiences during this summer helped me decide to transfer out of California Polytechnic. I applied for admission to Redlands University, a Baptist institution just outside Los Angeles, where I could major in theology, philosophy, and the humanities.

It took only a few weeks at Redlands to determine that I was where I belonged. I worked hard at public speaking—I surely had no natural talent for it—and made the debating team. I was also elected president of a fraternity. More important, students who had problems getting along with their peers, with girls, or with their families, somehow tended to seek me out and ask my advice. When

I was able to help them even a little, it gave me an enormous feeling of satisfaction.

I was graduated from Redlands in June, 1951, and after a summer of work in a cannery to help cover school expenses, I enrolled in a seminary in Berkeley to begin my ministerial training.

CHAPTER 3

I wanted to combine my studies at the seminary with work in a nearby church but there was none that could find a place for me. Besides, the local vegetation was particularly bad for my allergies. I began to explore the possibility of transferring to a seminary in the east. I was accepted for transfer to the Eastern Baptist Theological Seminary in Philadelphia and was able to work part-time at the nearby Second Baptist Church.

The Philadelphia Baptist Association is the oldest organization in the American Baptist Convention, which includes some 6,000 northern Baptist churches. The American Baptists go back to Roger Williams, who, after a dispute with the Puritan theocracy in the Massachusetts Colony over religious freedom, led a group of English Baptists to Rhode Island in 1639. The land grant in Rhode Island was given to the Baptists, who established the first colony that guaranteed the principle of complete freedom of religion (the first synagogue in America was built in Newport, Rhode Island).

Most of these early Baptists were farmers, but they placed a high value on education and founded such institutions as Brown and Colgate universities. The Baptist movement also grew in Pennsylvania, and a group of its churches around Philadelphia formed the first Baptist associatiion. Baptists were active in support of the separation of church and state in the days of the Constitutional Convention in Philadelphia. The organization of Baptist churches was called an "association," to stress the fact that membership is voluntary and that its structure is democratic. The national organization, when it was formed, was called a "convention," since it was set up as a voluntary coming-together of delegations from all the local churches. This democratic tradition has been maintained. The national organization, and even the local association, cannot dictate to an individual church or congregation. It is felt that only Christ has the direct authority over as individual congregation. The ordination of a new minister can be authorized only by the local church, not by any other organization. Once the local church ordains a minister, however, the action is generally approved by the local association of churches and the national convention.

The Second Baptist Church, where I served as an assistant pastor, traced its origins to 1803. It was in a neighborhood from which many of the white residents were moving out to the suburbs because of an influx of black residents. The pastor, Reverend Robert Pierce, was for me the living embodiment of the Great Commandment of Christ. He never relaxed in his preaching of high ethical standards but, at the same time, he was a practical man, understanding, and forgiving. He seemed never to lose his temper. His guidance to me was invaluable. He encouraged me and other seminary students to come forward with new ideas and new programs in the belief that "nobody has a patent on how Christ's message should be interpreted."

Some of the churches in our area had already closed down or were in the process of doing so for financial reasons. As the more affluent people moved to the suburbs, church trustees often insisted that the church move out, too. The Second Baptist would have been shut down, too, were it not for the fact that Mr. Pierce wouldn't stand for it. If the church was to do God's work, he maintained, it shouldn't "run away" to green pastures. Instead, it had all the more responsibility to stay where it was and work all the harder to fight growing problems of crime, poverty, prejudice, and social unrest.

I doubt that Mr. Pierce—who is now retired and living in Pompano Beach, Florida—ever earned more than $4,000 a year as a clergyman. I have no doubt that he was a tremendous force in molding the lives of many fine people.

The feeling of love and faith that seemed to flow out from Mr. Pierce had its effect on the members of his congregation, who welcomed newcomers with the warmth and good will they showed toward one another. When hard times, illnesses, or family troubles victimized one of the members—or even a nonmember who lived in the neighborhood—they would immediately volunteer their help.

If there was a call for blood donors, a plea for emergency funds to help somebody who'd been in a fire or a bad accident, a request to take care of a sick woman whose husband had to go to work—the response would be prompt and the desire to contribute what one could would be a genuine one, without thought of compensation.

One of my assignments was to visit members of other Baptist churches that had closed down and try to get them to join the Second Baptist. My salesmanship was effective enough to get many of them to join, but it was difficult to dispel the bitterness many of them felt at being "deserted" by their own church. I was also assigned to work with a youth group and to help build up its membership. I was able to organize a basketball team that played teams at suburban churches with gymnasiums. I also persuaded a friend to teach wrestling, boxing, and tumbling. We managed to get some mattresses out of the seminary and we laid them out on the old wooden floor in the church basement. It was a makeshift arrangement but the boys didn't mind and the tumbling, boxing, and wrestling lessons we gave on Friday nights helped boost membership. Following the sports program, we would take the boys upstairs for religious songs, some religious instruction, and a devotional.

There were only a few black boys in the group when I started, and I was able to bring more in. This was considered somewhat revolutionary at the time because similar youth programs in the city at that time were invariably all white or all black. Those who had learned racist attitudes at home unfortunately absorbed these attitudes and would reflect them until they were able to see that this was wrong.

The incidence of juvenile crime in a city like Philadelphia was not as high then as it is now, but it was already on the rise. It was brought home forcefully to me one night when a policeman came to the church and returned a wallet that had been taken from one of our seminary students. It turned out that the thief was a boy who had come to the youth program and had picked the student's pocket. We worked with the boy, counseled him, got him active in the church, and were fortunate enough to be helpful to him. After that, I worked with several other boys who had already been involved—or showed signs of getting involved—with gangs and petty criminals, and under Reverend Pierce's direction I managed to run up a better than respectable batting average. In recent years, it seems to me, churches have been all too anxious to push the problem of juvenile delinquency into the laps of the police, the social workers, and the lawyers. I'm convinced their abdication of responsibility has contributed in an important way to the shocking rise in youth crime and drug addiction.

Drug addiction was not a serious problem when I was at Second Baptist, but alcoholism was. Time and again I saw Mr. Pierce work patiently to rehabilitate alcoholics. He refused to admit defeat even with the most difficult cases. Today, churches tend to resort to the cliché that "alcoholics are sick people"—as though this relieved them of their responsibility.

I was paid $600 a year for my work in the church and shared it with other seminary students who sometimes helped me. This didn't leave me with very much, but I felt the experience I was getting was beyond price. Besides, I cleaned people's yards for $1.25 an hour and also worked from time to time in the seminary dining club. In summers I worked in an ice-cream plant, as an elevator operator and a window-washer. Though I was frail physically, I could get along with only three hours of sleep a night—perhaps an example of nature's compensation.

One of the major reasons why my association with the Second Baptist Church turned out to be so important in my life was that it provided me with my one lasting romance. On one of the first Sundays that I attended church services there I found my eyes drawn to an attractive brown-haired girl who sang in the choir and did a solo. When I was introduced to her and the other members of the choir after the service, I learned that her name was Kathleen Van Canhegan and that she was president of the Baptist Youth Federation at the church. I subsequently learned that Kathleen's parents were divorced when she was about ten years old and that the church's pastor, Mr. Pierce, had been a kind of father to her ever since.

I attended the B.Y.F.'s meeting at the church that night and was impressed with the intelligent and efficient way Kathleen ran the meeting. I also was to get the feeling that Kathleen wasn't exactly bowled over by Andy Jensen. When I got a chance to talk to her later in the week I found I was right. She and the other girls in the choir had laughed when they saw the new seminary student from California come into the church vigorously chewing gum and they didn't much care for the way I broke up over their "eastern accent." (It didn't occur to me that I may have had a "western" accent.)

Fortunately for me, my relationship with Kathleen soon improved. She had been teaching one of the Sunday School classes but wanted to turn this chore over to somebody else. I was happy to oblige. Because of my assignment to the youth activities at the church, we often came into contact during these. Also, Kathleen's older sister would frequently invite some of us seminary students to her home. Kathleen was always there and we'd get into long discussions. I would see her at her own home, too, when she had gatherings for seminary students. We were also part of the group that would go out together after church on Sundays.

I didn't take Kathleen out on any individual dates for the first year-and-a-half after meeting her, other than to escort her to youth banquets or socials held under church auspices. Although I had dated several girls in California, these dates had been intermittent and had never grown into anything serious. This was partly because of my natural shyness toward girls and my conservative upbringing and training, but also because I simply had never met anybody in California who strongly attracted me. Moreover, as a seminary student and an assistant pastor, I felt I should be especially careful not to seem frivolous or appear to be using my position to start an intimate relationship with one of the girls associated with the church. I didn't want ever to be the subject of gossip. So I was careful not to touch girls or put my arms around them, as some pastors did, and I insisted on taking somebody with me whenever I was asked to make a pastoral visit to the home of a woman who lived alone.

I was anxious to see more of Kathleen and I was fairly sure that she returned my feelings and that she understood the reason for my caution—which she did. Toward the end of my seminary training, we finally started to go out on dates away from the church. Her sister and mother encouraged us. Apparently they could see we were falling in love and felt we were and would be very good for each other. When I graduated from the seminary and was ordained a Baptist minister in the spring of 1954, Kathleen helped me write the thank-you notes to everybody who had participated in the ordination. It further served to encourage our mutual attachment, and after this we actually talked about getting married, though we were still relatively casual and informal about it—particularly because I wasn't sure where my future would take me.

During the next few months I worked part-time in the office of a luxury apartment building in addition to my work at the church and also took on an extra job washing windows for tenants of the building—which enabled me to save up some $200. One day in October, I went to a jewelry store on Market Street and bought a ring. I called Kathleen at her job in the complaint department of the Philadelphia Transportation Company and told her it was important that I see her that night. When I walked into her house, I pulled the ring out of my pocket and literally thrust it on her.

"How out of character for you, Andy," she reasonably said. "When did old conservative you ever get so impulsive?" Then she came into my arms.

We waited until the next Sunday to invite the members of our church group over to the house to tell them the news. They were surprised. "We had no idea you were seeing each other regularly," they said.

One girl fixed me with a look and wanted to know why I hadn't been more open about my relationship with Kathleen. I got out something about trying to be a very proper minister.

"Silly," the girl remarked. "Ministers have the right to fall in love just like anybody else."

Looking back—and I know this sounds outrageously romantic—for Kathleen and myself it was far more than a "right." It was an inevitability.

CHAPTER 4

It was at about the same time that my relationship with Kathleen was becoming serious that I started to give thought to a career as a military chaplain rather than that of a civilian minister or pastor.

The fact that our churches were moving out from the inner city to the antiseptic suburbs was under constant discussion at the seminary. There was much talk that white pastors would no longer be needed or wanted in the city and that maybe this was a good thing because the work would be easier and the problems much fewer in those "good, middle-class sections" outside the city limits.

I felt the notion of choosing a nice, safe, easy place to serve missed the basic point of the Christian religion. Ministers of Christ were supposed to devote themselves primarily to people in need of their help; their mission was to go where there were challenges to be met, not where challenges and problems could be avoided.

I felt that service as a military chaplain—providing guidance to young men who had to leave their homes to serve under what might be extremely hazardous circumstances—would represent an important and challenging calling. The idea also appealed to my deep and natural sense of patriotism that goes back to my upbringing. Further, the Korean War had caused a sharp increase in the number of young men called into the service. In the future a large majority of the male membership in our churches would consist of veterans and I thought I would be able to relate to them better if I spent several years in the service myself.

Philadelphia was—in many ways—a Navy town with a large Naval Yard. One of my acquaintances there was a chaplain and through him I got some books on the history of chaplains in the military service. I learned that the tradition of having men of the cloth serve with military forces goes back to ancient times and the Old Testament. Moses seems to have been the first leader to have called on his priests to accompany fighting men in battle. The very first military chaplain, according to Hebrew records, was Phineas, who was dispatched by Moses with his religious equipment to join Hebrew forces in a battle against the Midianites.

The Hebrew priests were asked not only to lead their men in prayer and conduct services but also to try and secure information through divine channels that would help in winning the battle. Moses directed Joshua to make inquiries of the priest attached to his forces before beginning military operations. King David later credited his military chaplain, Abiather, with advice that caused him to change his campaign plans and win a great victory.

The priests were also charged with enhancing the effectiveness of the troops by demonstrating the justice of their cause and exhorting them to be loyal to God and country. The code of Deuteronomy included what has been referred to as "the law of the chaplaincy in the Hebrew Army." It included these words:

". . . And it shall be, when ye are come nigh unto the battle, that the priest shall approach and speak unto the people and shall say unto them, Hear, O Israel, ye approach this day unto battle against your enemies: let not your hearts faint, fear not, and do not tremble, neither be ye terrified because of them; for the Lord your God is he that goeth with you, to fight for you against your enemies, to save you."

The Greeks subsequently followed the lead of the Hebrews in their use of spiritual leaders to serve with battle forces and the example was also followed by Western countries. The use of the term "chaplain" seems to have originated from a legend concerning St. Martin of Tours, the patron saint of France. The legend describes Martin as a common soldier in the French Army during the Fourth century who one night met a beggar crying for alms. Martin had no money but he took off his cloak, slashed it with his sword, and gave one half of it to the beggar. That night he had a vision of Christ wearing the half-cloak and was so stirred by it that he abandoned his military career and devoted the rest of his life to the Church. The cloak, called a *capella* in French, was watched over by a special officer well versed in spiritual matters. The officer was known as a *chapellain,* and the place where he would perform religious rites was called a *chapel.* The English word "chaplain" was derived from *chapellain.*

Chaplains served at frontier posts in the New World in the earliest days when white settlers fought the Indians. They were active in the French and Indian wars and served with Washington's Army during the Revolutionary War as well as with the Navy. According to Colonel Roy J. Honeywell (Ret.), author of *Chaplains of the United States Army,* Revolutionary War chaplains were steeped in the Hebrew Scriptures and believed them to be a guide book for all times and places. "Many practices observed reverently by American chaplains [in the Revolutionary War era] grew directly out of the usages . . . of the prophets, priests, and judges of Israel," Honeywell wrote. A captain commanding a Connecticut company was reported to have changed his campaign plans at the behest of his chaplain in the same fashion that David changed his plans on the advice of Abiather.

A total of 179 chaplains served officially with Washington's forces. All were from Protestant denominations, although a French-Canadian Catholic priest ministered to a regiment of Canadian volunteers. Prayers for Jewish soldiers were led informally by one of their number. Three of the 179 chaplains died in battle and eight others died of illnesses caused by their service. (According to Colonel Parker C. Thompson, historian for the U.S. Army Chaplaincy, 272 Army chaplains have been killed in all United States wars to date. The number of Navy and Air Force chaplains killed is estimated at 100.)

General Washington's favorite chaplain was Reverend Israel Evans, who led the Army in prayers at Valley Forge. In 1807, when Evans was on his deathbed, a fellow minister prayed that he might be allowed to sit down with Abraham, Isaac, and Jacob in the Kingdom of Heaven. The dying Evans whispered, "And with Washington, too." Obviously a mutual admiration society—and understandably—had developed.

The vehemence of their opposition to British rule induced several Revolutionary War chaplains to go beyond the role of noncombatants. The pastor of a church in Concord, one of the first persons to join the Minutemen in the fighting at Lexington, carried a musket into the battle. The pastor's name was William Emerson, grandfather of the celebrated poet, Ralph Waldo Emerson.

Another of the warrior-pastors was James Caldwell, a Presbyterian minister who served as chaplain to Washington's forces when they wintered in New Jersey and also held a military combat rank. He was so hated by the Tories that one of them murdered his wife. Caldwell himself was shot dead by an American soldier on guard duty who claimed he mistook him for an enemy. It was found later that the American guard had been bribed by the Tories. He was hanged. Caldwell's orphaned son was adopted by Lafayette and educated in France.

Caldwell had his counterparts in the War of 1812. Samuel Livermore was serving as chaplain aboard U.S.S. *Chesapeake* when the ship had its epoch battle with H.M.S. *Shannon.* It was during this battle that the dying Captain James Lawrence voiced his memorable slogan: "Don't give up the ship." The inspired Chaplain Livermore led a desperate American attempt to beat back a boarding party from the British ship and even engaged in a personal duel with the captain of the *Shannon.* Another fighting chaplain, Thomas Breese, helped Commodore Oliver Perry load and fire the partially damaged guns on his flagship in the battle of Lake Erie. And when the U.S. navel ship *Essex* captured several British prizes at sea and ran out of available officers, its chaplain, David Adams, was pressed into service as commander of the ship. He remains the only Naval chaplain in history to have commanded a U.S. warship.

The Civil War had such a chaplain as Milton L. Haney of the 55th Illinois Infantry, who won the Medal of Honor for leading a Union counterattack against Confederate forces outside of Atlanta. In another battle in Georgia, two combat chaplains—one from the North, the other from the South—were killed nearly at the same time. And Chaplain Arthur Fuller of the 16th Massachusetts Infantry led a group of volunteer sharpshooters across the Rappahannock River in Maryland in an attempt to wipe out a Confederate patrol. He had just got to the other side of the river with his riflemen when a Confederate marksman spotted him and shot him dead.

As the War went on, there was a growing realization on both sides that it was inconsistent with the special calling of chaplains for them to carry arms and to kill. Orders were issued for all chaplains to turn in whatever weapons they carried. And both Union and Confederate commands put out directives that captured chaplains were to be immediately exchanged, thereby permitting them to stay with wounded men without fear of retaliation.

Catholic priests joined the Chaplain Corps of the armed services in substantial numbers for the first time during the Civil War. This reflected the increase in immigration from Catholic countries in Europe, and the increase in the number of Catholic draftees and volunteers. In 1862 the Army got its first official Jewish chaplain—Michael M. Allen of the 5th Pennsylvania Cavalry. He was followed soon by a second, Rabbi Arnold Fischel.

The Chaplain Corps in the years preceding and during the Civil War expanded its military-backup function to achieve important advances in human relations. A Navy chaplain, Charles S. Stewart, led the successful campaign to outlaw flogging on American ships. Chaplains crusaded against excessive drinking and gambling in Army camps and aboard ships and launched a drive against corrupt money brokers who were bleeding naïve recruits. They also started basic education programs for illiterate soldiers in the camps. Catholic and Protestant chaplains working together in the Civil War years helped break down much of the bitter prejudice existing among soldiers and sailors on the same side of the fighting. And when the war ended, they were active in advancing Lincoln's policy of healing the wounds between North and South.

I was impressed by the many heroic acts performed by chaplains in our various wars. There was Chaplain Charles McCabe, who helped save the lives of Union soldiers with whom he was imprisoned in a dank Confederate jail. McCabe also gained fame as the first to sing "The Battle Hymn of the Republic" in the army camps. Eight chaplains assigned to Marine and Army units fighting at Château Thierry in World War I were decorated for their "unbelievable" courage in rescuing wounded men amidst machine-gun and shell fire. The most famous of the World War I chaplains, Father Francis Duffy of New York's "Fighting 69th," was also noted for his disdain of enemy fire while crawling to forward trenches to aid the wounded and retrieve the dead.

It was a Navy chaplain who keyed the American response to Japan's sneak attack on Pearl Harbor by exhorting the exhausted crew on the cruiser *New Orleans* to "praise the Lord and pass the ammunition." His name was H. M. Forgy and his plea was turned into a song that helped galvanize the entire nation. The nearby battleship, U.S.S. *Oklahoma,* was wrecked by torpedoes, and Chaplain A. H. Schmitt, serving his first tour of sea duty, helped several sailors crawl through a porthole to safety. When they called for him to follow, he stepped back to let others through and was drowned.

A Naval chaplain aboard U.S.S. *Houston,* George Snavely Rentz, gave his life jacket and his life to save another when his ship was sunk. Army and Navy chaplains who took part in the notorious Bataan Death March and were later imprisoned were beaten when they refused to tell their captors how medicines were being smuggled into their prison camp. Eighteen of thirty-three chaplains in the main prison camp at Cabantuan died before MacArthur was able to make good his pledge: "I shall return."

Joseph T. O'Callaghan, senior chaplain aboard the carrier U.S.S. *Franklin,* won the accolade of his commanding officer—"the bravest man I've ever seen in my life"—and the Medal of Honor for his exploits on that stricken ship. The *Franklin* was turned into a torch by bombs from a Japanese suicide plane, but Chaplain O'Callaghan kept dragging out sailors and beating out the flames. Even while the ship was being rocked by explosions, he organized and led fire-fighting crews to prevent the engine and boiler rooms from being destroyed. He manned a hose to wash down armed bombs that had come loose from their racks and were rolling dangerously on the listing deck and directed the jettisoning of live ammunition overboard. Officers on the ship officially credited the chaplain's "courage, deep spiritual strength and profound faith in the face of almost certain death" with inspiring the extraordinary efforts to keep the ship afloat. Tentative orders to abandon ship were cancelled, and when the last fire was put out, it was towed safely to port.

A modern miracle was performed by yet another Navy chaplain, Frederic Gehring, who became known as the "Padre of Guadalcanal." Chaplain Gehring, who won the Legion of Merit and a Presidential Unit citation, saved the life of a five-year-old girl during one of the crucial battles on the Canal. She had been brutalized by Japanese soldiers and left for dead. Her terrifying ordeal had washed out her memory; she couldn't remember who she was or what her name was. Chaplain Gehring gave her a made-up name—Patsy Li—and flew her from Guadalcanal to an orphanage in the New Hebrides. Years later, a woman in Singapore named Ruth Li wrote Chaplain Gehring about a daughter she had lost at sea named Patsy Li. Could the chaplain have inadvertently given the child found on Guadalcanal her real name? It seemed impossible, particularly since the daughter had been lost off Singapore harbor, 4,000 miles from Guadalcanal. Yet, as Chaplain Gehring wrote in a book called *A Child of Miracles,* the impossible turned into reality. Mrs. Li traveled to the New Hebrides and discovered that the child was indeed her daughter.

The spirit of brotherhood fostered by chaplains of different faiths in the Civil War was further accentuated in World War II and in the Korean War. I learned of Protestant chaplains who crawled through heavy fire and at great risk to themselves, comforted and prayed for dying soldiers of the Catholic and Jewish faiths. Catholic chaplains did the same. Two Jewish chaplains were killed—one by shellfire, one by flying shrapnel—while holding crucifixes to the lips of wounded Catholic GIs.

Perhaps the most stirring example of brotherhood-in-action was demonstrated in a group sacrifice in the North Atlantic during World War II. Four chaplains—two Protestants, one Catholic, and one Jew—were aboard an Army troopship, U.S.S. *Dorchester,* when it was torpedoed by a Nazi submarine. The four chaplains all moved to the forward deck to hand out lifebelts and give spiritual comfort to the men leaving the sinking ship, but there were not enough lifebelts for all. The four chaplains removed their own lifebelts and handed them to others. As the doomed ship sank, the four clergymen stood with arms linked and with voices raised in joint prayer.

The four chaplains—Reverend George L. Fox and Reverend Clark V. Poling, Father John P. Washington, and Rabbi Alexander D. Goode—were posthumously awarded the Distinguished Service Cross and a special Congressional award equivalent to the Medal of Honor. Their sacrifice struck a special response in the churches of Philadelphia, because Clark Poling was the son of the Reverend Daniel Poling of Philadelphia, one of America's most prominent clergymen. Daniel Poling helped organize a drive to build the Chapel of the Four Chaplains in Philadelphia as an interfaith memorial.

I was already familiar with the story of the four chaplains but it was a stirring experience for me to read the graphic details of their sacrifice. It wasn't long afterward that I made a firm decision to apply for a military chaplaincy. I preferred the Navy because I had served for a short time in the Naval Reserve after graduation from high school and liked the Navy tradition.

In order to be accepted into the Navy, Army, or Air Corps Chaplain Corps, a minister must be endorsed for the Corps by his religious denomination. Shortly before I was scheduled to be graduated from the seminary I contacted an official representative of our Baptist denomination and told him of my interest in Navy service. He told me I would have to serve three years in a church after ordination before I could even be considered. This didn't square with other reports I had heard about pastors going into military service immediately out of the seminary. Another denominational representative who came to our seminary one day told me it was proper for me to put in a formal application to the Navy, with a copy to the denominational board that acted on endorsements.

What followed was a rather classic bureaucratic snafu. I was given the Navy's test for admission to the Chaplain Corps and passed it. A chaplain from the Corps then called me and said I would be acceptable to the Navy after ordination, providing the endorsement was forthcoming. When I told him that one local denominational representative wanted my endorsement held up until I'd served three years in a church, he suggested I contact the American Baptist Convention for the endorsement. I did this, but when letters went up and back between the Convention, the Navy Chaplain Corps and the local denominational representative, it created bruised feelings and insinuations that protocol was being violated. I was given to understand there would be no endorsement.

I was disappointed, of course, but Kathleen and I both decided to make the best of it and go ahead with our wedding plans, and we were married in December of that year by Mr. Pierce. (When I repeated after him, "With all my worldly goods I thee endow," there was laughter from some of our friends who knew what little *that* amounted to.) My parents came in from California for the wedding and I was greatly pleased when two black employees from the seminary staff came. After honeymooning in California, we set up a little apartment on Roosevelt Boulevard. Kathleen went back to her job while I continued my part-time work for the church and also worked as an elevator operator in an office building. I enrolled in the graduate division of Temple University for an advanced course in counseling and canvassed churches in the area for pastoral openings.

After I'd finished my course at Temple I got an unexpected call to go to the headquarters of the American Baptist Convention in New York for an interview with the board that passed on endorsements. One of the ministers on the board had apparently been impressed by the recommendations I'd received from the Second Baptist Church and felt the question of endorsement for me should be reconsidered. A month later I was informed that the board had rated me highly after the interview, that I was to be formally endorsed, and that the Navy had agreed to commission me. Furthermore, the Convention had decided to change its procedures so that any candidate for endorsement could appear before the full board if he desired. No longer could an individual denominational representative reject anyone on his own initiative.

For all the fine and glorious history of the chaplaincy, it appeared that a bureaucracy was a bureaucracy—especially at the top. And no matter whether it was a school principal or the U.S. Navy Chaplains Service.

CHAPTER 5

During the years before my assignment to Cecil Field I also served with destroyer squadrons, on a survey ship, a seaplane tender, and a giant carrier, such service interspersed with short duty at Marine bases and at the Naval Training Center in San Diego. I made four trips to the Vietnam area and was on seaborne missions that took me elsewhere in the Far East and around most of the world.

I found that what I had been told about the "sea-going" Navy—particularly aboard the larger ships—was true. Life was different from the "land-based" Navy. The most conscientious, the most dedicated and understanding officers seemed to be those who did long tours of sea duty or served with the Fleet Marine Forces. They were not as petty, as bureaucratic, or as obsessed with the social niceties as those who spent most of their careers on shore. They even saw some value in a chaplain willing to take on additional duties. And since they were well aware of how their mission could be imperiled by discontent aboard ship, they gave good marks to chaplains who devoted time to the problems and grievances of enlisted men.

My promotions came mostly from my sea-going service and from my good fortune in serving under some outstanding commanding officers and executive officers. I continued to get intermittent heckling over my "Protestant work ethic," my nondrinking, and my refusal—good-natured, I hope—to join in romantic diversions in various ports. As I developed a sense of ease, I learned not to be overly sensitive and to handle the gibes with some sense of humor. I found that holding a glass to join in toasts at ceremonial functions went a long way toward dissipating resentment against me from those who saw my nondrinking as an offense aganist Navy tradition. Not to mention—in the vernacular—a drag.

I suppose the high point of my Naval career was from 1967 to 1969, when I served aboard the carrier *Ticonderoga.* The responsibilities were large, the work schedule tough, but the experience was unforgettable. A carrier at sea is a floating city that never sleeps, churning with machinery and energy, crowded with jet planes, helicopters, electronic and computer gear—and people. It was like a community of nearly 4,000 with only one Protestant and one Catholic pastor.

I conducted three services aboard ship on Sundays, the last one at 11 P.M. At first I would prepare my sermons in advance, but later I'd do them extemporaneously. Destroyers in formation with a carrier usually ask for a chaplain on Sunday and I would fly over during the day in a helicopter and conduct one or two services for them. I suppose I made more 'copter flights than anyone on the carrier. I held devotional groups three times a week and evening services twice a week, as well as choir rehearsals and special religious services. I took turns with the Catholic chaplain reciting an evening prayer over the intercom system each night before taps. Since I was in charge of the overall religious program aboard ship, I had to insure that all minority groups such as Latter Day Saints (Mormons) had the opportunity and facilities for worship, though one of their own laymen ran the actual service.

Counseling aboard ship never seemed to end. Men came to me with problems of loneliness, marital situations, sex problems, difficulties in adjusting to shipboard duty, religious concerns, need for emergency leave, and alleged mistreatment by petty officers. Toward the end of any period on the line, tempers became hot. Complains about harassment by petty officers built dramatically. My job was to support the enlisted man with counseling until he was able to understand what was going on and work it out if the complaint was justified. When men developed hostile feelings toward their superiors, I preferred to have their anger channeled against me rather than have them nurse a grudge against superiors who could and would hurt their careers.

The complement of a carrier consists of the ship's company, which operates the vessel, and the air wing, which comes aboard just before a cruise begins. The wing is made up of two attack squadrons, two fighter squadrons, and some supporting detachments. When there are bad feelings between the wing and the ship's company, you have fights, recurring conflicts, and an above-average quota of accidents. The *Ticonderoga* was always so crowded that it was a considerable challenge to maintain reasonable peace and harmony.

When disagreements occur, men tend to split up in a number of ways—by division, by compartment, or by race. The worst threat is the one of a racial fight, such as the ones in recent times on the carriers *Kitty Hawk* and *Constellation.* I managed to intercede in a few situations to help cool tensions that threatened to explode into racial conflicts. Often this kind of tension was and is generated by antiblack slurs by crewmen or petty officers or by discriminatory practices against blacks. But I must also point out that I have seen fights precipitated by blacks cursing out a petty officer as "southern white trash." And I really believe that so-called black studies programs on a ship—however well-intended—serve in part to accentuate a feeling of racial division.

One of the *Ticonderoga*'s executive officers I served with, Captain Thomas Loomis, flew from Washington at his own expense to testify as a character witness for me. A second one, Captain Reuben Prichert, would have done the same except for some apparent skullduggery. When he heard that I was to be tried, he went to the Chief of Chaplains in Washington and offered his services as a character witness for me. The Chief told him his offer would be passed on to me, but I was never informed of it until *after* the court-martial.

On the *Ticonderoga* the men involved in the primary operation were those who flew the planes that attacked the Communist forces and installations in Vietnam. It was an odd kind of situation because, in a sense, our pilots commuted to war. Though we were always on guard against attack on our ship, no serious attack ever came. Fliers went off on combat missions, then returned to a floating base that, for all practical purposes, was outside the war zone.

The most difficult job was to perform religious services for the dead. We lost only a few of our pilots to enemy fire and in accidents, but of course every death was one too many. I still remember every one who was lost, but one etched most deeply in my memory was a young pilot who was the first I saw die. Something went wrong with his plane and he had to bail out. He was returned to the ship alive, and I thought the doctors could save him. Then I saw his face turn ashen as life ebbed away. I was angered by my sense of inadequacy. Why couldn't I do something for him? There are times when even a chaplain forgets that such things are in God's hands, not his.

The service for the dead was a memorial, not a funeral, since we buried no bodies at sea. Either no body was recovered, or the remains were sent back to the States.

The Commanding Officer of the ship as well as the C.O. of the squadron officiated at these services along with the chaplain. Typically a service would be followed by a rifle salute and the playing of taps. Then we would throw a wreath into the sea. Once when we had no floral wreath, an imaginative chief steward fashioned one out of dyed vegetables, potatoes, and apples.

As controversy grew outside—and inside—the service over America's role in the Vietnam war, I wrote two pamphlets defending our position and circulated them among the men on the carrier. I wrote the pamphlets on the basis of research and information available to me and on the basis of my honest convictions at the time. I believed in the much publicized concept that if we allowed South Vietnam to fall under Communist control, the Communists would then take over the rest of southeast Asia. I also believed that we had pledged our support to South Vietnam against aggression and so were duty-bound to honor our commitment.

I was upset by some of the press reports that accused American fliers of indiscriminately bombing hospitals and massacring defenseless civilians. I knew that the Navy fliers on *my* carrier were honorable officers with humane values who would never deliberately murder civilians and I felt they deserved a defense against a "bad rap." It is also true that their "gung-ho" attitude about bombing missions and the way they would use football-style comparisons in measuring one squadron's "score" of death and destruction against another seriously disturbed me. But I told myself that their aggressive habits and language—bluster, if you will—were part of the American jet pilots' style and did not necessarily represent a "killer" instinct. All the pilots I knew were patriotic men who felt obliged to carry out missions assigned to them by a democratically elected government. They were not exactly deep thinkers, perhaps, nor were they astute students of foreign affairs, but this had never been part of their job requirement. I could understand some of them being careless in emptying their unused ordnance on their way back to the carrier but I could never see the ones I knew deliberately choosing women, kids, and hospital sites for target practice.

My pamphlets drew a good deal of flak from younger members of the crew who had come to believe that our Vietnam adventure was a ghastly mistake, and I got into several frank and open debates with them. I did change my views on the war—though not, to be sure, until sometime later.

One of my most rewarding accomplishments aboard the *Ticonderoga* was that I was able to cultivate a deep interest in religion among a sizeable number of crewmen. I would try to get at least one man from each department to join a religious nucleus, to help form choirs, and to let me know how well I was doing in serving the spiritual needs of the men in their departments. On one cruise I had nineteen men whose absorption in religion reached such a stage that they told me they intended to go into full-time religious work after they finished their hitch. On the second cruise I had eleven more who told me the same thing.

The spirit of ecumenism also came abroad our carrier. As I have mentioned, I found this spirit observed mainly in the breach during my early years as a chaplain. The advent of Pope John and his refreshing approach to the brotherhood of man contributed a great deal to a change of attitude in the Navy as well as elsewhere. Many Catholic chaplains who had displayed hard-shell anti-Protestant attitudes adopted a new approach. Some of our Protestants who had been just as antagonistic to Catholic priests and their doctrines also switched and at least met their Catholic confreres half way. On the *Ticonderoga,* ecumenism took on its warmest meaning in the person of Lieutenant Jim Doyle, a Roman Catholic chaplain. He was to be an important character witness for me at my court-martial. Jim seemed to be as well versed in Protestant as in Catholic theology. He was anxious for us to conduct a joint service, and we finally decided to do it for the Sunrise service on Easter Sunday. We combined parts of the Mass with parts of the Protestant service and I hope did not sacrifice the reverence of either one.

Our plan was to hold the service on the flight deck at 6 A.M., but the weather was unusually cold that morning in the Tonkin Gulf and so we moved it to the hangar deck. We had more than a thousand, including many crew members who had not gone to any kind of religious service in years.

My service on the *Ticonderoga* seemed to have aged me ten years in two. The pressures, long hours, the periods of sleeplessness had their effect on a physique that was something less than Charles Atlas robust, and sustained periods in the sun on the ship's deck aggravated my skin-cancer condition.

I suppose I should have taken a long leave when I was reassigned from the carrier to a senior course of study at the Chaplains School in Newport, but my replacement arrived late and I had only a short leave before going on to the school and then to Cecil. My weakened physical condition and the medically prescribed rest periods at motels that were to be the basis of so much suspicion and the charges later brought against me were the result. As they say, I quite literally should have stayed in bed, and far from Cecil Naval Air Station. But hindsight, while helpful, is too easy . . .

CHAPTER 6

During these years I became aware of a trend that reached its low during my service in Florida—I mean the sexual, the overall moral behavior of many Navy personnel and their dependents.

I didn't go into the Navy a complete bumpkin. I knew that when men are sent away from their families to different parts of the world they become especially open to the blandishments of illicit sex. I was aware of the endless stories of Navy men involved with prostitutes and bar girls in ports from Naples to Hong Kong. I did find many officers and enlisted men who stayed faithful to their wives no matter where they traveled, but it was also common for married personnel to patronize prostitutes, to "shack-up" and have arrangements with women abroad who served as "second wives." I doubt if officers in general behaved more nobly than those in the lower ranks, but I know they always came out much better in the V.D. statistics—mostly because the medics listed V.D. for what it was when enlisted men were treated, but the ailment became a "bad cold" or a "flu infection" when the patient was an officer.

Chaplains might try through formal preaching and informal persuasion to discourage these widespread sexual forays, but I doubt that we were a formidable influence. Those who could not be swayed by appeals to moral principles sometimes did take the medical warnings seriously. But often they just took precautions against infection.

A few chaplains got involved in affairs themselves. They then would often try to induct their clerical confreres into their "swinging" circle. Some officers urged chaplains to join them, and others merely expected the chaplains to help them. On one occasion when we came into Yokusaka, Japan, an officer asked me to lend him a civilian suit for Saturday night ashore. I obliged him and he returned the suit the next morning. "Suzy San sure appreciated your lending me a suit for our night," he told me. He added he was going to take a short nap and would appreciate it if I'd wake him for church service. Quite a sport.

What happened overseas involved a "double-standard" long tolerated by many Navy wives as long as they weren't obliged to confront it personally. A recent proposal, though, that female Navy personnel be assigned to ship's crews triggered a vociferous protest by a group of Navy wives who said this would convert the ships to "floating whorehouses." This was clearly an instance of the old double standard being flaunted in their faces, and they weren't having it.

In recent years I've seen a severe breakdown of this "double standard." In years past, Navy wives would set their teeth and generally stay faithful even when they suspected their husbands were misbehaving abroad. But lately they have begun to adopt an attitude of "what's sauce for the goose . . ." And often—despite or because of their abrupt liberation—they have seemed to suffer guilt feelings they later frequently reveal to a chaplain in counseling sessions.

Behavior varied at different bases. The increasing number of wives who took on jobs seemed to be reflected in a higher degree of sexual activity. The ease with which extramarital arrangements could be made at different installations also had a bearing on the number of wives who decided they were no more bound than their distant husbands by marriage vows. The amount of peer pressure from friends who were doing it was also an important influence. And so was the attitude of the C.O. or his wife. If the C.O. himself had a reputation for promiscuity, it would encourage those who had compunctions to put them aside. He was the leader in more ways than one. Frequently the wives of officers would take their cue from the wife of the C.O. or squadron commander.

At bases in the southern California area, particularly around San Diego and Long Beach, I became especially aware of how this so-called new morality was permeating Navy life. A Navy man would ship out and his wife would naturally become lonely. A friend might be seeing another Navy man who would have his own male friend available to the lonesome wife. There would be double dates, and the girlfriend would begin a sexual liaison with her partner—if she hadn't already—and soon the lonesome wife would tend to follow the example with the Navy man's friend. She might start this way, then move on to new admirers or become involved in a relationship with the friend until it was his turn to ship out.

There were a number of bars that catered to "overseas wives," as women with husbands at sea were called. These were bars which catered to Navy wives who were willing to be picked up. Later, when I heard of them in the Jacksonville area, they were called "body shops" or "body exchange shops." The owner of one of these bars in the San Diego area is an intimate friend of a high-ranking admiral and a senior chaplain. Both admiral and chaplain talk of themselves as being near moral puritans, yet they also maintain this close friendship with a man who operates a known pick-up spot, featuring Navy wives as bait.

The Naval caste system also seems to operate in these extramarital relationships. Wives of officers tend to go to places to be picked up by other officers; wives of enlisted men to be picked up by other EMs. There is tacit agreement that each should stick to his or her "own kind." Some officers' wives who have affairs boast that they advance their husbands' careers while they have their fun, because they cultivate relationships with senior officers who can arrange promotions; and I've heard of young officers who supposedly obtained advancement through sexual liaisons with the wives of C.O.s.

Sometimes, of course, officers and EMs cross caste lines, which can cause trouble. At one bar, known to be a place where EMs picked up Navy women, a brawl developed one night because several officers came in to pick up women the enlisted men felt were their "property."

Husbands returning from sea duty often came home to find their wives had been doing unto them what they had traditionally been doing unto their wives in various ports-of-call, which provoked indignant squabbling and divorce. But in the majority of cases, surprisingly, I found the wives breaking off their outside liaisons completely and returning to the role of faithful spouse, at least until the next time their husbands shipped out. It would seem that the condition had much to do with the degree of fidelity, and that for many wives, at least, marriage with their husbands at home was still considered a monogamous affair. Many—but not all, by any means, as Cecil Field made clear.

For me, one of the most appalling aspects of life at some Naval air bases was the treatment directed at widows of men killed in action or accidents. While the men of the squadron were overseas, the other wives would treat the widow with sympathy and understanding. But as soon as the men returned, the wives would tend to shun her and phase her out of social activities. It seemed they feared she would begin to attract their husbands. I even saw wives of Navy POWs in Vietnam treated in this fashion. Sometimes a POW's wife would receive only a perfunctory few weeks of friendly attention before being treated as a pariah. The widows and POW wives I saw tended, understandably, to be sad and lonely, and as such were considered fair game by many Navy men, who thereby lived up to their wives' worst expectations and fears. The loser, of course, was the victim—guilty or not.

Not all the extramarital sexual activity involved intra-Navy relationships. Some Navy wives would take up with civilians who had a close association with the base or air station—such as doctors who treat Naval dependents, civilian technicians, or civilians the wives would meet at work.

In my counseling, I have encountered situations in which a Navy wife would not be unfaithful to her overseas husband but would insist on "confessing" to her husband on his return. These bizarre episodes usually occurred when the wife wanted, consciously or unconsciously, to break up with her husband but for psychological, moral, or religious reasons would not and could not actually participate in extramarital affairs. In a few cases, I suspect, the wife felt she *should* have had an affair to get even with her husband, and so she believed, through the conviction of her fantasies, that she actually *did* have one.

Although a laissez-faire attitude seemed to prevail around most bases, the brass became disturbed when racial lines were crossed in sexual affairs. At one Marine installation, no questions were raised about pick-up bars, "body shops," etc., until it was learned that white girls were being picked up by black Marines. Then there was a hurried crackdown, with place after place being declared "off limits." Moral indignation and rectitude seemed prompted by visible breakdown or violation of a presumed condition of proper servitude, inferiority, and segregation between blacks and whites. The blacks heard about it first, and suffered most and most lastingly.

Reports of homosexual behavior also caused consternation and speedy crackdowns. Homosexuals who found young Marines or sailors willing partners were dealt with severely. It was also suggested that I should report personnel who confessed homosexual desires for prompt prosecution. I refused to do this because I insisted that their weakness did not call for criminal penalties, but rather for psychiatric treatment, and probable quiet discharge. It would have been disgraceful to treat them as criminals.

I also found in my overseas towns that not all Naval chaplains lived above and apart when it came to succumbing to immorality. I found that this was also true Stateside. Some chaplains had discreet affairs with officers' wives; others were not so discreet. One of the first scandals reported to me in the Navy involved a Catholic chaplain who took off with the wife of a Protestant chaplain—a rather questionable example of ecumenism. The amorous activities of some chaplains were widely known and they didn't mind talking about them to confreres who were "understanding," but they were noticeably uncomfortable when they were around "square" chaplains like myself.

At one installation a group of Catholic ladies came to see Kathleen and me to complain about a Catholic chaplain. They said he was going with the wife of a neighbor who had been sent overseas and whose quarters were near ours. This was long before I myself became the target of charges, but my position then was the same as the one I was to take in my own case—namely, that the moral behavior of a chaplain is not a matter for military investigation and judgment but an ecclesiastic matter that should be brought before the chaplain's religious authorities. I also told them how priests and ministers were often subjected to charges of adultery that were made out of whole cloth and that they should be certain of their facts before taking any kind of action. They told me that this was not a matter of a complaint by neurotics, that the chaplain's conduct had been well substantiated and that he had admitted to friends what he was doing. They said they had already been to his religious superior but had been laughed out of his office. Kathleen and I knew the woman allegedly involved, but the chaplain was not part of my command or of my religious discipline and I insisted to them I had neither the right nor the duty to intervene. Whether he was guilty or not, I felt I had acted—or not acted—properly, although I am afraid these ladies never really understood why I so believed.

Since Catholic priests are required to be celibates, there were always more rumors about them than about chaplains of other denominations. But errant chaplains were certainly not confined to any faith. Some of the chaplains who became involved in adulterous liaisons were, for example, from fundamentalist Protestant sects.

Even when they transgress, however, some chaplains seem to maintain special status and esteem. A young sailor told me he had had sex with a nurse who told him she had also had an affair with a chaplain. I expected that the sailor would be angered and made cynical by the chaplain's behavior. Instead, I was amazed to learn that he was *flattered.* "It makes me feel very important to know I was able to make out with a woman who's been going to bed with a chaplain," he said. This for me was more a testimonial to the built-in advantages for setting a good and instructive example that this particular chaplain had squandered than to the good sense of the rather perversely impressed sailor who derived a feeling of importance by sharing with a man who had defaulted on his vows and his obligations.

Obviously, though it needs saying in the context of this discussion, the number of Navy chaplains improperly involved is a very small percentage of the entire chaplaincy. For whatever reasons this comparatively small number of so-called rogue chaplains do fall from propriety—"new morality," cynicism, or commanding officers favoring them over the so-called squares, etc.—the climate in which they and their nonministerial counterparts seemed to flourish was especially pervasive, it seemed to me, in the Cecil Field–Jacksonville area of Florida.

CHAPTER 7

Cecil Field—a picture of contrast.

The facilities were better than at any of the other bases where I had served, the climate was good most of the year, and there was a good school near the base and excellent recreational opportunities for our young boys. The chapel was modern and I was provided officer's quarters nearby. We found a nucleus of fine Navy families —officers and EM and their wives—who were members of the chapel and sincerely concerned with Christian ethics. A feeling of trust and friendship soon developed between Kathleen and myself and these Navy families— a trust destined to be put to an agonizing test when Mary Ann Curran and Lora Gudbranson made their scandalous attacks against me and these families found they had to risk future careers if they were to stand up for their accused pastor.

As opposed to our new friends, the C.O. of the field quickly let me know his distaste for me. He had heard I was a Baptist, a non-drinker. One who'd been there before apparently was a pleasure-bent sort, most friendly with the female residents of the field and perhaps more committed to socializing and golfing with the C.O. than with maintaining a full program at the chapel. Apparently—even understandably—the C.O. was upset when he didn't get one cut from the same mold. He told me from the start that the only reason I'd gotten my house was that a pilot who had originally been earmarked for it had decided it was too small. Then he began a pattern of bypassing me on chaplaincy matters by pointedly going to one of my assistants, thereby putting me in the embarrassing position of passively submitting to insults or making noises about chain-of-command and seeming to be more concerned with position and status than with result.

My compulsive work habits—I take no special credit, it's just the way I am—at the chapel pleased many families, but some officers let me know via feedback that I was doing "too much" for the so-called lower ranks. The word was passed to me that they should get beer parties—no serious stuff.

In any case, it wasn't long before the chapel was busy every night with activities for all ranks, men and women, that went on until eleven or so. I also sought out each new family that came on the base to encourage them to join our programs. If parishioners missed Sunday services, I called to ask if anything was wrong and said I hoped I'd see them at the service the next Sunday. No doubt a few felt annoyed by this, but most didn't, and anyway it was my job to do it; the net was that regular attendance at services doubled.

My assistant Protestant chaplain, Joe Simpson, and the young Catholic chaplain who helped on scheduling, Paul Gerlock, grumbled just a bit about the pace but they were very good and conscientious men. They also went along when I aked them not to take days off to play golf and to do a minimum of social drinking on the base, so as to set an example. I told them they were, of course, not obligated to follow me as a teetotaler, but I felt it would help the image and effectiveness of our chaplain's service if they were moderate in this area. Paul was also every bit as ecumenically minded as Jim Doyle had been and was very helpful when I began programs for church-related family outings involving both Protestants and Catholics.

My programs at Cecil Field were noticed by church and civic organizations in Jacksonville, and I accepted invitations to speak before these groups and take part in some of their programs. This didn't go down too well with Captain John Danielson, senior chaplain at the Naval Air Station, Jacksonville, and the senior to all chaplains at satellite units such as Cecil Field. Word got back to me that the captain felt somehow upstaged by my participation in Jacksonville functions and by the many ongoing programs at Cecil. He dropped hints that he preferred the facilities at Cecil to his in Jacksonville. However, I always ignored the hints. Nobody said it then —that I'd be sorry later, or at least be made to pay. Meanwhile, I kept at it and wondered a bit—never out loud—about some of the activities Danielson might be involved in. During the week he lived alone at the bachelor officers quarters in Jacksonville—which usually was only to be used for visiting officers. His family was at Ocala, where he maintained a dairy farm, and where he would go only on weekends.

The strict schedule I put in to make maximum use of my time became extremely important because of the heavy load of counseling that had to be carried. Before I left Cecil Field, about 75 percent of my own schedule was taken up with counseling, much of which involved problems that seemed to come out of the rising new wave of open sexuality among Navy people around both Cecil Field and Jacksonville.

The so-called body-exchange shops near Cecil and in the Jacksonville area moved one town cynic to describe them as "Jacksonville's biggest growth industry." The officers' clubs, the chief petty officers' clubs, and the NCO clubs were rumored to be used as such shops. The action was fast. One officer told me that after meeting the wife of a civilian at one of the shops he had consummated the new relationship in less than a half hour, something in the fashion of New York's much publicized Eastside swinging singles bar.

Groups of officers and enlisted men were renting apartments for a variety of sexual activities. The beach-and-resort complex and the presence of so many Navy men were an attraction for girls from other parts of Florida, and from neighboring southern states, who were becoming sexual nomads, highly exploitable, as they left their homes at an early age and roamed through the Jacksonville area. Parties would start on Friday nights and go on throughout the weekends. The use of marihuana seemed relatively slight—mostly alcohol was the lubricant.

When one squadron would deploy, several wives of departed pilots would become regulars at the parties held at the apartments of bachelor officers. The PX's and the commissaries often served as meeting places where party arrangements were made. Some officers of a squadron that had remained behind at Cecil were openly moving in with wives from a squadron that had gone overseas or was assigned on a mission elsewhere. Some of the wives said they were sure their husbands, during weekend flying trips, had sexual relations with women in other cities and therefore they had the right to do likewise. But usually one heard of more wives cuckholding their husbands than vice versa. Women's "liberation"—in at least one narrow area—was having a field day. The double standard was in full retreat, if not routed.

The question remains—was anybody really happier, more fulfilled? I'd suggest not. For example, there were wives who broke down in remorse and guilt when they talked to me of their infidelities. But there were also others who discussed them with me with the apparent nonchalance of an announcer reading the weather report. The ones who were afflicted with guilt feelings usually wanted to know if they should confess to their husbands when they returned to the base. I usually suggested that they should not; my principal concern was to keep marriages intact. If a woman honestly felt she could take up again the role of faithful wife and mother when her husband came back, why should she subject both of them to a recital of her infidelity? Why risk an unnecessary break-up of a salvageable and in many real ways healthy marriage?

Of course in those instances when husbands heard rumors that seemed to have substance and demanded that the rumors be confirmed or denied, I would advise their wives to tell the truth and try for understanding, to openly work it out if possible.

My primary awareness of wife-swapping, "open" marriage, and the like was not based on gossip or rumor but came from actual counseling sessions. By this time I was probably more involved in marriage counseling than any other chaplain in the area and I had arranged, on my day off, to take an additional weekly course in clinical pastoral education. Yet nearly every day I listened to painful revelations beyond anything I had ever previously encountered or even imagined.

Captain Coleman did seem more interested than his predecessor in the programs we had going at the chapel as well as in the intensified counseling work. He said he'd recommend me for accelerated promotion to the rank of captain, but on the question of behavior at and around his base his approach struck me as being rather on the far side of the angels. I want to emphasize at this point that despite my built-in personal, professional, and deep opposition to erosions of the traditional moral codes, I am not—I hope—a holier-than-thou. But I also can't pretend to be what I am not. I do believe that more misery than meaningful liberation has resulted from the so-called new morality. That is partly why I speak at some length about the prevailing breakdown in the old codes among Navy personnel and others. My overriding reason, though, is to offer some insight into the probable motivation for the remarkable actions against me of certain of my colleagues and others in the military and the chaplaincy service. "Square Andy" was rocking the boat—out of conviction and without public broadcast. But to them he no doubt seemed a disruptive element, even a threat.

Take, for example, Captain Coleman. He had been married two times, and although he told Kathleen and myself that his second wife would soon be coming down from Washington to join him, she never appeared. Instead, he began seeing an attractive divorced woman, some twenty years his junior. She was at his home when Kathleen and I were invited there for dinner and a social gathering one evening in January, 1971. Following dinner, the C.O. brought out a suit bag and suitcase, and told all of us at the gathering to remain while he and his friend left. His parting comment, heard by several officers' wives, was, "I may be too old to fly but I'm not too old to R.O.N. (remain overnight)."

After this the captain and his friend were seen together often and it became apparent that she was spending time on weekends at his quarters. She indicated this herself in talks with Kathleen, and we often saw her car there early on Saturday mornings. Talk of the married C.O. and his lady friend became common around the base and I suspect it's reasonable to assume it lent encouragement to others involved in infidelity and experiments with "open marriage." The C.O. and his friend even signed in as "Mr. and Mrs." at the Navy Regional Wives Club social in the spring of 1971, although he was still married to his second wife.

Both Captain Coleman at Cecil Field and Admiral Geis in Jacksonville further gave a license to immorality, in my view, by approving the employment of Go-Go and "exotic" dancers at the officers' and EM's Clubs, some of whom performed in the nude.

I made numerous complaints about these goings-on; they were brushed aside. I especially protested the employment of the Go-Go dancers on the base—particularly after an incident in which one of them, while—as was not unusual—lounging about one of the swimming pools on the base during the day, bared her breasts to a young child approaching the pool. I was told that the girls boosted the sale of liquor at the clubs and thus helped the clubs meet their expenses! I also complained that at some of the squadron and departmental parties drinking went on to great excess and that alcoholic beverages were being served to persons under twenty-one. I tried to make clear that I was not making complaints simply on my own behalf, but that many decent families at Cecil Field were most concerned that the rising tide of immorality would take over their children and eventually cancel out their training in good moral behavior.

The response, in effect, was, "Why don't these people mind their own business?" The word to me personally was, "Stick to your preaching, chaplain, and don't make waves." When I suggested that the Naval Investigative Service could be used to investigate the situation and the commercialization of it, I was told, "The N.I.S. doesn't concern itself with such things unless somebody wants to bring specific criminal charges." I was told that the body-exchange shops in our areas had become so well-known that a couple of prominent figures in the defense establishment were coming down from Washington from time to time for personal "observation." The officer who told me this actually seemed to consider such visitations from on high an honor.

The question of adultery as a legal offense came up just once prior to the time it was raised against me. The case involved a group of sailors who had picked up the drunken wife of a civilian, driven her with her consent to their apartment, and had taken turns having intercourse with her. The woman's husband came to me and asked that the Navy prosecute the sailors on adultery charges. I told the civilian that I shared his outrage and that I deplored any violation of the commandment against adultery. However, I felt, as I always had, that social transgressions of this kind should not be the basis of criminal proceedings. I felt that much more should be done to discourage the atmosphere around naval bases that encouraged immoral practices and that we needed a concerted educational and spiritual drive to persuade people to live more by the moral concepts advanced by all our religious faiths. I still, though, didn't believe in handling cases on a criminal level where there had been mutual consent.

The civilian pressed the legal argument, however, so I took it up with Lt. Bob Ford, the Cecil Field legal officer. He told me, "There's no question of rape here, so we can't take this thing seriously. If the guy's wife wants to behave like a bum, that's her problem and his, not the Navy's. Civilian courts don't prosecute for adultery anymore. The law is a dead letter, for all practical purposes. So the Navy surely won't prosecute for such an offense. What does the guy want us to do—court-martial half the fleet?" (This was the same legal officer who, when directed by his superiors, would suddenly find that the regulation against adultery—when leveled against me—was no longer a "dead letter" but rather a heinous offense against Navy laws and traditions and deserved to be prosecuted to the hilt.)

I tried to devise more church-related programs and "family retreats" to counter the pleasures of the Go-Go shows and the body shops, but I really could do no more than I was already doing and even was having difficulty maintaining the schedules I had set for myself. I had never really recovered from the strain of those two years aboard the aircraft carrier, and I found myself increasingly subject to periods of exhaustion. My convenient home near the chapel became a virtual adjunct of the chapel office, with people constantly coming in and out to discuss their problems. Our phone was tied to the base phone system and it rang incessantly, even on Friday evenings, when we had always tried to maintain a private family night at home. I found that in the warm-weather months in Florida my allergies and asthma were particularly bad. Moderate physical exercise quickly wore me out. I was given EKG tests after nearly passing out a few times.

Dr. Roger Shetterley, the Navy doctor who treated me in the dispensary for exhaustion, was the first to urge me to get away from the base for short rest periods. He said if I couldn't manage a long rest leave, it was urgent for me to shut myself away from the local pressures for short "breathing spells" in order to avert a physical breakdown. He knew that as a chaplain with regular Sunday duties it would be difficult for me to take weekends off, but suggested I get away for a day, or even part of a day, whenever I could. He wrote down the names of motels spread out over this forty-mile Jacksonville resort area, especially those with pools that were shaded or kept open in the evenings. I had found swimming to be very relaxing for me, but my skin-cancer condition prevented me from swimming when the sun was out and our pool at the base was closed down in the evenings. The first motel Kathleen and I tried was the Ramada Inn, and we had such a restful day there that I decided to follow Dr. Shetterley's advice to take these short breaks as often as possible with Kathleen accompanying me whenever she could manage it.

Physical weakness wasn't my only handicap. The organization of our chaplain's office at Cecil Field had also been affected at this point by problems that had surfaced around Joe Simpson and Paul Gerlock. I hadn't known that Joe was dating a parishioner named Mary—who was married and whose husband was away at sea—until another parishioner complained about it to me. Shortly afterward, Mary's husband came back to Cecil Field and demanded an inquiry. When I took the subject up with the C.O. and the executive officer, it turned out that they had known of Joe's dates for some time. My predecessor as senior chaplain had also known but had never told me and had done and said nothing. Joe asked that I counsel him as his senior, and it developed that his case was distinctly not one of the cheap affairs that were common to our Naval environment. Joe and his wife had had marital problems for some time. Mary had also been unhappy in her marriage. She and Joe had fallen in love; they wanted to divorce their spouses and marry in an honorable way. The situation was, of course, complicated by the fact that Joe was a chaplain. Also heard voiced against him was that he had violated the unofficial Navy rule of "class" in his social associations—he was an officer and should never have taken up with Mary because she was an EM's wife, not an officer's wife!

Despite my disappointment over what had happened, I felt convinced that Joe was a conscientious chaplain and could still render good service at another base. Mary's husband kept pressing for disciplinary action, however, so at the C.O.'s suggestion, I flew to Washington for a meeting with the chief of chaplains. I found his attitude cold and callous. He indicated that when a chaplain became a source of trouble, the best thing was to get rid of him quickly (in retrospect it seems he was also talking about me) and not try to counsel him and salvage him for the use of his talents. Later a staff member would tell me that the chief held a grudge against me because I didn't bring formal charges against Joe, turn him over to the command, and have him thrown out. I might add that the chief seemed unconcerned about less talented, less conscientious chaplains who were far more flagrant and casual than Joe and who sought no honorable divorce and remarriage. As long as nobody else made their actions a source of official complaint to him, it didn't seem to bother him. Once a complaint was on his desk it became a problem, and the source of the problem—regardless of context and quality—was the object of official wrath.

The chief finally used a letter written directly to him by Mary's husband to ask for a line investigation himself and to bring the Naval Investigative Service into the picture. An N.I.S. agent who visited me at Cecil Field gave me the first inkling of how this service sometimes tries to manufacture a case once given its head by higher command. When I told the agent I could not tell him what had been confided to me by Joe in counseling—even though it was not in any way incriminating—he angrily accused me of trying to arrange a "cover-up." I also found he was trying to twist statements that I and others had given to him, in an effort to turn idle gossip into evidence.

Since the only information the N.I.S. had was that Joe had had several dates with Mary, and since no other accusations were made, the matter finally had to be dropped at that level. The chief had grudgingly allowed Joe to transfer to the Great Lakes Naval Training Station. But he'd made it plain that he had no more use for him as a chaplain, so Joe accepted an honorable discharge from the service and the chaplaincy and he and Mary did get their divorces and did marry. But a cloud continued to linger over our office.

The cloud grew with Paul Gerlock's departure. Paul confided to me that he disagreed with some of the tenets of his Roman Catholic doctrine—such as the prohibitions on various birth-control devices, which he felt too dogmatic and caused unhappiness and privation in some families. He also felt that the celibacy rule for priests was unwise and not even in accordance with the original Catholic faith—some of the early Popes, he told me, had been married men.

Paul began to date quietly but his situation as Catholic chaplain became untenable when he fell in love with a Navy widow at the base. He opted to leave the priesthood, go on to graduate school, and be married. His loss was accentuated by the fact that the replacement we eventually got just did not measure up to him, which added to my pressures and work load.

Joe Simpson's departure also created problems. His first replacement, Lt. Robert Hubbard, was a fine young chaplain, but he was soon ordered to Vietnam, and the man who followed him—Lt. Commander Hoyt Swann—was, in my opinion, highly ineffective. Swann was a Baptist from the south. He talked a great deal (mostly about sex and his desire for promotion) and apparently had little interest in his job. I'm not partial to the role of carping critic—especially with a colleague—but in Swann's case, there seemed little alternative. One of the early assignments I gave him was to visit in the EM's housing area to see if there were problems we could help with, and to encourage their increased attendance at our religious sessions. Weeks went by and he still had not gotten around to all the housing units. His personality also seemed to give the men a chill rather than a feeling of warmth. One chief told me our office was doing more harm than good in sending him around. When he took over a Sunday-school class or a devotional group, attendance always seemed to drop.

My stormiest session with Swann came just before I left on my fateful leave in Philadelphia–South Jersey, in August, 1971. A young pilot and his wife had asked to have their child baptized in our chapel during the week I would be away. As Baptists, neither Swann nor I performed the baptismal rite on babies, and I would usually ask Chaplain Richard Boyer at the Naval Aviation Training Center, who was Lutheran, to perform the service when we had a request for it. Usually we scheduled such baptisms on Mondays between three and seven P.M., but this particular couple was anxious to have it on Sunday because it was the only day the pilot's parents could attend. Swann arbitrarily refused the request to have the rite performed on Sunday. It so happened that the pilot's squadron commander was my friend and neighbor, Dick Coleman, so the pilot's young wife called Dick and Jeanine Coleman and asked that they intercede on their behalf.

When the Colemans relayed the request to me, I immediately told them that of course we'd have it done on Sunday, if that was their wish. I chewed Swann out for his captious treatment of the couple, reminded him that Dick Boyer had always been accommodating in the past and undoubtedly would oblige us now on a request for a Sunday baptism. "This couple doesn't even come to chapel," Swann argued. "I saw no reason for our office to go out of its way for them."

"We're here to give service," I told him. "Even if the people aren't regular parishioners, it's our business to accommodate them in their religious request."

Dick Boyer was as accommodating as I'd expected and performed the rite on a Sunday when I was away. A few months later Dick Coleman's squadron was deployed overseas and the young pilot was killed. If we had failed to serve him and his wife with this baptismal rite before his untimely death, it would have been an irremediable stain on my conscience; I suspect that for Swann the only unforgivable thing was the way I had dressed him down for his indifference.

Swann's consequent resentment of me, the apparent if rather wrongheaded—after all, he outranked me considerably—jealousy of Captain Danielson, the attitude of the Chief of Chaplains, the cloud over our chaplain's office at Cecil Field, my need for rest from my workload, and the climate of immorality in our Naval environment were all to become elements in the storm that was to strike me and my family without warning. Another factor, which seemed innocuous at first, was the arrival of a new executive officer at Cecil Field who came on the base with the announcement that he was going to "clean things up around here" and also meant to make a record that would insure his succession to C.O.

But the catalysts that precipitated the storm were the accusations brought against me by Mary Ann Curran and Lora Gudbranson.

CHAPTER 8

In the opening chapter I briefly sketched something of my relationship with these two women—as well as elements of their backgrounds that seemed to impinge on their accusations—at the same time that I told of the rush of events that was to change my life and my family's so drastically. It now becomes possible and, I think, appropriate to develop further some details that may throw additional light on their motives for bringing charges that seemed to compromise them as much as they maligned me.

I've already mentioned Lora's determined involvement in the affairs of our chapel, incongruously—to me at the time, at least—with her simultaneous advocacy to me of such arrangements as open marriage and outspoken disbelief in the tenets of Christianity. Her persistent use of these discussions to be around me culminated, about the time my wife was due to go to Philadelphia in July of 1971, in her making an unmistakable gesture toward me in my office which, as I've also said, I tried to handle in a fashion so as to discourage but not offend her. It seems obvious that I was something less than successful. She began calling at the office, and when I avoided her calls there she called me at home during the evenings with open invitations. On the Friday before the weekend of July 16 and 17, when Kathleen as well as Lora's husband were to be away, she called on Friday night to tell me she would put her children to bed early and invited herself over to our home. I thought my refusal was as firm as possible, but the next evening she repeated her suggestion and when this time I was even stronger in my reaction she made a threat to the effect that she would fix me. The threat developed into a promise to "destroy" me when she learned that I had heard of her and her husband's mate-swapping activities—despite the fact that I repeated over and over that I had no intention of publicly exposing them—however much I disapproved of what they and others were doing. I also assured her I had no interest in compromising in any way her husband's chances for promotion, which he and she were so concerned with. Again it seems that I failed to convince, and that Gudbranson's subsequent violent threats against me and Lora's involving herself in the scandalous charges she and Mary Ann brought against me were at least in part motivated by their fears that I would eventually publicly expose their behavior and jeopardize his career. It wasn't so much that their actions were a secret, but rather that if made officially public they would force the C.O., Captain Coleman to recommend against Gudbranson's promotion. It therefore may have seemed imperative to discredit me before I could make otherwise damaging accusations.

This I can say in retrospect. It was not so clear then, and certainly the likelihood that Lora would actually accuse me as she did never occurred to me when I went on leave. I simply refused to take her threats seriously, convinced as I was that nobody would believe anything she might say or do to compromise me. Clearly I underestimated the nature and degree of her anger—as I did that of Mary Ann Curran.

As I tried to indicate earlier, Mary Ann Curran communicated much more at the level of her emotions that Lora Gudbranson, and at her husband's request I became involved in marriage counseling with the Currans. Lt. Larry Curran came to see me about such counseling shortly after he was transferred to Cecil Field in the spring of 1970. He told me his wife was still in Beeville, Texas, winding up her duties as a nurse at a nursing home, and he was having difficulty reaching her. When she arrived at Cecil Field about two weeks later, she came in to see me and immediately proceeded to tell me that the reason her husband couldn't locate her and was upset about their marriage was that she had been having an affair with a man who had an interest in the nursing home and who came to Beeville from time to time to see her. She seemed amused by her husband's frustration in trying to locate her as well as by an incident in which she also managed gratuitously to frustrate her friend in Beeville. It was her first indication to me of her pleasure in manipulating men to their discomfort. Later she would be more explicit in her feelings about men, opening saying that she really hated them—as she apparently had hated her father for what seemed to her his mistreatment of her mother. As for her relations with her husband, she said that they were bizarre, that he was sadistic in achieving satisfaction with her.

Without attempting to find out the truth of her marital sex life, I did respond to her more prosaic complaints about lack of attention from Lt. Curran. I suggested to him that he try to open up more with his wife and to be more solicitous. He agreed that he would, but Mary Ann complained that he did not, and he, in fact, stopped coming to the counseling sessions. She continued them alone, and seemed to be making some progress. She decided that the man in Texas had merely been using her and she would not make such a mistake again. She took a job as director of nursing at Trowbridge Nursing Home in Jacksonville. For a while she and her husband came to church on Sundays, and during this period she became quite friendly with Kathleen. She said that since Kathleen had divorced parents and had grown up with her mother she too could understand what it was like to have a "bad father." As I have mentioned, she volunteered to help take care of our children when Kathleen was sick and in return we would allow her to stay a few nights when her husband was away as she seemed terrified of being alone.

It was after Mary Ann began her job at the Jacksonville nursing home that she and Lora Gudbranson apparently developed a close friendship. Lora had volunteered to become director of our missions projects and decided that visiting with the elderly people at the home would be a worthwhile project for the women of our chapel. She led a group on Thursdays to play bingo with the patients and generally socialize with them.

I knew from conversations with Lora and Mary Ann that they thought alike on such matters as sexual freedom and at the same time shared a highly moralistic attitude about the behavior of others. Mary Ann, as mentioned, was especially critical of the C.O.'s keeping company with a woman who was not his wife, and when her husband told her that the C.O. had shown interest in a go-go dancer she told me I should make an official complaint against him and have him relieved (apparently for her I was either God or—failing that—the Devil). Taking a similar high moral tone, Lora Gudbranson was one of the Navy wives especially critical of the C.O.'s conduct when he left the party at his home with his friend and announced he was going to "R.O.N."

By hindsight, Mary Ann's manipulative approach to men makes some incidents involving her seem somewhat more significant than they did at the time. For example, there was the night when she called me at the chapel with a long tale of woe about how her dog had been messing up in the house all day, she couldn't reach her husband, she had no cleaning gear, and her father refused to come over and help her. She said the dog was a German shepherd, that she'd like to get rid of him and wondered if somebody from the chapel wanted him. I happened to be counseling a young couple at the time and mentioned the dog to them. They were interested. Mary Ann called again a while later, still very upset. I told her there was choir practice that night—it was a Thursday night—but if it would help I would drop off some cleaning gear from the chapel after practice. When I got to her place with the cleaning gear, I found no mess; instead, I found she was loading up her car and wanted me to help. Larry Curran arrived soon after, doubtless and not unreasonably wondering why I was there. Later Mary Ann was to say I had come to her apartment to help her move out.

It was at about this time that in counseling sessions she told me she had become attracted to a young married doctor named John Blanc who had recently served in the Navy Medical Corps and had become visiting physician at the Trowbridge Nursing Home. She made it plain she was transferring the feeling she had had for her lover in Texas to this doctor. At the same time she told me sex was most satisfying to her when she visualized herself being in bed with a woman instead of a man. As a young girl she rarely dated or went out socially because, she said, she felt more at ease with girls than boys. She talked again about her pleasure in manipulating men attracted to her and how she used men.

As mentioned, I have never considered myself an expert in psychiatry despite my counseling experience, but I could recognize the symptoms of somebody with strong homosexual inclinations camouflaging them both to themselves and the outside world by a display of heterosexual relationships—including flagrant extramarital displays. This might, I decided, help explain Mary Ann's quick—even boastful—early recital to me in counseling of her affair in Texas and her approval of open sex.

Still, along with my limited insight was the realization that I was clearly out of my field in trying to counsel her further and so I recommended a psychiatrist—at which point she promptly erupted with indignation. There followed my attempt to reassure her that mine was only a suggestion, hardly a prescription obligating her; my proposal that she and her husband see a family counseling service in Jacksonville, which she accepted as preferable to the stigma—by her lights—of seeing a psychiatrist; my formal referral to the counseling service in July of 1970, after which I no longer acted as her counselor; and separation, during which she moved first to a motel and then an apartment, and her husband took up residence at the bachelor officers' quarters—a rupture precipitated, she insisted on telling me in detail, by her commencement on Sunday, August 9, of an actual affair with the young doctor. Despite the fact that I was no longer counseling her, she would call and tell me such intimate details and demand emergency appointments at the chapel, during one of which she told me she suspected the doctor was using her, her marriage counselor in Jacksonville was of no help, and she was certain her husband was ignorant of her affair, being "too dumb to be able to find out on his own." It was at such times that she told about being intimate with friends of her husband as well as drug-supply salesmen who called at the nursing home where she worked. After each of these revelations she warned that I was not to disclose anything she said or let the doctor or her husband find out she was seeing other men (which, considering her behavior, seemed rather ironic).

In first talking about her relations with the doctor, she said they were characterized by the same abusive treatment of her as those with her former lover in Texas. Again, I am no psychiatrist, but the pattern seemed fairly clear: Mary Ann apparently was unable to handle her anger against her father, felt so guilty about it that she used substitute fathers to punish herself, thinking all the while that she was manipulating them, whereas she was being manipulated by emotions she could neither understand nor even acknowledge. But the hate was there, along with the guilt, and she seemed determined to make them pay and pay.

Mary Ann was especially concerned about the doctor. She said he had already become suspicious of her because somebody identifying himself as "Dr. Santos" had called Dr. Blanc's office numerous times asking for her. She also said that the caller had once left a number which the doctor had discovered was a public phone at the bachelor officers' quarters. Since her husband was staying there and most of the help was of Spanish descent, I suggested to her that it was possible the caller was her husband using the name of one of the stewards. She dismissed this, saying that her husband was too naïve to be suspicious. (Later she was to testify that *I* had made those calls as Dr. Santos.)

Dr. Blanc shortly thereafter became busy on the phone as well. He actually called our home one evening asking to speak to me. When Kathleen told him I was not home he suddenly became abusive and suggested I had been in a mental hospital. After I arrived home he called again and said something to the effect that if I knew what was good for me I would keep my mouth shut about him and Mary Ann, that I was not just dealing with her now but with somebody who could make a great deal of trouble for me if I should ever talk about them.

Apparently Mary Ann had told the doctor she had confided in me about their relationship, which understandably upset him and prompted his phone call. As for her motive, I can only surmise it was of a piece with other behavior in which she seemed determined to play one man against another, to manipulate, to take revenge. In any case, I called her the next day to tell her of Dr. Blanc's threatening calls and that I would stand for no more of them, that I would, if necessary, make a complaint to the phone company. In retrospect this seems a bit foolhardy, but I was especially upset because of the way his calls had frightened Kathleen.

Mary Ann eventually decided that not only was the doctor using her but that he had no intention of leaving his wife for her, even after she had begun divorce proceedings aganist her husband, apparently with such expectations firmly in mind. By November, in fact, she had told Kathleen that she had decided to go back to her husband and wanted to thank me for working so hard to reconcile them. I suspected the reconciliation was on rather flimsy grounds—her sense of rejection by Dr. Blanc—but I took it at face value until a few months later when she called to say she was having "problems" again. The problems were that she was seeing Dr. Blanc once again and was being used by him again.

She herself was no longer working at Trowbridge Nursing Home, having left, she said, because of the administration there. Most serious, she told me that she had gone past the stage of visualizing sexual relations with a woman while with a man and had in fact had become close with a woman whose husband was overseas. She mentoined the motels they went to and her appreciation of this relationship.

I again recommended a psychiatrist—though more strongly than the first time—and her reaction was more extreme than the first time. She accused me of wanting to shame and destroy her and said that "I'll destroy you first." (One remembers such words, especially in the context of accusation and trial.) Despite my assurances to the contrary, she seemed convinced that I would—if I hadn't already—betray her confidences. Instead of her civilian counselor, whom she said reminded her of her father, it was now Chaplain Jensen who did so. She said I sat and lectured her as if I were Jesus Christ himself and that if she got into trouble she would "blame everything on good old Chaplain Jensen."

It seemed that her greatest concern was a public revelation of her lesbian tendencies—something which I certainly did not condemn her for and had no intention of revealing—and that she would go to any lengths to offset such disclosure. In a sense, her concern was realistic. The Navy might be indifferent to "normal" infidelity, but homosexuality was considered a social stigma. Further, a nurse thought to be homosexual would have great difficulty finding a job. What was unrealistic about her concern was her worry that under the circumstances I would betray her confidence. When I did finally speak up, it was for the sole purpose of defending myself and my family against destruction by her false accusations.

Despite her threats and opposition to the notion of a psychiatrist, Mary Ann did seriously consider psychiatric treatment. When she said she was concerned about the cost, I told her that under a Navy medical program 80 percent of the expenses would be covered by the government. This, together with my urging that she be good to herself and get the best help possible seemed to calm her some and by the time I was about to go on my leave she had promised she would take advantage of the Navy program.

The fact that Mary Ann's threats came at about the same time as Lora Gudbranson's had no significance for me, and I regarded them no more seriously than I had Lora's. The reason for my miscalculation was basically the same in both instances—I simply could not believe anybody would seriously listen to any compromising accusations made against me. I believed this not out of any smug sense of the absurdity that I felt and which I assumed others would share at the notion of Andy Jensen being involved in such wild happenings. To them I would surely not be the type, if they knew me at all. To myself, it was ludicrous and impossible.

It was to take time and the perspective of hindsight before I perceived the common interest in my being disgraced and discredited shared by such disparate people as fellow chaplains, naval officers, a civilian doctor, and two women whose motives singly and together were uniquely their own.

CHAPTER 9

After hearing that Mary Ann and Lora had actually signed the formal charges against me, Kathleen decided to return immediately with me to Florida. She felt that if we could both have it out with them they might be shamed into withdrawing their charges.

She was also very worried about Commander Gudbranson. I tried to make light of his threats and argued that Gudbranson had been making them for theatrical effect. Actually I was nearly as worried as she was. Gudbranson had the reputation of being a drinker and, as I've mentioned, his loud arguments with his wife were the subject of gossip around the base.

As we drove to the airport, Kathleen said, "Andy, I've got an awful premonition that he knows you're coming down on the plane today and he'll be waiting at the Jacksonville airport with a gun."

I tried to reassure her. "He has no idea we're coming back today and he wouldn't be standing around at a public airport with a gun anyway."

While waiting for our plane, I suddenly decided to call the judge I knew in Jacksonville and ask his advice about legal representation.

The judge advised that I immediately get a competent civilian attorney in Jacksonville to represent me in any dealings with the command at Cecil Field, and warned me that I couldn't know what they might be hatching or what sort of legal trap they might set up for me. He gave me the names of a few Jacksonville attorneys who were well versed in criminal law and recommended that I talk to one of them before setting foot back on the base.

When Kathleen and I got to the Jacksonville airport, we both glanced around for Gudbranson, then almost laughed at one another for giving in to jumpy nerves. I called the first lawyer on the judge's list, and although he was in court, his partner told me to drive out to their office. We had left our car with friends before going on leave, and so we rented a car and reached the office in fifteen minutes. It turned out to be a brief and disappointing session. The partner said he knew very little about military law and had no interest in taking on the case. However, he did make one useful suggestion as we were leaving. "If you're as innocent as you say, ask your naval authorities to give you a lie-detector test."

Kathleen immediately agreed that this could be the quickest and simplest way for me to establish my innocence and avoid the nightmare of a public scandal. *We* at least knew I was telling the truth and that Mary Ann Curran and Lora Gudbranson were lying. If the three of us were put to a lie-detector test and if the test were properly run, the charges would have to be withdrawn. I called the exec officer to let him know that I insisted on my legal right to go to my quarters on the base and that I would gladly submit to an examination by lie detector.

I might as well have been talking into the wind. I absolutely could not go on the base at least until the C.O. returned and had a chance to study the whole question. Didn't I have sense enough to realize the order was for my own protection? Commander Gudbranson, he said, was "wild and uncontrollable" and his threat to kill me was very real. But why wouldn't he take any action to restrain and disarm Gudbranson, I wanted to know. My question was brushed off with the intimation that an aggrieved husband has a moral right to avenge himself. And my request to submit to the lie detector was also brushed off. It seemed obvious I was dealing with a man who believed without question that a chaplain accused of such misconduct must *ipso facto* be guilty.

I felt as if the ground had fallen away from under my feet. The idea of going out to the base, of facing down my accusers, and of convincing them to take back their words no longer seemed practical. The exec had made it plain that Gudbranson was still waiting out there for me and that the law would not be brought in to stop him. We decided to check into a local motel and try to figure out what to do next.

Kathleen and I both desperately felt the need to talk to people we thought might throw new light on this whole business whether they were sympathetic or not. First I called my assistant, Hoyt Swann. I reached him at choir practice and the first thing he said was that he'd been praying for me, that he was still shocked over the whole thing. Then he added that it looked very bad for me, and that if I wasn't going to resign, I'd better get a very good lawyer.

His attitude infuriated Kathleen even more than myself, and she took the phone away from me. "Chaplain Swann, do you *really* think Andy could have done anything like this?" she demanded. He said he didn't know, that he didn't have anything to do with it and that it wasn't the chaplains who were pushing the matter but Mrs. Gudbranson and her husband. "By the way, Kathleen," he finished, "how are the kids?" She blew her stack at him.

I took the phone back and could hear Swann still protesting that he was praying for me and had no information about how the whole thing had started. "You and the other chaplains know more than you're letting on," I told him. "I already know that John Danielson and Lew Allred are involved in this thing. You knew what was happening and you didn't have the decency to let me know about it."

"I was sworn to secrecy. I couldn't say anything. I'm still praying for you." I hung up.

"Let's call Chaplain Elliott in Pensacola. He was at the chaplains' conference along with Allred. Maybe he knows something about this," I said.

Elliott knew all about it. He told me he was well aware of the dangerous role neurotic women could play in the church. He and several other chaplains were angered by Allred's gossiping about me during the chaplains' conference. It was Allred, he said, who had told Admiral Francis Garrett, the Navy's Chief of Chaplains, about it, and Garrett, I learned later, had recommended that the command investigate me rather than have the case handled as an ecclesiastical matter.

I also was able to make contact with Paul Gerlock, the Catholic chaplain who had served with me at Cecil Field until he decided to leave the priesthood. He was stunned when I gave him the news. "I could sooner believe that the Pope had gotten married!" he told me.

There were also words of reassurance and support from Chaplain Ronal Mudd, the civilian chaplain at the Methodist Hospital in Jacksonville. And Mudd was able to help me get legal representation. He knew a couple of young lawyers in Jacksonville who practiced from a storefront office and were interested in civil liberties. One of them was named Lyman Fletcher.

Lyman Fletcher turned out to be a tall, personable young man with eyeglasses, long hair, and a generally so-called mod appearance. He saw me as the underdog against the establishment and he would go all out for me. We agreed that he would get a fee of thirty dollars per hour for his time. He was not well versed in military law and procedures, however, and so it would be necessary for me to get military counsel if the command pressed for a formal investigation. But he didn't think the case would get that far. He felt that the command would come to its senses and realize how ludicrous it would look to try a chaplain for alleged adultery committed off the base. Adultery and fornication were so common around Naval bases that he found it hard to imagine that the Navy would start bringing such cases to trial. He felt he could talk to the two women who had accused me and convince them to withdraw their charges.

"Once they realize that you're not going to be scared into a resignation, that you've got a lawyer and are going to defend your legal rights, they're going to have second thoughts about this whole thing," he said. "And even if they don't, their husbands certainly will." He would make them understand, he said, that to make a legal case against me they would have to proclaim themselves publicly as adulteresses. He couldn't imagine them willing to expose themselves like that. And once they charged me publicly, I would be free to disclose everything they had ever confided to me in private counseling sessions.

Kathleen pressed him to tell us what would happen if the women and the command refused to back down and did force a court-martial. He looked at us for a moment and then acknowledged that would be very bad. He said that from all he knew about military courts-martial, the accused had very little chance. The military judge was beholden to the command and so were the officers who served as the jury. Any military counsel who would be assigned to me served under the Staff Judge Advocate of the command and was dependent on him for recommendations for promotion. If he cared about his career and didn't want to play hero, he'd give me a weak defense. Fletcher said that the records would show that when the command wants a court-martial, it gets a conviction nearly every time.

He could see that both of us were upset and quickly added that no matter what his opinion of the court-martial system, he was confident that my case would never reach court-martial. "They court-martial people for rape, or assault, for failing to salute, or maybe for refusing to obey an order, but they don't court-martial for adultery."

Fletcher suggested that we fly back to New Jersey and wait at least until the commanding officer got back. We did, but I kept talking about the case so much to my brother-in-law and sister-in-law that I finally had to apologize. I called Fletcher twice, and went out to the Philadelphia Navy Yard to consult with the Navy lawyer I mentioned before. He repeated his belief that the O'Callahan decision would act as a bar to a court-martial.

Luckily for me, another Navy lawyer at the Yard that day knew the people at the law center at the Jacksonville Naval Air Base, which would have jurisdiction over my case if it stayed with the military. When he heard what I'd been charged with, he found it hard to believe. He warned me not to accept an inexperienced, promotion-minded young lieutenant as my military defense counsel. "Try to get a lieutenant-commander named Charles Pope to represent you," he advised. Pope was an outstanding trial lawyer, he said, with a good deal of experience in both civilian and navy courts. And he had recently been passed over for promotion to commander, so he would have no hopes for future promotion and no compunctions about taking on the command.

I received word that the C.O. was due back at the base that night. Kathleen asked Frank if he would fly down and help us convince the C.O. of my innocence. She felt that as a minister, his testament to my character and moral conduct would carry some weight.

When we arrived in Jacksonville I went through the same ritual of calling the exec and demanding permission to return to our home on the base. I told him that Kathleen and I were back with the children this time and that my brother-in-law was with us. He told me to call back in an hour so he could discuss this with the C.O. On my second call he told me that I could go back but that the command would take no responsibility for protecting me against Gudbranson. And I was to report to the C.O.'s office the first thing in the morning.

No sooner had we opened the front door of our house than the war of nerves began again. A light went on immediately in the Gudbransons' house across the street. We had hardly unpacked when the phone rang. When I answered it, I heard nothing except heavy breathing and then a click. A few minutes later it rang again and Kathleen grabbed it. Again there was nothing. The phone rang six more times that night. Each time we answered, the same thing happened.

Frank wanted to know what my relationship had been with the C.O. I told him that, unlike Captain Shute, he at least knew me. I also pointed out to Frank that the C.O. was a man with a tangled marital history. I mentioned that I had restrained some Navy wives who wanted to make it public that he was going with a woman who was not his wife.

"Well, in view of all that, he can hardly sit in moral judgment, especially not against *you.* He's got to take your word against the word of two apparently neurotic women," Frank said.

As Frank and I entered the passageway to Captain Coleman's office at eight the next morning, we came face-to-face with Gudbranson. He was with Chaplain Swann. I stopped, unable to control a tingling sensation of fear. I looked at his hands, perhaps expecting to see a gun, but the show of violence was in his words. As I looked away and went past him, he muttered, "You dirty son-of-a-bitch." Swann, in his fashion, called out, "Good morning, Andy. How are Kathleen and the kids?"

The C.O. was with Lt. Bob Ford, a young legal officer at Cecil Field.

"You've been charged with adultery and sex offenses with the wives of two of our officers, Jensen," Captain Coleman said. "The executive officer, with my approval, has requested a full investigation by the N.I.S."

I answered by telling him that I was innocent of the charges, that I had never been involved with either of these women, and that I had had a good record during all my years of Naval service.

"That's in the past, Jensen. What concerns us now are these

charges. You'll have a chance to defend yourself during the investigation. You can request any lawyer you choose from the legal staff at N.A.S., Jacksonville."

"I've asked a civilian attorney to represent me," I told him. That angered him. He probably expected me to go along with the command, not rock the boat. "I would like to talk to you alone and in private, man to man," I said. "You can only talk to me officially, and anything you say can be used against you," was his reply.

"Then I'd like officially to request a lie-detector test," I said.

"The results of lie-detector tests are not acceptable in courts of law so there's no point in your taking it," he said. He went into a tirade about how he'd expected this, his last hour of duty, to be smooth and harmonious and how I was "messing it up." It seemed clear to me that he had already prejudged the case against me in the interests of his own comfort. He kept calling me "Jensen," not "Andy" and not "Commander." I brought my brother-in-law in to speak for me, and Frank told him that he believed my character was above reproach and that he knew as a minister that there were disturbed women who often made false charges against clergymen.

The C.O. heard him out without interruption but without indication that he was accepting any of what Frank was saying. I told him I wanted to see just what evidence Lora and Mary Ann were offering against me. The C.O. acknowledged that he hadn't had a chance to look at the evidence himself, but after a glance from the legal officer he insisted that the exec and the legal officer had gone over the sworn statements carefully and that the women were very specific about their charges.

No evidence was shown to me that day, but later on I was allowed to look at copies of the statements the women signed on August 11th. I read Mary Ann's first:

> I, Mary Ann Curran, make this sworn statement voluntarily. I first met Chaplain Andrew Jensen on 5/12/70. My husband had gotten him as a counselor for both of us, since at this time we were having marital problems. He counselled both my husband and myself frequently. Some time about the end of July he took me into the other chaplain's office (I had come for counseling) and proceeded to kiss me, saying, 'how did this happen to us?' I never knew this was going to happen or that I had enticed him whatsoever. The relationship continued, as

I became emotionally involved. (I don't think I need go into the details.)

Dates of my involvement:

Aug. 12th, 13th, 14th—Gator Lodge
Aug. ——? Jamaica Lodge
" Fox Meadow Apt.
" Holiday Inn at the airport
Sept. Carriage House Apts., University Blvd.
Jan.-March (approx.) Ramada Inn, airport (this could be April and May)
Airport Inn
April-May-June Howard Johnson's Golfair

I was also given a key to the chapel, which I returned in December.

During this relationship, I left my husband and lived with him for two weeks in August while his wife was gone to Philadelphia. He told me he would leave his wife in a year.

The relationship continued until Aug., 1971. There were various times I tried to break it up and failed to do so, due to the emotional involvement."

Mary Ann Curran
8/11/71

On the bottom of the page there was a notation that the statement had been witnessed by "Hoyt M. Swann, LCDR. Chap. Corps, U.S.N." My assistant chaplain, who had pretended to know nothing about the charges until the exec officer had told him about them, who had not called me on his own to let me know what was happening, had accepted this statement and witnessed it without any attempt to question Mary Ann Curran or to see proof.

It was apparent that Mary Ann had picked the names of motels and dates or approximate dates from the information my wife had given her when she had told her about my visits to motels on doctor's orders. The Fox Meadow and Carriage House Apartments were places where she had lived when she separated from her husband. It also seemed obvious that she was substituting me for the man she had actually had an affair with—Dr. John Blanc of Jacksonville—when she wrote, "He told me he would leave his wife in a year." She had mentioned that affair often enough in our counseling sessions.

I then read Lora Gudbranson's statement:

I, Lora Gudbranson, certify that this statement is voluntarily made.

Cdr. Andrew F. Jensen and I met when he and his wife first reported aboard Cecil Field in February of 1970. Beginning soon afterwards, Cdr. Jensen would telephone often and regularly invite me into his office to talk. The relationship became closer as time went by. Sometimes Cdr. Jensen would call me at the Environmental Coordinating Office where I am a volunteer. Twice he came there. He sometimes invited me to meet him somewhere for lunch. I did not meet him at those times.

The relationship culminated in sexual relations between us finally—once in May at the Howard Johnson Motel on Golfair Boulevard, once in June at the Gator Lodge on Phillips Highway, and twice at his quarters in July—once on July 16 and once on July 17.

At no time did I approach Cdr. Jensen in any professional capacity as a counselor or advisor. I make this statement only in the hope that he will not be able to carry on the same activities as a Navy Chaplain in the future."

Lora Evelyn Gudbranson (Aug. 11, 1971)

Witnessed by:
Hoyt W. Swann
LCDR. CHC, USN

Here again were the names of motels and approximate dates that had been learned from Kathleen. But I was stunned at Lora Gudbranson's saying she had sexual relations with me in my house. "Can you believe this?" I said to Frank. "She picks dates when Kathleen was away but she says we carried on an affair right in the house—a house that's always been so open that everybody knows when the chaplain is there, and where people from the chapel come in and out all the time! What kind of fool would I have been to do such a thing there? How could I possibly have thought it would go unnoticed? What kind of minds do these men have—the exec, Swann, the C.O. and the rest—to *believe* such garbage?"

Frank shook his head and said, "Your C.O. no doubt thinks this reflects on his command. But his attitude toward you will have to change when he finally learns what kind of women he's dealing with. He'll *have* to accept the truth."

CHAPTER 10

The encounter with the C.O. was followed by more bad news. I called Lyman Fletcher to tell him what happened and learned that his attempt to "talk sense" to Mary Ann Curran and Lora Gudbranson had ended in failure. When he called Mary Ann, she told him, "It's in the hands of the N.I.S. and the command," and would not discuss the matter further. Lora had launched a tirade against me, claiming I was "dangerous," could destroy a lot of people, and had to be put out of the Navy. If it was necessary to go to a public court-martial to get rid of me, she would be ready, willing, and able to do it and it didn't matter what she would have to admit about herself.

Fletcher warned me not to say anything to her or Mary Ann if I ran into them. "People like this will twist and distort anything you say to them, no matter how innocent your comment may seem to you," he cautioned. He also told me to say as little as possible to the command and to the chaplains working with the command and to let my legal representative do the talking for me. He suggested that the C.O. had now made it plain that he too was unsympathetic. He also suggested that I try to have somebody with me wherever I went in case they tried to entrap me in a compromising situation.

Fletcher agreed that the circumstances now made it necessary for me to get a military counsel. I decided to call on the legal officer whose name had been recommended to me in Philadelphia—Lieutenant Commander Charles Pope. I went over to the chapel first to take out my current appointment book, my old appointment books, and my monthly calendars. I felt I would need these records to help establish my innocence. I had always been meticulous in setting down dates, times, and events in my records and diaries, though I never dreamed I would have to use them to help prove my innocence of a crime.

I asked Frank to come with me to Pope's office in the Jacksonville law center. Instead of waiting for the receptionist, who had stepped away from her desk, I barged right into the inner office with Frank following behind me. A short, stocky, red-faced man in his early forties looked up at me in surprise.

Here are some notes Pope wrote describing that first meeting:

> Chaplain Jenson first came to my office at the Law Center at N.A.S., Jacksonville, on August 17, 1971, accompanied by his brother-in-law, Frank Lamania. I had no idea who either of them were. I knew Chaplain Jensen was a chaplain by reason of the cross insignia on his shirt collar. Perhaps this is why I did not question the fact that he came in unannounced and without an appointment. This was fortunate for him. If I had known in advance about the purpose of his visit, I would have asked Captain Bob Lee, the Staff Judge Advocate, and he would have told me not to discuss anything with Chaplain Jensen and I never would have been his attorney. As it was, before I knew what was happening, he had told me substantially all that he knew about the case.
>
> When he first began talking about the two women and their accusations, I thought he was talking about somebody else. Chaplains occasionally would come to see me for legal advice regarding men whom they were counselling, and I assumed at first that this was what Chaplain Jensen was doing. When it dawned on me that it was actually he, himself, who was involved, I was flabbergasted. Here before me was a relatively short, wan, not unpleasant-looking, rather kindly fellow of my own age—43. He seemed an unlikely person for the exploits he was being charged with, hardly strong enough. And yet two women had come forward at the same time to accuse him. That such accusations would be made by women at all stupefied me. And how could they ever do so unless what they said was true? My reaction (to what he was telling me) was, I suppose, the natural one: he must have done it because the women said that he did. . . . So I addressed myself to him along purely legal grounds and stated that, in my opinion, the military had no jurisdiction over his alleged offenses. My first advice to him was, don't worry. . . . As it later turned out, the "don't worry" advice

was bad advice indeed. . . . Had I, and others associated with his defense, had any inkling of what lay ahead it might have led us to visit the local psychiatrist. . . .

When I say that it is fortunate for Chaplain Jensen that he came to see me unannounced, thereby committing me to his defense, I mean to imply no self-adulation. I only mean to say that, looking back on the entire case, I am absolutely certain that I was the only attorney in the area at that time who could have given him the type of representation that he needed. I say this because of many reasons: First of all, I had returned to the Navy within the past five years after extensive civilian practice in law. I also had experience as a newspaper reporter and was able to give Chaplain Jensen a sophisticated view on the matter of publicity, which disturbed him greatly. I was able to reassure him that unless the matter got to the court-martial stage, he need not be concerned about any publicity.

In addition, I had been passed over for promotion from lieutenant commander to commander and felt that my future in the Navy was nil. As a result, I had no fear of any effect that a spirited defense of Chaplain Jensen might have on my career. I have to make this point in all honesty. There are those who have made reference to my courage and determination in the Jensen case. However, I must say that while I did all that I did with sincerity and conviction in his cause and while I believe I would have done the same even if my promotional chances had been good, I still must admit that I had little to lose.

The "don't worry" advice that Pope gave me was based on the precedent of the O'Callahan case—the same case that the legal officer at the Philadelphia Navy Yard had cited to me. The O'Callahan case had established that any offense committed in a civilian setting or that did not relate to a military function or activity could not be prosecuted in a military court by military authorities.

But why, I wanted to know, were both the exec officer and the C.O. threatening me with a court-martial? They perhaps weren't aware of the O'Callahan case precedent, Pope said. He also said he would see that they were made aware of it. Also, they were undoubtedly enraged by charges that a respected chaplain in their command was involved with officers' wives and wanted to make things as rough as possible for me so that I would resign. But they couldn't legally force me to resign.

I told Pope that I had asked the young civil liberties lawyer, Lyman Fletcher, to represent me for a thirty-dollars-an-hour fee for whatever time he put in. He suggested that I continue this arrangement with Fletcher, and that in the event the case went on longer than he expected, Fletcher would do some of the legal research that he wouldn't have time for. He explained that he had a good deal of legal work to handle at the Law Center and would only be able to devote a limited amount of time to me.

Pope told Frank and me to wait while he went in to the Staff Judge Advocate to tell him that I had come to see him about my case, that he was interested in it and had agreed to act as my military counsel. When he returned a few minutes later he said, "I'm afraid I jumped too fast. My superior doesn't want me to represent you—says I have too many other things to do."

I told him that Captain Coleman had said I could have any military counsel I chose. "I've been falsely acused, humiliated, threatened with murder. . . . How much more do I have to take? I have nearly seventeen years of service, a clean record, commendations—"

My outburst seemed to startle Pope and persuaded him to go back to Captain Lee's office. When he returned the second time, he had better news for me.

"I pointed out to my boss that based on all the things you've told me about your case, I've already given you some preliminary legal advice," he said. "I therefore couldn't have anything to do with your case other than as a defense counsel and he's agreed that since I've gone this far, I might as well become your counsel. He's going to let your C.O. know that I'm representing you. The Staff Judge Advocate, though, is very upset about your case," he told me frankly. "He feels you must have been involved with these two women, otherwise they would never have come forward and accused you. And he feels that such behavior by a chaplain is reprehensible." (I could understand the reaction, but I won't pretend it didn't anger me, especially since my disapproval of such behavior hardly stopped with chaplains.)

Pope went on to say that he subscribed to a different standard of morality. He felt that any chaplain or clergyman had the same right as any other man to "screw around" and "take his pleasures where he finds them," so long as he didn't force himself on anybody or take advantage of anybody who was ignorant or under-age. The implication, of course, was that I'd been taking such pleasures.

I told him as forcefully as I could that I had never touched either of these two women and that I had never committed adultery with anyone. "I'm not only legally innocent of these charges they've brought. I believe I'm innocent morally and ethically too. And I'm not saying this because my wife's brother, who also happens to be a minister, is here with me. I'm saying it because it happens to be the truth."

Pope smiled. "Look, Chaplain, if I'm going to be your lawyer, I feel you should level with me. I want you to tell me everything, even though things that are told me in confidence will never be disclosed to your detriment." He went on to say that he was a graduate of Notre Dame, had a brother who was a priest, and had a close friendship with many priests. He said he knew that some of them drank heavily and even had affairs with women, but he did not blame them even though this violated the edicts of his church. "Priests are human beings and are entitled to human pleasures," he said. He was sure many Protestant ministers behaved the same way and no doubt some rabbis too. He went on to quote passages from Shakespeare and Shaw about the weaknesses of the flesh and the sexual temptations that man cannot resist.

"When you say that *some* clergymen can't or won't resist sexual temptations you're right, of course, but it's wrong to generalize. Anyway, it just *doesn't* apply in my case," I said.

"All right, Chaplain, I'm not going to doubt your word." But I felt he still didn't believe me.

He went on to explain that the investigation by the N.I.S. was for the purpose of gathering evidence and statements for an "Article 32" investigation. That is a procedure similar to a grand jury hearing in civilian courts. At the end of the "Article 32," the hearing officer reports whether he feels that a *prima facie* case has been made and a court-martial should be convened. A report that a *prima facie* case has been made is equivalent to an indictment handed up by a civilian grand jury. An indictment usually leads to trial. In the military, the decision to convene a court-martial (trial) is up to the commanding officer, who presumably bases his decision on the hearing officer's recommendation. Since Cecil Field is under Commander, Fleet Air Jacksonville, the final decision on a court-martial rests with that Commander, who at that time was Rear Admiral

Lawrence R. Geis. If the Article 32 investigation resulted in a recommendation for court-martial, and if the C.O. at Cecil Field approved it, then the admiral would probably give final approval.

"But based on what you've told me, I'm confident—as I told you before—that this thing will be shot down long before it gets to such an advanced stage," Pope said. He also assured me that N.I.S. investigations and Article 32 investigations are kept secret and that there was no danger that the charges against me ever would be made public unless a court-martial was ordered.

When I left Pope's office I was convinced I was getting a good legal advocate but I was still disturbed that he did not believe me. When I got home, I found Kathleen nearly hysterical. Anonymous phone calls had come in about every fifteen minutes or so, with no sound on the other end except breathing, and then the click. Even as Kathleen was describing these calls, another one came in. I picked up the phone, and when there was only silence I shouted, "Who are you and why are you doing this to us? We're going to notify the authorities!"

It was an empty threat, of course, and both Kathleen and I knew it. "The authorities are on *their* side, not ours," Kathleen said. She was upset not only by the phone calls but also by the report I had given her of the C.O.'s attitude. She had counted, even more than I had, on the belief that he would support me or at least authorize a lie-detector test.

I called the switchboard operator at the base to complain about the calls and to find out where they came from. She listened in on the next call and reported that it had not come from the outside but had been made from somewhere on the base. But she had no way of stopping these calls or of finding out who was making them.

During the next few days, the pressures on Kathleen and myself mounted. First Danielson called me to his office and said that Chaplain Ralph Hopkins, Staff Chaplain, Naval Air Force, Atlantic Fleet, had come down and wanted to see me. Kathleen and Frank went with me. With both of them sitting there, Danielson said, "Let's face it, your effectiveness at this station is over. You're going to have to move no matter how the command investigation turns out." He also said that he and the Navy's Chief of Chaplains, Admiral Francis Garrett, had pressed the command to make a full investigation of the charges against me. His explanation was, "If you're innocent, this is the one sure way to prove it."

Frank demanded to know if he turned in every charge against a chaplain to the command for an investigation instead of first checking the charges out with all parties and then handling it on an ecclesiastical level. He also wanted to know if he hadn't heard of cases of unstable women who invent accusations against clergymen. Danielson agreed that there was something in what Frank said, then added, "The charges in this case are far more serious than anything I've heard of before. They were so serious they had to be turned over to the command. Besides, Lew Allred had been informing me for weeks what Mrs. Curran was saying about you before it was decided that something had to be done."

(We later found out from official records that Allred, the chaplain Mary Ann Curran had seen at the Navy hospital in Jacksonville, had had only two sessions with her and just a week before the charges were made. We also learned that Danielson had been to the C.O.'s office at Cecil Field that very morning to urge that the investigation against me be "pressed hard, to the court-martial stage if need be," and that "nothing should be swept under the rug.")

Danielson said that the Chief of Chaplains had assigned him to act as my pastor in this case and that I could confide in him. Here was a chaplain determined to have me prosecuted and yet seeking confidences from me by acting as my minister. I told him that even though I had nothing to hide, I had been advised by counsel not to discuss the case with him. He and Chaplain Hopkins became upset at this. When the meeting ended, Danielson said he'd been told to assign me to an office. It turned out to be more of a warren than an office.

Later that day I headed back to the Chapel at Cecil Field to see if there were any more records and papers I might need to take. I saw several N.I.S. agents on the grounds. I recognized one as an agent who had been involved in the investigation of Chaplain Simpson and who had accused me of "covering up" when I had refused to recommend a court-martial for Simpson. When I got to my office, I discovered that my desk had already been searched, and a pocket flask, which I'd kept in the back of one drawer, had been removed.

I had found the flask on the grounds outside the chapel some time back when Chaplain Gerlock, Chaplain Robert Hubbard, and myself had been cleaning up the area. I had seen flasks and liquor bottles left around the chapel area before. I had told them I wanted to keep this particular flask and try to find out who it belonged to, so I could warn the owner he'd be reported if he were caught drinking around the chapel again. It seemed to me the chapel area deserved a little more respect than that. Now, I thought, the N.I.S. agent would probably try to use the empty flask as evidence that I was a self-proclaimed teetotaler but a secret drinker.

I explained to Mrs. Lucy Whitbeck, the secretary of the chapel, that I was being temporarily shifted to Jacksonville, and why. She was flabbergasted. She had never heard any rumors involving me with Mary Ann Curran, Lora Gudbranson, or anyone else.

While I was talking to Lucy, Lora Gudbranson suddenly appeared at the open door to my office. "Andy, I want to talk to you," she said. I had never been so tempted in my life to curse and denounce someone, but I managed to hold back. I'd also been warned that she might twist anything I said, so I just stared at her and told her that on the advice of my counsel I wasn't able to talk to her. She turned abruptly and left.

I showed Lucy exactly which papers and records I was taking with me, and left the office. I spoke briefly to Swann in his office, but then he came after me as I was heading down the corridor. "Andy," he said suddenly, "you're being relieved as the senior chaplain on this base and I've been assigned to take over."

I stopped short. "Who gave *that* order?"

"The C.O.," he said. "He told me you can't ever come back here anyway, whether they find you legally guilty or innocent. I think you'd better turn over all your schedules to me."

"I'll wait till I get a direct order on that," I said.

Outside the chapel, I found Lora Gudbranson again, waiting. "Andy, I want to talk to you," she repeated. And again I told her I couldn't speak to her on the advice of my counsel. She walked to her car. I waited until she got in, then went to mine. She suddenly stepped out of her car and said to me, "Andy, get out of here. Take your family and get out of here."

Still mindful of my lawyer's advice, I said nothing. Then she said, "You think I'm crazy, don't you?" I just kept on walking to my car, got in, and drove off without saying a word.

The anonymous phone calls continued through that day and the next. Pope called me to say he'd had a call from my C.O. accusing *me* of making annoying calls to Mrs. Gudbranson and Mrs. Curran. I was also accused, he said, of having confronted Mrs. Gudbranson outside the chapel and having made obscene remarks to her.

I told him that *we* were the ones who'd been getting the calls and what had really happened outside the chapel and that I now strongly suspected that it was Lora making the calls to us.

Pope couldn't quite believe what I told him. "You're sure you didn't say anything to her at the chapel that she could have misconstrued?"

I repeated emphatically that I had said nothing to her and wanted to know what he, as my military counsel, could do to stop this harassment of my family. He said he'd see. Then he said that the C.O. had added another proviso to his order shifting me to Jacksonville. I was to be off the Cecil Field grounds every working day at 7:30 A.M. and would not be permitted back till 4 P.M. in the afternoon. I was not to go to the chapel again without permission and I would have to be searched on entering and leaving my office.

There was more insult to come—this time felt especially by Kathleen. One night when she was making a call, the wires apparently got crossed and she heard Lora Gudbranson telling somebody that she and her husband were invited to a "shivaree" (a Navy party to welcome new officers assigned to a base) being given by the C.O. We had not been invited. Kathleen was certain it was not an oversight but a direct slap at both of us. As far as the C.O. was concerned, we were to be outcasts, but two women who had asserted that they had committed adultery were quite acceptable. And they could continue to attend church and chapel activities while I, a chaplain and a minister, had to get special permission and be searched.

Because Kathleen was suffering from the awful tension, I made arrangements for us to go to St. Augustine for a holiday weekend and then to move off the base into the guesthouse at the Jacksonville base. I told Kathleen to rest while the children and I packed. She took the pill the doctor had given her to relax her nerves, but it didn't help. I soon heard her crying in the bedroom. When I went in to her, she said, "Andy, I've decided you should give up the fight and resign. There's not going to be any end to this thing here. It's not only affecting my health but it's got to affect yours too. If this pressure keeps up, it's going to break you down completely."

I tried to reassure her and told her about the decision in the O'Callahan case. I said that this nightmare would end as soon as I was cleared legally.

She shook her head. "The command is siding with those two. You'll be crucified in the papers and you'll have to leave the church.

Our only chance is for you to resign now from the Navy and for us to go back home to Philadelphia."

At that point, what Kathleen was saying seemed more an expression of the shock she felt at the charges than of a realistic view of my situation. Both the law and the truth were on my side, and I still believed it was only a matter of time before the command would recognize that I was being wronged in a terrible way. What was happening to us simply was not the way the Navy or the world worked. . . .

CHAPTER 11

If the command continued to pursue its present course, however, I might have to go on trial. And if a military court decided to take the word of these two women, the result would be disastrous for the Jensens. I might be cashiered from the service and even sent to prison.

As Kathleen had said, an immediate resignation would at least insure me against these awful possibilities. There would be no record of the charges against me if I resigned before formal hearings were held. For the record, I would be resigning for "personal reasons"—to return to the civilian ministry. There would be gossip, of course, at Cecil Field about the puritanical chaplain who was exposed as an adulterous swinger, but that would be the extent of it. We would be somewhere else, in Philadelphia, or perhaps in some ministry in California. If anybody ever heard of my case, we could say—truthfully—that false statements had been made against me but that no official charges were ever filed.

This would be the easy way out of the crisis, but the more I considered it the less I liked it. As a little kid I had been pushed around by bullies and I defended black, Chicano, and Japanese kids. But I had also learned to stand up to them. Now there were grown-up bullies pushing me around, and the thought of submitting to *their* muscle went down hard. I also felt I had an important function to perform as a Navy chaplain and it would be wrong to desert my calling. I was still devoted to the service and to its patriotic mission. And on a purely personal level, we would miss the friends we had made at Navy bases and the security we had felt. I felt, too, that if I resigned I would be sanctioning falsehood.

I decided to have Chuck Pope talk to Kathleen and convince her that my case would never go to court-martial. I explained that I wanted him to assure my wife because she was close to a breakdown and wanted me to resign rather than face a court-martial. He did speak to her at length and was patient with her even when she interrupted him with weeping. He said he had checked out military legal sources and had found that there had never been a court-martial of a chaplain in the entire history of the United States or a court-martial of any Naval officer only on a charge of adultery. He was sure that reason would finally prevail and that they were not going to set a precedent with me.

Pope was only half-successful in calming Kathleen's fears, but she agreed at least that I should await further developments before considering a resignation. That night in thinking back over events I wondered if perhaps I had been too preachy, too intense in dealing with Mary Ann Curran. She had revealed a deep hatred for moralistic authority figures who, as she said, "tried to act like Jesus Christ." Maybe she wouldn't have identified me as such an object of hatred if I'd used a different manner. And maybe I had waited too long in telling her I could no longer help her and in recommending psychiatric help. Perhaps I was so anxious to achieve success in counseling this troubled woman that I delayed in admitting failure. And as for Lora Gudbranson, I probably should have recognized earlier that her domineering and possessive attitude could cause harm. I had encouraged her to play an important role in our chapel activities because I was anxious to use her energies and skills in behalf of our programs. If I'd been less success-minded, she might have been less involved in our activities and have had even less plausible grounds for her fears and accusations. But such thoughts—however valid—could not undo the past. Kathleen criticized herself again for having been so open as to share confidences with Mary Ann, and in addition to her earlier explanation, I expect that perhaps she was also trying—through these disclosures—to establish a greater closeness to Mary Ann.

The weekend of rest and relaxation in St. Augustine, away from the base and the tyranny by telephone, helped to restore us to some extent. On the first day of our stay in the Jacksonville guest quarters, I went into the library at the Law Center to study past records of court-martials. I was disheartened to find that about ninety-five percent of all military court-martials ended in convictions.

When I next spoke to Chuck Pope he told me that Lts. Ralph Levy and David Schraver had just been assigned by the Navy as prospective trial counsel and assistant trial counsel on my case.

"This is outrageous," I said. "The command has just started the investigation, there have been no formal charges filed yet, and already they've appointed counsel for a general court-martial."

Pope agreed that the command's action was wrong and that he would object to it. He also said it was improper for two young lieutenants to be assigned to the prosecution of a Navy commander, but he kept insisting that this wasn't serious, that it was a matter of over-eager beavers jumping the gun rather than a deliberate effort by the C.O. and the Staff Judge Advocate to humiliate and degrade me. And he reaffirmed his belief that my case would not reach the court-martial stage.

In the little room to which Danielson had assigned me I found myself in isolation, cut off from any function relating to the chaplaincy. Danielson made light of the charges against me and told others that I was being kept under wraps because of sexual misconduct. He freely talked to the N.I.S. men although he was supposed to be my pastor and to keep anything he might know about me in confidence. I heard from a chaplain who had served with me in California that Danielson was telling other chaplains, "They caught Andy shacking up with two women." To my face, Danielson had said the charges against me had to be investigated, but behind my back he was acting as if they had already been proven.

Again I called Pope in some anger, and he erupted at me. He didn't care for Chaplain Danielson, he said, and what the man was doing was wrong, but there was nothing he could do about it and it would have no bearing on the legal outcome of my case. Furthermore, he was busy with many other things and he was "damned annoyed" at my calling him so often. He said if I didn't think he was doing all he could to protect my legal rights, I should get myself another lawyer.

That night, Pope called me to apologize. He said he could understand that my whole career and way of life were at stake and that I couldn't think of anything else all day. He sympathized with my feelings of anxiety and my worries over my wife.

I was glad to hear from him, but my problem remained: I could not complain directly to any member of the command at Cecil Field since they had isolated me and would only deal with me through my attorney. And each new order that came down to me through my lawyer seemed designed to humiliate and insult me. Pope, though, made no strong objection and seemed to feel the command had the right to do these things as part of the investigation. When I showed my bitterness at being barred from my chapel and from base activities, he said the command was doing me a favor by keeping me from close contact with Gudbranson. I was nagged by the thought that Pope was reacting this way not only because I called him so often but also because of his belief that I had indeed had a sexual involvement with my two accusers. I considered whether I should take him up on his offer to look for another counsel, but then I dismissed the idea. If I got another military counsel, he probably would be an inexperienced lieutenant controlled by his superiors. Lyman Fletcher had already told me that because of his unfamiliarity with military law, he could only assist in the presentation of my defense, not serve as chief counsel. And the cost of getting a civilian attorney with substantial courtroom experience as well as knowledge of military law would be too prohibitive.

One day I was ordered to report to the N.I.S. office at the Jacksonville base for questioning. I had never "pulled rank" in the Navy before but I felt this was a propitious time to do it. I asked that the N.I.S. agents come to my office since I outranked them. Back came the order from the command, as relayed by Pope: If Jensen doesn't get right over to the N.I.S. Office, he will be locked up in the hospital until he's ready to do as he's told. So much for the old military tradition that rank has its privileges, at least when the rank was that of a chaplain whom the command had decided was already bucking the system and therefore outside its pale.

Pope advised me to be polite to the N.I.S. men but to tell them that I had the legal right not to answer any of their questions. I was taken into a small room with a one-way mirror—I could be observed from the outside but I couldn't look out—and was confronted by Arnold Sleeper, the agent who had wanted me to press for a court-martial against Chaplain Simpson. Another agent joined him and sat down near me in an overstuffed chair. He introduced himself as another of the agents at the Jacksonville N.I.S. office. Sleeper told me he had taken a detailed statement from Mary Ann Curran about adulterous relations with me in motels, hotels, and her apartment in Jacksonville. His agents had copies of motel registrations, he said, and now he wanted a statement from me.

"On the advice of my attorney, I have nothing to say to you," I said as politely as I could.

"Then you're wasting our time," he said angrily. "Do you want to terminate this interview right now?"

I said nothing, so he went on. "We want you to write your name, and then you might as well go."

I assumed he wanted my signature to check it against the motel registrations, and since I had done nothing wrong in those motels, I gave it to him.

Later that same day I received an order to return the appointment books and the calendar I had taken from the chapel along with my key to the chapel. The order was accompanied by the same threat I'd heard the day before: failure to comply would result in my being placed under house arrest in a hospital room. I quickly made copies of all the dates and notations in these books that I felt would be pertinent to the case. I had always kept a detailed personal diary at home, too, and I thought the notations in this diary and in other personal records might help me.

As soon as I had copied what I thought I would need from these books, I went back to the N.I.S. office to turn them over along with my key. The girl who worked there said I would have to wait for Sleeper. When he came out, he just grabbed the books out of my arms.

"I'd like a receipt," I told him.

"Sorry, I won't give you any."

"Don't you give receipts when records are turned over to you?"

"Not if I don't want to."

When I asked once more for the receipt, he actually made a fist and said, "Try and get it."

When I went to Pope's office the next morning, he told me that he had heard some disturbing reports from the Staff Judge Advocate. Apparently the women were now supplying information of adulterous activity in or around my chapel office as well as in motels. This would provide the command with a service-connection for the charges against me and thus circumvent a defense based on the O'Callahan decision. Also, he'd been told that Mary Ann Curran had turned over love notes supposedly written by me to her. Pope assumed these notes had been signed by me and mailed to her, and warned that this could be used to support a charge of improper advances to another officer's wife.

"I never wrote a love note to Mary Ann Curran, and I never mailed anything to her of such a nature. If they've got any kind of notes or letters, they're obviously papers which were taken from my desk. I told you that my folders had been rifled. There also may be notes Mary Ann took from my wife's personal effects when she was at our house—notes written by me to my wife."

Once again Pope cautioned me to level with him. "I've got to have the complete truth from you, chaplain, if I'm to do the best I can as your counsel," he said. "If you're not telling me the whole story because of shame or embarrassment, you're only going to hurt yourself, because it's sure to come out."

I could hardly keep a lid on my temper as I repeated my denial that I'd ever had any kind of intimate relationship with either Mary Ann or Lora. "If you're not going to believe me, who will?" I asked. He told me he wouldn't doubt my word—but, as on previous occasions, he left me convinced that he did.

I had another worry. Perhaps someone induced by the N.I.S. had forged my signature to love letters purportedly written to Mary Ann. I was coming to believe that they were capable of doing anything once they made up their minds they had to get rid of a potential troublemaker. Pope wouldn't hear of any such possibility. "They would never do a thing like that," he insisted. I wondered, however, if he was too trusting. I had noticed that despite his somewhat maverick reputation he still tended to be very deferential to superior officers. It was part of his Navy training and discipline, no doubt, but I felt he might be allowing that to keep him from perceiving some of these superior officers as they really were.

The mystery of the "love notes" was cleared up when I was ordered to report with Pope to my Cecil Field C.O. to see the evidence gathered by the N.I.S. and hear the formal charges against me. Captain Coleman and his legal officer greeted Pope warmly, shook his hand, and said they were glad that a Navy career officer was going to be my counsel rather than an outsider. They wouldn't, however, shake hands with me, and the C.O. again referred to me coldly as "Jensen." I was being charged with adultery resulting in violations of both Article 133 and Article 134 of the Uniform Code of Military Justice, he told me. He had the legal officer, Lt. Ford, spread out copies of statements signed by Mary Ann and Lora for the N.I.S. agents, six registration receipts signed by "A. F. Jensen" at motels in the Jacksonville area, a bill for some purchases, and those "love notes." I could hardly contain my feelings of relief when I saw those notes. They were exactly what I'd suspected. None of them was addressed to Mary Ann—or to anyone at all—and there were no stamped envelopes to indicate she had received a single one in the mail. At least they didn't concoct any forgeries.

Captain Coleman, however, behaved as if he had been given ironclad proof of my guilt. "Because of the preponderance of evidence against you, I ask that you resign," he said curtly. Pope told him that I had no intention of resigning. The C.O. retorted that I would then have to take my chances in court. When Captain Coleman left the office, Pope and I read over the "evidence." "If that's all they've got on you, you're home free," Pope told me with a smile. He had helped the legal officer get his assignment at Cecil Field and so he felt he could talk frankly to him. "This comes as a big surprise to me because I thought you really had something," he said. "This evidence doesn't amount to anything. You can't make a case if this is all you have."

He asked the legal officer for permission to have the statements, registration receipts, etc., duplicated on the Xerox machine. This was always done routinely, as a matter of courtesy, but when Lt. Ford went to the C.O. for permission, he was told that no Xerox copying would be permitted. Instead, Pope had to copy everything laboriously by hand, with Lt. Ford detailed to sit and watch us in the event I tried to destroy the evidence. Pope, who had been so respectful to superior officers, now threw up his hands and said, "How picayune can a man get?"

The statements by the two women were scandalous on their face and would look damning to anyone who was unfamiliar with the circumstances and did not know the principals. Since I had refused to resign after they first made brief statements against me, the N.I.S. had apparently told them that a good deal of specifics would have to go into their formal charges. So now they had specifics, but the distortions and lies were obvious to me, and Pope was quick to detect discrepancies in their statements. Mary Ann's read as follows:

> I, Mary Ann (GLASS) CURRAN, dependent wife of Joseph Laurence CURRAN, Jr., hereby made the following voluntary statement to Mr. A. C. SLEEPER and Mr. S. D. WHITE, who have identified themselves to me as Special Agents of Naval Intelligence.
>
> During the latter part of 1969 and early 1970, my husband and I were having marital difficulty. At the time we were assigned

at Beeville, Texas. We were reassigned to NAS, Cecil Field, Florida, in May 1970, and at that time my husband and I decided to seek counseling regarding our problem. On 12 May 1970, I had my first meeting with Chaplain JENSEN for counseling after my husband had met one time with him previously. I had one meeting a week up through the end of July 1971. At the outset of our meetings, Chaplain JENSEN told me that he understood my problem, that is, I needed attention, money to be spent on me and that my husband should spend more time with me. I must add, that during the first few counseling sessions I told Chaplain JENSEN about a sexual affair I had in Beeville, and the reason for the affair was because my needs were not being met at home. Chaplain JENSEN stated that he understood.

On the last Friday of July 1970, I went to Chaplain JENSEN's office for a counseling session. He took me into another office which he said belonged to Chaplain SIMPSON. After we entered the office he put his hands on my face and kissed me on the lips. He then said, how could this happen to us. I was surprised, perhaps shocked, so I sat on a chair. I think probably to avoid his advances more than anything, but I must admit that at the time I needed someone, or at least felt that I could not stand being rejected. He sat next to me in the chair, put his trms around me and again kissed me on the cheek. I can honestly say that I in no way enticed him nor did I do anything to promote him to make such advances. The following Monday I contacted Chaplain JENSEN and told him I was leaving my husband and moving to the Gator Lodge on Phillips Highway. He said he was sorry, he wished he could be with me that night. His family left the next day, Tuesday, and that evening he visited me at the Gator Lodge. As soon as he walked into the room he put a chair against the door and turned the lights out. He kissed and embraced me and finally engaged in a normal act of sexual intercourse. He didn't stay with me that night because he had the duty and he was afraid his neighbors would say something. The next night, and every night for the following two weeks, he spent the night with me at my room. The first two nights we stayed at the Gator Lodge, the next three at the Jamaica Lodge, Friday and Saturday at the Holiday Inn at the International Airport, then back to the

Gator Lodge for the remainder of the two-week period. Chaplain JENSEN registered at the Gator Lodge the last time under the name Francis Smith. I then moved to the Fox Meadow Apartments on Jasper Avenue for about two weeks, then to the Carriage House on University. Chaplain JENSEN continued to visit me frequently, almost every night. While at the Carriage House, September, October, and November, we had sexual relations nearly every day. These relations consisted of oral genital stimulation by both Chaplain JENSEN and myself, then sexual intercourse.

Toward the end of October and early November, I wanted to sever the relationship because I began to believe Chaplain JENSEN was not being sincere in that things he said were not consistent with what he told me at the outset of the affair. I mean he first told me he was going to leave his family because he loved me and planned to marry me. I finally told him I didn't want to see him anymore.

Chaplain JENSEN, whom I of course by now referred to as Andy in private, began frequently calling me at my apartment, work, and at my mother's, to whom he always said he had an appointment with me. I had an answering service at the time because of my work as a nurse. During this time I would receive numerous calls through the answering service from a Doctor SANTOS. One day I returned a phone call at a number left by SANTOS and the BOQ at Cecil Field answered. I was sure in my own mind by this time it was Andy who was making the calls. I finally told him to stop making the calls and accused him of being Doctor SANTOS. He denied using the name and said, prove it. The calls finally ended after John BLANC, a doctor with whom I worked, finally told Andy to stop making phone calls for me at work. I received no more calls from Doctor SANTOS. I did, however, continue to receive calls from Andy, as Andy, who wanted me to go back with him. In December I told Andy I was going back with my husband. Andy then said that was fine, anything for me to be happy.

My husband and I went on a two-week vacation beginning the 11th of December. When I returned from vacation Andy again started calling me on the phone. I returned his calls because by this time I was, as I told Andy, emotionally dependent upon him. He said, when I told him this, that he hoped I was emotionally dependent upon him. In late December we again saw each other, my thinking it could be a close personal relationship without sex. For the next four months, up through April 1971, the relationship culminated into a sexual affair and more motels. We spent nights at the Ramada Inn at the airport, Airport Inn, Howard Johnson's on Golfair Boulevard and on Phillips Highway and at my apartment. He had a fear of being caught and was very apprehensive about fully disrobing at any time during our relationship. After periods of impotence Andy, who was not circumcized, during sexual acts would discuss and ask about certain men with whom I worked and whether or not they were circumcized and whether he was better in the act than the others. He always demanded an answer. Another thing, about seven times Andy and I engaged in various sexual acts in his office at the NAS Cecil Field Chapel. Andy also drank alcohol often and excessively, even after telling me he was a tee-tottler. He did admit that drinking was one of his problems and that he was not allowed to drink at home.

This past Sunday, 8 August 1971, I went to the chapel for the first time in a long time. After church we went to Fellowship Hall for coffee and donuts. Lori GUDBRANSON was there and we began talking about forming a group at the chapel for purposes of engaging in various educational discussions. In discussing topics and books for the group a woman present mentioned *The Intimate Enemy* and I said Lori, you should read it. It tells you how to fight fairly in marriage, how to get a good fight started, how to fight about extramarital affairs and also how to fight about other affairs. About 1400 that afternoon Lori called me on the phone and asked me if I had heard any rumors. I said I'm sorry, I don't know what you're talking about, you'll have to explain more. So she said, at the bowling alley. I said, what is the rumor. She said the rumor is about Chaplain JENSEN and myself. It seems that was all I needed because I had to talk to someone, and I told Lori everything about JENSEN and myself. The following Tuesday, 10 August, Lori called me again wanting to discuss JENSEN. Later that evening she told me about her two affairs with JENSEN at two different motels. The next morning Lori again called me and wanted to know if I wanted to bring everything out in the open. I went to Lori's house and talked and she told me then that CDR GUDBRANSON knew about and had reported the incident to someone. That night, Wednesday 11 August, I was called to Capt. SHUTE's office, where I partially told him about the incident.

At my request, Mr. SLEEPER typed this statement for me which consists of two pages, and which I freely and voluntarily make, with no threats being made against me or promises extended to me. I have read this statement, corrected and initialed mistakes, and it is true and correct.

(Signature)________________________________

This was Lora Gudbranson's statement:

I, Lora Evelyn (SNIDER) GUDBRANSON, dependent wife of CDR. Larry Gene GUDBRANSON, 543997, hereby making the following voluntary statement to Mr. A. C. SLEEPER and Mr. S. D. WHITE, who have identified themselves to me as Special Agents of Naval Intelligence. I make this statement freely, with no threats having been made against me or promises extended to me. At my request, Mr. SLEEPER is typing this statement for me as we discuss its contents.

Chaplain JENSEN and his family arrived at NAS, Cecil Field, Florida, in February 1970. Almost immediately Chaplain JENSEN and I became mutually attracted toward one another. I would say at the outset the attraction was more intellectual than anything else. I had been and continued to be involved in Chapel activities, in addition to other voluntary activities in the community. By the nature of my activities, Chaplain JENSEN, who I shall refer to as Andy, shared a general interest. These interests oftentimes brought us together at various meetings. Around December 1970, I felt that both of us were becoming strongly attracted to each other physically. In November 1970, I became a staff volunteer in the Environmental Coordinating Office, which was not a chapel activity. I began receiving telephone calls from Andy suggesting he come to the office at 2123 Park, Jacksonville, Fla., to look it over. I feel that this was an opportunity for Andy to spend more time with me away from the chapel, and I wanted him to. In fact, Andy visited me at the office on two occasions.

In February and March 1971, I attended PTA meetings at Whitehouse Elementary School. Andy was also present at both of these meetings. After each of these meetings Andy and I went for a ride in his car which lasted twenty to thirty minutes. During this time we kissed and embraced each other. On the second occasion Andy suggested we engage in sexual relations, but I declined to do so in the car.

On 18 May 1971, Andy and I mutually agreed to meet at the Howard Johnson's Motel on Golfair Boulevard. When I arrived I found Andy had already checked into the motel. He said he registered under the names of Mr. and Mrs. A. F. JENSEN. We went to a room and engaged in an act of normal sexual intercourse. The next time we met was on 8 July 1971, at the Gator Lodge on Phillips Highways, where we again engaged in a similar act.

On 16 and 17 July 1971, both of our spouses were out of town. On both nights I met Andy at his home and we engaged in sexual intercourse.

Last Sunday, 8 August 1971, I attended a group meeting after church services at the Fellowship Hall. In a conversation with Mary Ann CURRAN, something was said which led me to suspect that she might know something about my relationship with Andy. After returning home I telephoned her to question her about what she said. She then told me something of a similar relationship she had with Andy, including some facts of sexual intimacy. At this time I didn't tell her anything about my relationship with Andy. However, the following day we met and confided in each other. We agreed to divulge our relationships with Andy because we felt he needed help and was in a position to damage too many lives. I then told my husband who reported the incident.

I have read the above statement, made necessary corrections, initialed mistakes, and it is true and correct.

(Signature)________________________

How and why Lora and Mary Ann had got together in their accusations was finally becoming clearer to me through their statements. I had no reason to doubt that the discussion they both referred to at the chapel had touched off a talk about details of their own sexual adventures. This may well have led to reinforced concern about how I might react to their behavior. They may also have spoken of Mary Ann's homosexual tendencies, and Lora's attitude toward sexual relations. The fear and guilt then likely to have been aroused could well have been the basis for their initiating their conspiracy against me.

In her statement, Mary Ann had clearly substituted my name for that of her actual partner, Dr. John Blanc, in the details she reported about her sexual relations—details she had told me about during counseling sessions. She probably added a few from her relations with other men. It was interesting that she mentioned Dr. Blanc in her statement not as her lover but only as a protector to stop me from making those alleged phone calls to her. Actually, as she had told me, it was Dr. Blanc who was hearing from "Dr. Santos."

I felt the N.I.S. agents probably had coached her in her statement. They obviously knew from their investigations into my working habits and procedures that the door to my chapel office was always open during the day. To make plausible a relationship in the chapel, they had to place it somewhere else, which is probably why they picked the office of Chaplain Simpson. I was certain, too, that some of the dates Mary Ann gave for our supposed adulterous sessions in motels were tailored to the dates of the registration receipts the Navy agents had found. But I didn't know whether to laugh or cry at her statement that I had taken time out from my long, fully scheduled work days to go to her Jacksonville apartment in September, October, and November, 1970, for sexual relations "nearly every day."

The accusation that during the late stages of this supposed affair we engaged "seven times in sexual acts" in my chapel office impelled me to ask, "Who could possibly believe such nonsense?" Presumably these sexual acrobatics were performed in the evening rather than during the day, except I had so many on-going evening programs and so many people forever coming in to see me at the chapel that the whole thing became ridiculous to contemplate.

The charge that I "drank alcohol often and excessively" was another grotesque lie that could easily be contradicted by anyone familiar with my habits. But I deduced—accurately, as it turned out—that the N.I.S. would try to represent me as a secret drinker by introducing as evidence the flask they had found in my desk.

Another obvious falsehood was that "Chaplain Jensen registered at the Gator Lodge the last time under the name of Francis Smith."

Where was the registration receipt signed by "Francis Smith"? The N.I.S. apparently had gone through the records of all the motels, but the six receipts they produced showed that I always used my real name.

Lora's sexual accounts were more limited, so there would be less to disprove. It seemed ridiculous for her to have picked my house as a site for our supposed encounters because, like my office, it was always open to neighbors and members of the chapel, who often dropped in. I also felt she had damaged her case by picking the nights of P.T.A. meetings in February and March as those when we had spent time together in my car. I was sure that some of the P.T.A. members must have seen me get into my car and leave alone on those nights, and I thought that they would be willing to so testify.

Lora's first statement on August 11th had accused me of having relations with her at the Gator Lodge in June, but in this subsequent statement she had changed the date to July 8th. Why the change? I had an infection caused by "chigger" bites during the summer that at its worst caused too much pain for me to engage in sexual relations. I knew the Navy medical office had a record of my being treated for this on June 9th. Perhaps the N.I.S. men had discovered this and had therefore convinced her to switch to a July date instead. Actually my infection had gotten much worse in July.

The "love notes" turned out to be a motley collection of non-evidence. ("Incredible couriers without luggage," Pope characterized them.) Some were on get-well and birthday cards. Not only was none addressed to Mary Ann but they had no signatures, except one signed "Andy"—a card I had once given Kathleen. I also recognized two sympathy cards my older son and I had sent her when she was ill. One note on foolscap had these lines from a "Peanuts" cartoon: "Happiness is two people together who love each other. Sadness is when that love is injured. Please love me!" Kathleen collected Peanuts expressions, and I remembered copying this one down and giving it to her.

There were also three rough drafts of notes that I had prepared in counseling sessions for sailors to copy in their own handwriting and send to sweethearts. I would sometimes put these drafts in folders on my desk. Mary Ann or even the N.I.S. men could easily have leafed through them when I was out of the office.

One draft was of something I had written with a sailor in a

"role-reversal" technique that we sometimes used in counseling to help release emotions from a troubled person. The person being counseled is told to be relaxed and encouraged to act as though he were giving the advice instead of receiving it. This can help him express his feelings more freely. In this instance the sailor was having problems with his girlfriend. He wanted me to help him express his real feelings for her. I couldn't remember offhand which sailor I had been counseling, but I was fairly sure I could remember if I reviewed my diaries. The paper I had scribbled this draft on was a messy piece of scrap paper and I had used the back of it to write down the order of religious service for use at church.

What Pope had expected to find in the N.I.S. "evidence" was some corroboration of the charges of adultery. "You rarely find an eyewitness to an act of adultery," he explained. "But, in my experience, I've learned that there are usually eyewitnesses who see the man or the woman leaving a questionable place at a questionable time. Here they have no reports of eyewitnesses, and they don't even present rumors about how you behaved improperly with one or the other woman even though your supposed affairs with them have been going on for over a year in motels, your house, one of the women's, and your own chapel office. A Navy officer with a cross on his uniform would be very visible and easily identified. Except from the mouths of these two women, we don't see a scintilla of evidence that you've been misbehaving. It's incredible!"

He had already learned enough about my work habits and chapel programs to appreciate that Mary Ann's account of day-in, day-out relations with me was at best wild fantasy. And he was amused by the fact that all the motel registrations that had been turned up were signed "A. F. Jensen." "Who ever heard of a philanderer taking another man's wife to a motel for an affair and registering under his real name?" he said.

The only detail he questioned was my using a Newport, Rhode Island, address instead of my Cecil Field address. I explained that some of the local motels customarily refused accommodations to local persons, particularly when they are heavily booked. In any case, I would have felt self-conscious about indicating a Cecil Field address and suggesting thereby that a chaplain was avoiding his duties—I could hardly, after all, fill in the clerks on my medical problems and the fact that I was taking these brief time-outs on prescription of my doctor. The address was the one I had had in Newport before

I was assigned to Florida. Anything sent to that address would have been forwarded to Cecil Field.

The evidence presented by N.I.S.—or, rather, the lack of it—completely changed Pope's view of my case. He no longer was the cynical attorney willing to defend a chaplain's legal rights even though he suspected the chaplain actually had succumbed to human temptations. He had wanted me to "level" with him. Now he finally accepted that I had done so from the start.

The reason Mary Ann and Lora gave for suddenly deciding to expose the facts of a sordid involvement with a chaplain just didn't make sense, he told me. "Here are two women who have known each other for over a year, who have both been active in chapel work, and whose husbands were in the same command, and they say they've both been having sex with the chaplain, only neither one knew the other was doing it. Then they read a book and get the urge to confess to one another, then confess to their husbands, then announce their shame to the world on the grounds they have discovered the chaplain 'needs help'!"

CHAPTER 12

Pope decided we should spend the next Saturday driving to all the motels and apartments mentioned in Lora's and Mary Ann's statements so that he could get a clear picture of what these places looked like and how long it would take to get to them from Cecil Field. He felt that we should pinpoint the time it would take to drive from my chapel office to some of these alleged sites. Then we could produce appointment records or statements from eyewitnesses about where I had really been at a certain time that might prove the falsity of some of the statements made in the accusations against me. We went to one of the motels near the airport where I had stayed with Kathleen a couple of times when she was returning from a visit to her parents, as well as to a motel at the beach area and one near the Methodist Hospital where I had been taking a weekly Tuesday course in pastoral counseling. Although these motels were all in the Jacksonville area, they were as much as forty miles away from my base. We also drove past the two apartments where Mary Ann had lived and noted that it took forty-five minutes to drive from the Cecil Field Chapel. We went by the hospital, the nursing home where Mary Ann had worked, and the Baptist Book Store, where I sometimes stopped to buy books.

During the course of the day Pope and I got to know each other much better. We had been "Chaplain Jensen" and "Lieutenant Commander Pope" before; now we were "Andy" and "Chuck." I was impressed by his range of knowledge and his cultural and family background. He had been brought up in his mother's Roman Catholic religion. His father was a descendant of the Pilgrims who came to New England on the *Mayflower*. His father was a doctor, and indeed the Popes for several generations had been either doctors or lawyers. They had mostly been Harvard men. Chuck himself had gone to Harvard Law School for two years before joining the Navy during the Korean War. When he had reverted to the inactive reserve, he completed his law studies at Notre Dame and went into practice in Chicago. His mother's family had long been active in Chicago politics and law and so had his wife's. In fact, his wife's uncle had been the prosecutor in the sensational Loeb-Leopold murder case.

My case had become a cause for Chuck, and that could not help but lift my hopes. I was still worried, though. He had thought the O'Callahan case precedent would rule out the possibility of my being tried by a military court. As for the charge of adultery committed in the Navy chapel as well as off the base, he conceded that he had not expected this. He thought it probably had been concocted for the very purpose of circumventing the O'Callahan ruling. "But I still feel they can't show this to be a service-connected case. The O'Callahan ruling will still hold," he insisted. In any event, he was sure that the Article 32 proceedings would not take too long, and that he would destroy the credibility of Mary Ann and Lora when he cross-examined them, and that the command then would drop the case.

When I brought the N.I.S. evidence to Lyman Fletcher, however, he had a different reaction. He agreed with Pope that there was no valid case against me and also was now convinced of my innocence. But he felt Pope was too sanguine about the reaction of the command. "You're not dealing with civilian justice here. The Navy can proceed if it wishes to on evidence so trivial it would be laughed out of a federal or state court."

The command's behavior proceeded to bear him out. We soon learned that the two junior officers who had prematurely been appointed trial counsel and assistant trial counsel in my case had been to see the Currans and Gudbransons to encourage them.

I was also ordered to undergo a psychiatric and physical examination with the now-routine warning that refusal on my part would mean confinement to the hospital. The psychiatrists' questions seemed aimed only at determining whether I was some sort of sexual criminal. The physical examination concentrated on the inspection of my penis and genital area. I was convinced its primary purpose was to confirm Mary Ann's report about circumcision. This seems to have been borne out later when we saw the official report of the examination. The report spoke only of circumcision, and—by Lora Gudbranson's own sworn admission—was disclosed by the command to her husband.

Kathleen now couldn't sleep at night. The doctor had been called three more times but all he could do was inject her with tranquilizers and try to ease the strain.

When I showed Kathleen the N.I.S. statements and evidence, she saw the same fallacies in them that I had seen. And since she took care of all the family records and finances, she knew exactly how much money I had and how I spent it. She therefore knew I could not possibly have spent money at motels without her knowing about it. And if I had really made all those twenty-five-mile daily drives to Mary Ann's apartment, she would certainly have seen this reflected in our gasoline bills. But Kathleen had now come around to Lyman Fletcher's view that a command that had already gone this far probably would simply blink at the legal niceties and insist on pressing the issue to the end.

She felt guilty all over again for having allowed Mary Ann and Lora to pry confidences from her that they now were exploiting—as she had feared they would—in their sworn statements. Kathleen was also concerned about what would happen when news of the charges came out and again appealed to me to resign rather than face this.

I was increasingly torn between my desire to stand up for what was right and my desire to ease Kathleen's agony. Finally, we agreed to leave it up to our parishioners. If they turned their backs on me, I would resign no matter what Pope said. If they backed me, we would stand firm.

We called first on our neighbors, Commander Dick Coleman and his wife Jeannine, and told them the whole story. Dick actually burst out laughing. Kathleen and I stared at him. "You'll have to excuse me, Andy," he said. "I know how terribly painful this has to be for both of you, but I can't help laughing at the idea of my asthmatic neighbor being charged with all these sexual activities. We've been worried about whether you could keep on with your work at the chaple without falling apart and here they're portraying you as the all-time sexual superman." Jeannine's reaction was that Mary Ann and Lora must be very sick to invent "such awful nonsense."

Bolstered by the Colemans, we next told the story to two others who'd been active in our chapel, Lt. Commander Frank McKean and his wife, Betty. They couldn't believe it at first, then became indignant at the command. Betty McKean told us that Lora Gudbranson had been at the meeting of the Protestant planning board of the chapel just the day after she'd signed her charges against me and had been "cool and unruffled." And Mary Ann Curran, "looking as if she didn't have a care in the world," had come back to the church for the first time in a long time and was talking of resuming active work on some committees.

Both the McKeans and Colemans urged us to move back to Cecil Field. When we told them about Larry Gudbranson's threats and the telephone calls, they said, "We'll let the Gudbransons know that your friends will protect you against this sort of thing even if the C.O. won't."

We then called on Joy Oneth, who lived with her husband and their three children in the enlisted men's quarters. She was active in chapel programs. Her reaction was the same as the others—at first disbelief, then outrage at the two women and the command.

Joe Simpson, my predecessor as chaplain who, as I mentioned earlier, had left the Navy after an affair, a divorce, and remarriage, offered to testify to a time when Lora Gudbranson had tried to seduce him. I believed him, but it was also—if unfairly—clear that the command could use his past to undermine his credibility.

I received some unexpected backing as a result of a tragedy. One of our pilots had been killed in a crash, and his squadron had scheduled a memorial service for him. His widow had been told tht Chaplain Swann would conduct the service. She didn't want Swann and asked for me. When she was told I was temporarily transferred to Jacksonville, she asked the wife of the squadron commander to find me. She called and I told her what had been going on. She said she know that the charges had to be false, and she asked me to conduct the service. I told her I thought it would be better to accept Swann. But the pilot's widow insisted on me. When the squadron commander's wife called Lora to protest, Lora told her that she now knew who the third woman was who'd been having an affair with Chaplain Jensen, but she generously wouldn't say a word to expose her. The wife's reaction was to call the C.O. to say that she was speaking for the widow in insisting that I be permitted to conduct the service. Both the C.O. and the exec called Pope to say that under no circumstances could I perform the service. Chaplain Carroll Chambliss was with me in Pope's office when the call came in. He said, "They're really asking for trouble when they forbid a chaplain to conduct a religious service for a parishioner who has called for him." Apparently the C.O. realized this and relented when the woman refused to accept another chaplain.

The mounting support helped Kathleen overcome the initial effects of the accusations. She now saw me in the Biblical role of Joseph, wrongfully accused by the wife of Potiphar, another officer. Joseph was finally cleared and Kathleen was convinced that I would be, too. She agreed that resigning would be cowardly and a betrayal of our convictions.

CHAPTER 13

I spent the last few days before the opening of the Article 32 investigation with my attorney helping prepare for our defense, but I resisted accepting the fact that official proceedings were about to begin. On the morning of September 13, 1971, I had to drag myself out of bed and force myself to get dressed. Since the hearing was like a civilian grand jury proceeding, it was not open to the public. Not even Kathleen could attend.

When I reached the headquarters of the Naval Air Technical Training Command in Jacksonville, where the hearings were to be held, I saw Mary Ann Curran, her husband, and her sister walking into the building ahead of me. Chuck Pope and Lyman Fletcher arrived soon after and went into the office of the investigating officer to discuss procedures with him and the legal officer. I sat for an hour in one waiting room while the Currans and Mary Ann's sister sat in an adjoining one. Finally I was called to be sworn in. The room I entered was a conference room with chairs ranged around a long narrow table. The investigating officer was Lieutenant Ernest Duncan, a 27-year-old, reddish-haired Texan with a soft-spoken, deliberate manner.

Duncan read the charges against me in a low monotone. I was informed that I was being accused of violating both Article 134 and Article 133 of the Uniform Code of Military Justice. Article 134 was a catch-all that vaguely proscribed "conduct which brings prejudice to the good order and discipline of the armed forces." Article 133 referred to "conduct unbecoming to an officer and a gentleman." My violations of these articles included the offense of adultery alleged by my two accusers. Then, for the record, Chuck Pope repeated each specifications of the alleged acts of adultery and had me enter a sworn denial of each.

This was a perfunctory process when Chuck Pope asked permission to read an opening statement into the record. As he read it, my old feeling that all this was unreal and would somehow blow away changed to the inescapable realization that it was all very real, and finally happening.

"At the outset of these proceedings," Chuck read, "it seems appropriate for the defense to make a short statement. Commander Jensen maintains he is absolutely innocent of the offenses alleged here. Defense to these matters necessarily places him and his counsel in the unfortunate position of calling to account the veracity and character of the wives of fellow Naval officers. Such a posture is abhorrent to a chaplain and his military counsel, who have dedicated their lives to the service of the line. Regardless of such considerations, legal contention of this kind with the gentler sex runs completely counter to the instincts of manhood and chivalry implanted from the cradle by our western civilization.

"The defense therefore approaches these mournful procedures with humility and sorrow. As a gesture of protection for the innocent as well as for those who falsely accuse him, Commander Jensen has offered to have this investigation and any court-martial completely closed to the public, thereby shielding from outside view scandalous matters which by their very nature can only cause hurt and operate against the best interest of the Naval Service. The defense wishes to emphasize that while it will vigorously contest the alleged offenses, nevertheless it is its earnest desire and intent that the proceedings at all stages be conducted on the highest possible moral plane."

Mary Ann was called as the first witness. They gave her a seat at the table directly across from me and my lawyers. She did not seem embarrassed in any way. In fact, after the oath, when she began giving testimony, her manner seemed almost buoyant.

Lt. Duncan first led her gently through testimony that repeated what she had sworn to in her N.I.S. statement. But even in her routine recapitulation of our supposed affair, she contradicted herself. Her first act of sexual relations with me, she said, was on the Sunday afternoon following the alleged kissing in the chapel office on the last Friday in July, 1970. She said that I went to her apartment on Shindler Drive in Jacksonville because I knew her husband had duty that day, that she offered me coffee, that I didn't want coffee, and that we were soon in her bed. The very next day, she said, she called and told me that she was leaving her husband and moving to a motel and that on Tuesday, August 4, I went to her motel room. Then came a run-down of adulterous behavior with me in four different motels in August and in various apartments and motels in the months thereafter.

Duncan apparently didn't notice that her written statement gave a different version of our first encounter, but Chuck, Lyman, and I did. When Chuck went into his cross-examination he pointed out that in her statement to N.I.S. she swore that the first act had not occurred until Tuesday and that it was in the Gator Lodge, not at her home. "Don't you think you should remember when the first act occurred?" Chuck asked her. "It would be a pretty important thing, especially when it occurred in your own apartment."

Mary Ann said that she was upset at the time she swore out her statement and that she had had a memory lapse. When the recess began Chuck said, "Can you imagine any woman of reasonably sound mind not remembering when or where she first began an affair with a man whom she says she was so emotionally involved with—and a *chaplain*, at that?"

Mary Ann followed up her first error with a succession of inconsistent statements, contradictions, muddled explanations, and plain lies. Her own mood remained high, and she blamed her many errors on the fact that she wasn't allowed to consult a calendar to compensate her poor memory. When Chuck Pope tried to pin Mary Ann down to the total number of times she supposedly had relations with me, she responded as though she were quoting statistics. (Later on, at the court-martial, she would claim she felt a great deal of tension during the Article 32 questioning, but in fact she seemed to be enjoying herself.)

Here is an account of Chuck's questions and Mary Ann's answers to illustrate that impression.

> DEFENSE COUNCIL: Now, how many different times do you estimate, the whole time-period involved here from beginning to end, that you and Chaplain Jensen stayed together at motels?
>
> MARY ANN CURRAN: Do you mean how many motels?
>
> DC: How many times you stayed at a motel.
>
> MAC: I would say approximately fifteen times.
>
> DC: Let's take August. You mentioned the Gator Lodge, then the Jamaican, then the Holiday Inn, then back to the Gator Lodge, and I gathered from the fact that we decided at least ten days were spent by you there together, therefore the number ten is correct for August as a minimum, isn't it?
>
> MAC: Okay.
>
> DC: Let me ask the question first. There were no other times in August that you stayed in motels?
>
> MAC: Not that I remember.
>
> DC: You say here in your statement now at the Carriage House in September, October, and November, you had sexual relations nearly every day. Now during all this time there are no times which you haven't mentioned a motel. Is that correct?
>
> MAC: Right.
>
> DC: So that takes care of September, October, and November, and in August we have the number ten so far. In December you say in your statement here that you took a two-week vacation beginning the 11th. Now, between the 1st and the 11th did you and Chaplain Jensen stay at any motels?
>
> MAC: I don't remember. We could have because I didn't leave with my husband until after that.

DC: Now, as I recall, you said you left on the 11th and came back on the 20th and you began talking to Chaplain Jensen between that time and the end of December. Now, during that time did you stay at any motels?

MAC: I don't remember. A lot of times he would come over to the apartment during lunch time and when my husband would have the duty.

DC: I see here where you say, "Towards the end of December we again saw each other, my thinking it would be a close personal relationship without sex. For the next four months, up through April 1971, the relationship culminated into a sexual affair and more motels." I gather now that isn't what you meant. What you really meant was through June 1971. Is that correct?

MAC: Yes.

DC: One time at the Ramada?

MAC: Yes. Between January and March, or December and March.

DC: And then at the Airport Inn?

MAC: Same time.

DC: One time?

MAC: Yes.

DC: Then you said the Howard Johnson on Golfair?

MAC: I'd say around February . . . between February and April and May.

DC: How many times?

MAC: I'd say once or twice, I'm not sure.

DC: At the Howard Johnson on Phillips Highway?

MAC: Between March and May.

DC: How many times?

MAC: Twice.

DC: Okay, now are there any other motel times? You also mentioned your apartment and during that time-period there were some other motels which aren't listed in your statement, so I don't see the point in adding them. How many times at other motels?

MAC: Twice.

DC: You mentioned one was the Francis Patio Court. What is the second one?

MAC: I can't remember, but it was in Callahan.

DC: So that would be a total of seven or eight times altogether the way I calculate. Then taking that ten we have seventeen or eighteen times in a motel. The chaplain paid for all of those with one exception, is that right?

MAC: To the best of my knowledge, yes.

DC: How come we only have—let me count the receipts—how come we only have eight receipts for approximately 15 occasions that you mentioned to the N.I.S. agents?

MAC: Because some of those motels I couldn't remember then and I left them off.

DC: Well, of course taking your testimony now, you didn't have that much sex with Chaplain Jensen from December through June, did you?

MAC: Yes, I did.

DC: Didn't you state earlier today that there were seven or eight times at a motel and that the rest of it was at the apartment at Yorktown?

MAC: Yes.

DC: How many times did you have sex with Chaplain Jensen at Yorktown?

MAC: A lot of times during lunch.

DC: Well, then there were seven or eight times at the motels and six or seven times at the office. Now, how many times at the apartment at Yorktown?

MAC: Two or three times a week.

DC: Well, let's take a month at a time. Now, how many times in December?

MAC: We were gone through the 20th, so I guess three or four times.

DC: What about January? Would it be three times a week in January?

MAC: Two or three times a week.

DC: That would mean about twelve times in January?

MAC: Okay.

DC: How about February?

MAC: Approximately the same.

DC: So that would be approximately ten or eleven times in February?

MAC: I would say two times a week because the other times were at motels, so that would be less.

DC: Say eight times in February?

MAC: Right.

DC: Ten times in March?

MAC: Yes, approximately.

DC: Five times in April?

MAC: I would say, yes.

DC: How about May?

MAC: I don't know. When did Chaplain Swann arrive?

DC: You said through June 1971.

MAC: In a motel, not in the apartment.

DC: We have then a total of thirty-nine or forty times during that time-period at the Yorktown Apartments, approximately?

MAC: Yes.

DC: Well, no, there was the six or seven times at the chapel at the base, so that would be a total of about sixty-three separate times that you were together during which times you committed one or more acts of sexual intercourse. Isn't that correct?

MAC: Approximately, yes.

When pressed, and without motel receipts at hand, Mary Ann couldn't cite one specific date for our alleged adultery. She was confused about the order of the motels and she sometimes changed the order around. She again talked of my registering at one of the motels as Francis Smith and had no explanation why there was no record of any Francis Smith having registered. Nor could she explain why the N.I.S. men who had scoured the records of the motels in the greater Jacksonville area had come up with only six that could be connected with me.

Whether by night or day, I always came to my assignments in uniform and with my chaplain's cross in place, according to her testimony. And it was not surprising to her that there were never any eyewitnesses and that I never worried about being observed. When Pope asked her, "Does it seem reasonable to you that a Navy chaplain would walk into a motel room with a woman who wasn't his wife in broad daylight, having registered under his own name?" she answered, "It strikes me as being quite reasonable because he did it quite often."

In detailing the many occasions when I supposedly saw her, Mary

Ann made only one attempt to establish corroboration. Patricia Franklin, a woman who worked with her at the Trowbridge Nursing Home, had come to her apartment at seven o'clock one morning because of an emergency involving a patient. According to Mary Ann, I was in the apartment with her at the time and although she did not allow the woman inside, she insisted the woman saw me and recognized me a bit later when I left the apartment.

Of course I knew I had never been in Mary Ann's apartment at such a time and that if Patricia Franklin testified it would likely turn out that she had seen some other man—if indeed she had seen anybody.

In her sworn statement to N.I.S., Mary Ann had been very specific in saying that during the months of September, October, and November, 1970, we had had relations nearly every day. In her testimony at the hearing, however, she continually reduced the number of acts during this period, and she could never satisfactorily explain why:

> DC: Well let me ask you this in light of what you just said in the statement, let's take September now. September is thirty days, October is thirty-one, November is thirty, that's a total of ninety-one days. You say here that almost every night you had sexual relations, which I think you have to agree is somewhat different from what you said previously here today. How many of those ninety-one days did you actually have sexual relations with Chaplain Jensen?
>
> MAC: Do you want me to give you an exact figure, because as I said before, I can't.
>
> DC: Well, I realize that on something like this you can't normally come up with a precise answer, but nevertheless you did say in your statement unequivocally that while in the Carriage House in September, October, and November you had sexual relations nearly every day. And I take it nearly every day, on the basis of ninety-one days, to be something like between eighty-five and ninety. Is that right?
>
> MAC: Well, that depends on how many times you want to say that somebody—how many times you had it on a certain day that he came to see me.
>
> DC: But you did say, you did put this on the basis not on the number of times per day, but on the fact that there

were, according to what you said, these sexual relations nearly every day. Now, I take nearly every day, referring to ninety-one days, to be somewhere between eighty-five and ninety-one days.

MAC: Mr. Pope, I can say this to you, that yes I did want to break it off. There was a two-week period during that time that I did not have sex with Chaplain Jensen; there were a couple of days in between there during November when I decided to go back with my husband; and it seemed that Chaplain Jensen could talk me into having sex. Every time he came over I'd say no, but by the time he finished I wound up in bed. Okay. That's not saying much for my will power either, but that is what happened. So to say that I wanted to end it is fine.

DC: Now let's take one month at a time. Let's take September. When did you move into the Carriage House?

MAC: I'm not sure, but I think it was September first.

DC: Was it shortly thereafter that you had sexual relationships for the first time at the Carriage House?

MAC: It was probably the first night I moved in. Maybe the first of September.

DC: Let's take September which has thirty days. That month in 1970 began on a Tuesday. Now how many of those thirty days in September did you spend with Chaplain Jensen when you had sexual relations?

MAC: I'd say approximately half of them.

DC: What about October? October began on a Thursday and ended on a Saturday, and it's thirty-one days.

MAC: I can't give you any estimate because I don't know.

DC: But you say here in your statement that you swore to that during September, October, and November you had sexual relations nearly every day. What reason did you have for saying that then if you can't say it now?

MAC: Because I believe in the beginning of October I did, and probably about half of October, but I could not . . . you are asking me to pinpoint days and I can't do that.

DC: I'm only taking what you said here, Mrs. Curran. You said unequivocally that nearly every day in September, October, and November, at the Carriage House. Do you think it might have been half of the days in October but you don't know. What about November? November has thirty days . . . I'm not trying to be facetious and I'm not trying to embarrass you, I'm only trying to get information so that I can properly represent my client.

MAC: I understand.

DC: I don't mean to be unkind, and I mean that sincerely. Mr. Duncan, if at any point you feel it necessary in light of our previous discussion, I certainly hope you indicate it to me. . . .

MAC: If you're trying to surmise that Chaplain Jensen and I didn't have sex during this time, I'm sorry then I'll have to disagree with you. I'll swear to that because we did and it happened quite frequently.

DC: I understand that you disagree with me, my only position is in the interest of my client. Now, didn't you say as far as October, that it might have happened half the days in October?

MAC: I remember around Hallowe'en. I'll have to go by holidays because that's the only thing that I have, there wasn't any.

DC: But you think that on all the other days there was?

MAC: I would say half of that month there was, maybe even more than half.

DC: You're not sure now. What about November? Did you continue to have sexual relations through the entire month of November?

MAC: No.

DC: When did it stop?

MAC: I would say towards the middle of November because I went back with my husband around Thanksgiving, because I remember we were together at Thanksgiving, on the 27th, I believe.

DC: Would that have been the time you went back to your husband?

MAC: A little bit before that.

DC: How much?

MAC: A couple of days. Probably the weekend before.

DC: That would be the 20th or the 21st?

MAC: Somewhere around there.

DC: To your knowledge, did you have sexual relations on the day that you went back to your husband or the day before?

MAC: That I can't answer because I don't know.

DC: So, it would be around the 15th of November that you broke off . . .

MAC: Approximately . . . It wasn't broken off. When you say that it was broken off . . .

DC: Don't let me put words in your mouth. What I mean to say, would it be around the 15th that you in fact went back to your husband, is that correct? At the Carriage House?

MAC: No, I did not leave the Carriage House. We stayed until the middle of November, then I moved into Yorktown around the first of December.

DC: Did your husband come over to the Carriage House?

MAC: He stayed for one night because his brother came in.

DC: You stayed at the Carriage House the entire month, is that correct?

MAC: Yes.

DC: When did you in fact leave the Carriage House and go to the Yorktown Apartments?

MAC: December first.

DC: How many days in November did your husband stay at the Carriage House?

MAC: I don't remember.

DC: Would it have been more than two days?

MAC: Yes, I would say so.

DC: Would it have been more than five days?

MAC: I don't remember.

DC: You have no way?

MAC: I have no idea.

DC: Would it have been more than seven days?

MAC: See, you're asking me something that I can't tell you. This was a time when I was very upset and I don't remember. Honestly, I just . . .

DC: Your husband would know, I take it?

MAC: I'm sure he might have an idea how many times he stayed.

DC: Now, am I correct in saying that you stated previously

here today that your last sexual relationship with Chaplain Jensen occurred somewhere around the 15th of November at the Carriage House?

MAC: At the Carriage House, yes, somewhere around there I think.

DC: And, of those fifteen days there in November, from the 1st to the 15th, do you have any idea how many of those days you had sexual relations?

MAC: I would say at least every other day. Maybe three times a week, sometimes even more.

DC: About half the time? In other words, is it fair to say that in November, out of the fifteen days involved, seven or eight of those days were days in which you had sexual relations?

MAC: Yes.

DC: All right. Now, this isn't what you said in your statement, because in your statement you said that at the Carriage House in September, October, and November, you had sexual relations nearly every day. That's pretty positive, isn't it? How can you account for the discrepancy between what you are saying here today and what you have said when you made this statement to N.I.S.?

MAC: Because you can say that a month or more has passed since that statement and a month or more has passed since this whole thing broke.

Reasonably, though, Mary Ann's memory should have been fresher a month earlier, and at a time when she had thought out her accusations and made her statement.

In his cross-examination, Chuck also brought out the inconsistencies in Mary Ann's account of our supposed affair in 1971. In the first statement she gave to the exec officer when the case broke, she said we had had relations from January to March. In her sworn statement to N.I.S. she said they continued through April. Under direct examination by Lt. Duncan, she talked of us having sex right on through June. Chuck Pope asked her if she had lied when she first said March was the cut-off date.

"No," she answered, "I wrote as much as I could remember that night . . . through thinking, later, I went back and told them that

I was wrong, that it was at least until April or May and I wasn't quite sure."

"And now you're saying through June," Chuck pointed out. "This is only forty days or so after the period designated, through June . . . and as I read this first statement."

"Well, Mr. Pope, I can say June because there is a motel that we went to in June in Callahan, Florida, and since the time of writing that statement I remembered it. I also remembered a couple of the others which I think you have in other statements." (No corroboration in the form of a receipt or eyewitness for the alleged tryst in the motel in Callahan was ever produced.)

Pope led her through an accounting of sexual acts in the latter stages of our alleged relationship, but Mary Ann could never give us a specific date so that we could directly counter with proof that I was elsewhere at the stated time and place. During this testimony, she actually broke out in giggles, and Pope asked that the record show the witness' mirth. Here is how the testimony went:

> DC: Well, taking your testimony now, you didn't have that much sex with Chaplain Jensen from December through June, did you?
>
> MAC: Yes, I did.
>
> DC: Didn't you state earlier today that there were seven or eight times at a motel and that the rest of it was at the apartment at Yorktown?
>
> MAC: Yes.
>
> DC: How many times did you have sex with Chaplain Jensen at Yorktown?
>
> MAC: A lot of times during lunch.
>
> DC: Well, then there were seven or eight times at the motels and six or seven times at the office. Now, how many times at the apartment at Yorktown?
>
> MAC: Two or three times a week.
>
> DC: June . . . so that would be six months . . .
>
> MAC: I would include . . .
>
> DC: Well, let's take a month at a time. Now, how many times in December?
>
> MAC: We were gone through the 20th, so I guess three or four times.

DC: December three or four times?

MAC: Yes.

DC: What about January? Would it be three times a week in January?

MAC: Two or three times a week.

DC: That would mean about twelve times in January.

MAC: Okay.

DC: How about February?

MAC: Approximately the same.

DC: So that would be approximately ten or eleven times in February?

MAC: I would say two times a week because the other times were at motels, so that would be less.

DC: Say eight times in February?

MAC: Right.

DC: In March?

MAC: Approximately the same amount of times in March.

DC: Ten times in March?

MAC: Yes, approximately.

DC: April?

MAC: At the apartment in April? Maybe a couple, maybe at least two or three, maybe five. I don't really know. I don't remember that.

DC: Five times in April?

MAC: I would say yes.

DC: How about May?

MAC: I don't know. When did Chaplain Swann arrive?

DC: How about June?

MAC: None.

DC: You said through June 1971.

MAC: In a motel, not in the apartment.

DC: Who saw Chaplain Jensen's car at your apartment?

MAC: A few girls who were at the pool at the time.

DC: Who?

MAC: Some of them, I don't even know their names, they just came up and asked me if anything had happened to my husband.

DC: Can you tell me the name of any of the girls who saw the Chaplain's car at your apartment?

MAC: Well . . .

DC: Were these officer's wives?

MAC: I don't know them that well. Some of them have moved in the meantime.

DC: We have then a total of thirty-nine or forty times during that time-period at the Yorktown Apartments, approximately?

MAC: Yes.

DC: Now, add to that the eighteen times at the motels?

MAC: That's all, Mr. Pope.

DC: Well, no, there was the six or seven times at the chapel at the Base, that would be a total of about sixty-three separate times that you were together during which times you committed one or more acts of sexual intercourse. Isn't that correct?

MAC: Approximately, yes.

DC: Now, taking this figure involving sixty-three visitations, did you have any idea of how many separate acts of intercourse or masturbation were involved?

MAC: No.

DC: Let's go back to the motels. There were seventeen or eighteen motel visits . . .

INVESTIGATING OFFICER: Excuse me, counsel. We're talking about seventeen or eighteen total motel visits. Now, what time frame are we speaking in terms of? From August on, or from December on?

DC: We're talking about the initial period, and this I get from what she tells me. We're talking about the initial period, September, October, November, and December, there were about ten times. Then after the first of the year during the period from—

MAC: Mr. Pope, what are you asking me? How many times out of this did the actual sex act take place and how many times did masturbation take place?

DC: Before we get into that I would like to tell Mr. Duncan what he wanted to know. Now, there were about seven or eight times after the first of the year and she seems to indicate now that some of these motel visitations occurred in June although I wasn't aware of this until she said it and I don't want to get into that right now.

MAC: I said one.

DC: Okay, one time in June, so there were seventeen or eighteen motel visits then. She said six or seven times at the chapel and thirty-nine times at the Yorktown apartment.

IO: What I had reference to here was really were we covering the Fox Meadow and Carriage House Apartments in this case.

DC: Okay, we didn't get to that. Now, how many visitations were there to the Fox Meadow?

MAC: Approximately every other day when his wife came back.

DC: Okay, I think we went into that. For two weeks every other day, that would be seven times at the Fox Meadow then, right?

MAC: Right.

DC: Then you originally said almost every day in September, October, and November for a period of ninety-one days at the Carriage House. Then I think you qualified that and an educated guess was forty to forty-five times or forty-five visits, is that right? You weren't sure about October, but you said fifteen times in one month.

MAC: It seems like a heck of a lot of times, doesn't it?

DC: Yes, it does. Now, can we round it off and say thirty-five times? I'm trying to get a figure and with that it comes out to 105 visits, but how many acts of intercourse and masturbation . . . how many times did the Chaplain actually reach a climax in those 105 occasions?

MAC: Approximately . . .

DC: Would you like to go back and try to figure it out?

MAC: Okay.

DC: Starting at the motel . . .

MAC: Okay, what about my apartment at Shindler Drive, why don't we start there?

DC: That was four times there, is that right?

MAC: Yes.

DC: Okay, that's plus three. Now, at the Gator Lodge?

MAC: I would say once each night.

DC: So, no addition there. What about the Airport Inn?

MAC: Once each night.

DC: What about Howard Johnson's?

MAC: Once, maybe twice. Which Howard Johnson's are you

talking about? There were two times at Howard Johnson's. Put once for all of them, okay?

DC: You did say that it happened twice at each Howard Johnson's, so that would be an additional two, is that right?

MAC: Okay.

DC: At the Gator . . . I believe you said that it was twice a night when you went back to the Gator Lodge.

MAC: I didn't say anything about that.

DC: What about the two motels that you didn't mention at Callahan and the Francis Motel? Was that once?

MAC: Once at Francis that I can remember. I can be off, but it could have been twice. I know it was at least once.

DC: Okay, now moving down to the chapel, I believe you already stated that it happened once each time at the chapel. The next figure we have here was at your apartment at the Yorktown. Was that once each time?

MAC: Sometimes more, but I . . . if you give it once each time it would round off because there were times when there wasn't anything.

DC: So that would be once each time there, right?

MAC: Right.

DC: What about at the Fox Meadow, we have seven times there?

MAC: There were two days that there was none that I remember and for the other five, one each.

DC: So that cuts down two. Now, what about the Carriage House? There were thirty-five days there.

MAC: I would say approximately twenty.

DC: That cuts it down by fifteen, and we added three, so that means twelve. Now, we take twelve from 105, and that leaves ninety-three times we're talking about. Is that pretty close to the right number?

MAC: Approximately.

The Article 32 hearings had only been on a couple of days when Lt. David Schraver, Lt. Levy's assistant, received permission from the investigating officer to sit in as a "government counsel." Schraver explained that he would be present to "comfort" Mary Ann Curran, whom he claimed was very worried and disturbed by the continuing cross-examination. My lawyers objected, pointing out that both

Schraver and Levy had already represented themselves improperly to my two accusers as court-martial prosecutors and that there was no need for a "government counsel." Lt. Duncan overruled them, however.

It was our feeling that Schraver's mission was less to comfort Mary Ann than to monitor and guide her so as to make her tesimoney more believable. Mary Ann, however, continued with her pattern of inconsistencies and contradictions. How was it she so quickly accepted my advances and gave herself to me in the first place, she was asked. Her explanation was that she felt she was in love with me—she wouldn't have sexual intercourse with a man unless they were in love, and I had told her of my love for her during that first kissing episode in the chapel office, she maintained.

Chuck Pope then wanted to know why she had said nothing about my profession of love in her sworn statement and why she had said nothing about it when she recounted the episode in her direct testimony before the investigating officer. Her answer was that she was "emotionally upset" when she wrote her statement. Chuck again read aloud her sworn account and repeated:

> "You were pretty specific about exactly what happened."
>
> ANSWER: "Yes."
>
> QUESTION: "Yet you say nothing about him saying that he loved you or he was going to leave his wife."
>
> ANSWER: "Mr. Pope, the way my morals are he would have to say he loved me for me to have done anything."

She went on to say that "when he took me into that office on Friday, no, I did not know there was any love. Yes, I was very shocked. No, I did not know what the heck was going on and that is why I moved to the chair because I felt a little uneasy and unsure of myself and I wasn't sure what was going to happen."

> QUESTION: "But you did say that he loved you and you didn't say it here in the statement?"
>
> ANSWER: "Right."
>
> QUESTION: "In spite of the fact that you were very specific about everything else?"
>
> ANSWER: "Right."

QUESTION: "You said he [Chaplain Jensen] wouldn't have kissed you unless you felt that he loved you?"

ANSWER: Yes."

QUESTION: "Do you actually recall him saying 'I love you' that afternoon?"

ANSWER: "He had to have said it."

QUESTION: "Do you actually recall having heard him say, 'I love you'?"

ANSWER: "I can't remember."

Chuck next questioned her about her relationship with the man in Beeville, Texas, the first week of May, 1970.

QUESTION: "What about the man down in Beeville? Do you remember anything about him?"

ANSWER: "I wasn't with him long enough to know."

QUESTION: "Did you love him?"

ANSWER: "I felt that I did."

QUESTION: "How long had you known him before you went to bed with him?"

ANSWER: "A couple of months—about three months."

QUESTION: "Did he say that he loved you?"

ANSWER: "Yes."

QUESTION: "Did you love him in June?"

ANSWER: "I don't know."

QUESTION: "Did you love him in July?"

ANSWER: "I don't know."

QUESTION: "Did you love him in August?"

ANSWER: "I felt that by then I loved Chaplain Jensen."

QUESTION: "Okay, so somewhere between May and August you fell out of love with this one man and fell in love with the other, and you're not really sure if you fell out of love with this man from Beeville until the end of July, right?"

ANSWER: "I'm not sure."

She had acted as something less than a woman in love when Lora Gudbranson told her that she too had been having an affair with Chaplain Jensen and prevailed on her to join in her accusation. Wasn't she angry with Lora for having been intimate with the man she supposedly loved? No, she said, she wasn't angry. (Could it have been, perhaps, that Lora and her wishes were somewhat more important to her than anything she could possibly have with Chaplain Jensen?)

Still contending that her affair with the chaplain had been true love, she cited the "love notes" she had received, except she couldn't explain why none of the letters and cards was addressed to her by name and she was vague about the circumstances under which she'd received some of them. Chuck Pope responded to the vagueness by pointing out that she had been alone in my office at times when she had ready access to papers and notes on top of my desk and that she easily could have taken personal notes belonging to Kathleen on the occasions she stayed overnight in our home. She seemed to do a double-take when Chuck told her that Kathleen—whose sincerity and truthfulness she said were beyond question—would say that she actually discussed some of these notes and cards with her. And she admitted that certain intimate facts about me which supposedly came from our physical contact—even about circumcision, had gotten sun rashes, and a painful infection from "chiggers" while on a family outing—could all have been told to her by Kathleen during their numerous talks about personal and other matters when she was alone with Kathleen in our home.

She also seemed surprised when Pope told her that Kathleen knew when I had been at motels and would testify to that effect. "Would it surprise you to know that on this night (when Mary Ann said she'd been at the motel with me and had taken the receipt), Mrs. Jensen planned to come to the motel herself but changed her plans because of illness?" he asked her. She paused and then said, "Yes, it would surprise me."

She didn't want to do anything that would hurt Mrs. Jensen, she went on, but had no response when Chuck pointed out that this hardly squared with what she was doing to Mrs. Jensen—after all, a guilty verdict against Chaplain Jensen would destroy the Jensen family.

Neither could she reconcile my being in love with her and failing—as acknowledged in her own statement—to discourage her from returning to her husband, telling her, in fact, that I was pleased when she did reunite. And why hadn't she told her husband about her affair? She had a most bizarre explanation: she had wanted to, but "my husband's brother is in a mental hospital. He's an acute schizophrenic. When I asked Chaplain Jensen about telling my husband he said that, through counseling, he knew Joe and that Joe would end up just like his brother, so there was no way that I could tell him."

Chuck decided it was necessary to put her—and thereby myself and Kathleen—through the ultimate test: a rigorous interrogation about what she really knew of my genital organs and a detailed accounting of what we had been through in the alleged adulterous encounters that formed that basis of the charges against me. Her explicit responses made for the most sensational—and appalling—phase of the investigation. I knew from our counseling sessions that Mary Ann seemed to enjoy describing all variety of sexual intimacy. I would have expected her, though, to be considerably more restrained at an official tribunal. I was quite wrong, and although I tried to convince myself of the necessity for it—basically to undermine her false testimony against me—it still shocked and sickened me.

It went this way:

Q: Have your duties as a nurse in the past required you to observe unclothed male bodies?

A: Yes.

Q: In what respect would you observe male bodies unclothed?

A: In taking care of them, nursing care, operations. But you don't view the whole body as a body.

Q: I understand. This viewing of male bodies would include, I take it, the groin area. Is that correct?

A: Yes.

Q: Now, when you bathe male people, you do bathe male bodies, is that correct?

A: Yes.

Q: Would this be patients who are unconscious or conscious?

A: If a patient is conscious we try to get them to bathe as much of himself as possible.

Q: Did you in fact ever bathe the genital areas of a conscious man?

A: That depends on what you term conscious. There are varying degrees of consciousness, but, yes, I have.

Q: There were some occasions?

A: Yes, and also at the nursing home there were men.

Q: Aside from whether you bathed them or not, did you in

fact in the process of bathing have occasion to view the male organs?

A: Yes.

Q: Isn't it a fact—and I'm drawing on my own knowledge, coming from a medical family, my father is a doctor and my sister is a nurse—isn't it a fact that there is a set procedure nurses follow when a patient is being bathed and has an erection?

A: Yes. He is usually covered with a sheet.

Q: Isn't it a fact that occasionally male patients will have erections when they are being bathed?

A: A lot of the older men will and a lot of the neurological patients will. One of the nerves, the sex nerve of the nervous system is damaged and they will have an ornamental erection.

Q: You have had in fact an occasion to view quite a number of male organs in the erect state. Is that correct?

A: Not very many.

Q: About how many?

A: Three.

Q: So you do have, aside from your own husband and Chaplain Jensen, and I believe you stated that you had an affair in Beeville, aside from those three individuals and from those three occasions, you have also had occasions to on those three times, is that correct?

A: Yes.

Q: Therefore, you are in some position to make a judgment on . . . well, for instance, the average size of a male penis in the erect position. Is that correct?

A: I never really thought of it like that.

Q: Well, you must be able to make some comparison between the size, for example, of Chaplain Jensen's male organ and other male organs that you have seen?

A: I hate to tell you this, but no. I never thought of it like that and I never got down and looked and said that's about how many inches. They didn't turn me on to go down and look. If I could help it I always kept my mental patients covered with a sheet. Always, even when I was bathing them, just hold the sheet up and bathe, just make a cradle out of the sheet, drape it over him and come up from underneath. It's just for their own comfort and mine. Another thing, if you're in an open ward why expose him to people and visitors walking by?

Q: How many uncircumcized male organs have you seen?

A: I don't know. I've never even thought about an uncircumsized male or a circumcized one.

Q: Have you any way of telling us how you would rate the male organ of the chaplain in comparison to others you have seen?

A: No, I don't because I'm not that well experienced with genital organs of men.

Q: Well, in view of your statements as to the manner in which you performed the sex act with Chaplain Jensen, don't you think you could give some notion of the size?

A: No, I couldn't.

Q: You said your mouth was involved?

A: How big is my mouth, though?

Q: On the occasion of using your mouth, did the organ go all the way in or just part of the way, or what? I realize this is a very delicate situation, I'm just thinking what . . .

A: What do you really want me to say? Do you want me to really get down and tell you exactly?

Q: Yes.

A: Okay. If you put a penis in someone's mouth different ways it will go in, sometimes all the way, sometimes not. How do you want me to explain that?

Q: Just how did it occur in your situation?

A: I don't remember, to be honest with you.

Q: You don't remember whether it went in all the way or not?

A: I don't think it did all the way.

Q: But you don't remember?

A: I don't think it did, but what I am trying to explain to you is that . . . I don't know how to explain it except to be blunt about it.

Q: Well, I guess that's the way you'll have to be.

A: Okay, if you take . . . can I use something besides the male organ to explain what I'm trying to explain?

Q: Yes, I think it might be better for everybody here.

A: If you take . . . can I use a carrot?

Q: Yes.

A: If you take a carrot and you put it back in your mouth it will go in a certain distance and if you take it and put it toward the side it will go a certain distance, all right? But it would probably go different distances, in fact maybe you can get an inch more of the carrot going the other way than you can get going straight in. Do you see what I mean?

Q: Yes.

A: That's why when you say did it go in completely . . .

Q: What I mean is, you still don't know or remember whether it did or not?

A: As far as I remember, it didn't.

Q: Can you give us any notion of the thickness of the male organ in the case of the Chaplain?

A: Erected or not erected?

Q: Erect?

A: Normal size. I don't know really. Do you want me to show you or what?

Q: I don't know. I suppose you could indicate with your finger.

A: I don't know . . . about like that.

DC: I guess we'll have to say that you're indicating with your index finger and thumb, the tip of the index finger touching the joint between the front and middle sections of the thumb. Is that correct, Mr. Duncan?

IO: Yes.

Q: All right, I'm going to make a suggestion. Mrs. Curran, I wonder if you would draw . . .

A: I hate to tell you this, but I think this is really . . . you want me to draw a circle?

Q: I want you to draw inside the area that you indicated before by tracing that area.

A: You know, I don't think this shows anything. First of all I don't know how to draw.

Q: Let's see.

[The defense counsel took the drawing from the witness.]

Q: Now, does this thickness, is this thickness uniform throughout the entire length of the male organ, or are you referring to the base as it comes out of the body, or the front part?

A: Front part, I would say.

Q: Is the front part thicker than the back part?

A: I would say so, a little bit. I am just . . . from the top of my head, like if someone was asking me about someone else, I'd just be guessing. I don't feel that that is just from the top of my head, it's just not that close or accurate. It's just that you wanted it so I drew it.

Q: It gives some notion, though, doesn't it?

A: Yes, but a man varies in size very little from one to another.

Q: How much?

A: Well, if he's like seven-foot-something . . .

Q: How do Chaplain Jensen's dimensions in this regard compare with your husband's?

A: My husband is six-foot-five, Chaplain Jensen is how tall? Five-foot-something.

Q: But this is assuming that the size of the male organ varies with the body of the man.

A: Well, that's an assumption. Some people say it does and some say it does not.

Q: I understand that there is not necessarily a correlation to the bigness of a man's body and the bigness of the male organ. I may be wrong on that, but let's assume that there isn't necessarily any relationship. Let me ask you again, how does the Chaplain's compare with your husband's?

A: I don't know.

Q: You have no idea?

A: I don't know.

Q: And yet you performed the same act of oral-genital stimulation on your husband as you did on the Chaplain?

IO: Counsel, I think we've just about exhausted this area basically in terms of . . .

DC: Well, we still have a few more questions to ask.

IO: I think she has answered the question about her husband. Let the record reflect that a sheet of yellow paper with the mark made by Mrs. Curran on it has been marked as IO Exhibit 21.

Q: There are no distinguishing marks other than the lack of circumcision of the male organ that you can otherwise identify? Is that correct?

A: That I remember.

Q: Have you any notion on how the size of the male organ of the Chaplain would vary in its flaccid state, that is, no erection, compared to when it was erected?

A: Very small to me.

Q: Would it be half the size or a third of the size?

A: Just small, very small. It's much smaller than my husband's.

Q: The flaccid state of your husband's, is that correct?

A: Yes.

Q: Is your husband circumcized or uncircumcized?

A: Uncircumcized.

Q: You stated, I believe, and I want to be sure that we have this correct, that in the nonerect, flaccid position the Chaplain's male organ appears to be much shorter and less thick than your husband's. Is that correct?

A: Yes.

Chuck Pope needed to press Mary Ann especially for details of the sex acts we supposedly committed in my chaplain's office—since this accusation was the most ridiculous of all that had been made. He needed to get her on record as to the time and the circumstances of these acts so I could secure rebuttals from parishioners or members of the chaplain staff who might have been at the chapel at the same time. Chuck began this line of questioning by asking if these alleged acts with me in my office always occurred after hours. She answered that they did. He then attempted to develop the specifics:

Q: As to the alleged acts of intercourse in the Chaplain's Offices, they never occurred before four o'clock in the afternoon?

A: No.

Q: Would you always arrive at the Chapel around four o'clock on these occasions?

A: No, sometimes late at night.

Q: Like when?

A: Seven, eight, sometimes nine.

Q: All right, now was there anyone else . . . you said there were six or seven times this happened in the time period alleged. You don't recall the exact month or the exact date or anything, do you?

A: No.

Q: Of these six or seven times, how many times did you arrive at four o'clock?

A: I'm not real sure. Maybe about three, half of them, I guess.

Q: Then the other three or four times, when did you arrive?

A: After working hours. I'm not sure of the times.

Q: Around five o'clock? Can't you give me any idea at all?

A: (No response to the questions.)

Q: You do know that sometimes you arrived at seven or eight o'clock, right?

A: It could have been that late, it was dark. I don't remember but I think it was the time of the year it gets dark early, around five-thirty.

Q: I think we'll all agree that this would have to be sometime after six-thirty, at least, during the winter. Isn't that when it gets dark?

A: It gets dark around five-thirty in the winter.

Q: It does?

A: When we have daylight-saving time it does.

IO: When we revert back to normal time it does get dark quite early.

DC: All right.

Q: Now, was anyone present when you arrived on those three occasions at four o'clock, other than Chaplain Jensen?

A: Maybe the guy that picked up the garbage. That would be it.

Q: Are you sure of that?

A: Yes.

Q: When you arrived at four o'clock, was there anyone in the process of leaving, or anyone who saw you come in at that hour?

A: Not that I remember.

Q: Now, was there anyone around when you arrived later on, say five-thirty or six o'clock?

A: Sometimes Chaplain Hubbard would be there.

Q: Did you always have an appointment with Chaplain Jensen on the books when you arrived on these six or seven occasions when intercourse was allegedly committed?

A: No, not always.

Q: Well, how would you know you would go there and find Chaplain Jensen?

A: Because he would call and tell me to come.

Q: Would he call you at work?

A: He would call me at work, at my apartment while he was at work.

Q: Now, to your knowledge . . . now, when you went into the office and these acts occurred, was the door always shut?

A: Yes.

Q: Was it locked?

A: To my knowledge it was. I saw him go over there and lock it.

Q: How do you lock that door?

A: I think you just push and turn the little . . . I don't know, I never locked it.

Q: Did you ever unlock it?

A: Yes, I remember doing that, turning something.

Q: All right, would you explain, please, how you were able to, how you did commit these acts in the Chaplain's office. Where did they occur?

A: On the floor.

Q: Do you recall, was it always on the same part of the floor?

A: Yes.

Q: Were the acts all normal acts of sexual intercourse?

A: It didn't always happen on the floor. Chaplain Jensen would turn off the lights and make sure that the blind was pulled, and I think about twice or three times it happened on the floor, the other times it was manual masturbation.

Q: Was this when he was supposedly impotent?

A: No.

Q: Why did he ask you to manually masturbate him? Did he say he got more pleasure from this than from . . .

A: I didn't always do it by myself. Chaplain Jensen helped too.

Q: But did he tell you why he wanted it done this way?

A: He said that he needed it.

Q: Did he say why?

A: He said he was going to crawl the walls.

Q: According to your statement on the second page, I'm now referring to Exhibit 4 . . .

A: I know what I said.

Q: You say in that statement that during the period, this

period refers to late December through April 1971, which you now say is June 1971. You say "During this period he became impotent for periods up to three weeks. He pleaded and begged for me to masturbate him and [. . .] out of pity I would perform the acts." To my knowledge in this statement you don't mention masturbation except in relation to this impotency as a way, possibly, to bring him out of the impotent state.

A: There are a lot of things in that statement, Mr. Pope, because I was under great emotional strains at the time.

Q: I certainly think, Mrs. Curran, that . . .

A: How would you? You have never been in that predicament.

Q: I suppose not.

A: You should be thankful.

Q: I think you can sympathize with us when we wonder why you don't remember some of these things and when you bring these things in after the very detailed three-page statement . . .

A: Mr. Pope, it could have been a book.

Q: So you say that of these six or seven times, three times involved masturbation only and not intercourse.

A: Three times there was masturbation, and intercourse happened about three times.

Q: When there was masturbation there was no intercourse?

A: True.

Q: When there was intercourse there was no masturbation?

A: Not that I know of.

Q: When there was intercourse did it happen more than once or only once?

A: I don't understand.

Q: On each occasion did it happen just once or more than once?

A: Just once.

Q: Was there only one act of masturbation on each day?

A: Yes.

Q: How long would it take for the completion of the masturbation?

A: A fairly good length of time.

Q: Could you give me an approximation?

A: Ten or fifteen minutes.
Q: Would you use your hand, is that it?
A: There was [. . .].
Q: I take it when you refer to masturbation then it was manual [. . .]?
A: Yes.
Q: Was the completion outside of the female organ?
A: Yes.
Q: Now, when the masturbation occurred, how would that occur? Where would he be and where would you be?
A: Standing by the light. There was a light to the right of the door in the office and he would stand right next to the light.
Q: Was the light on?
A: He would turn it off.
Q: Would he disrobe completely?
A: No, he wouldn't disrobe.
Q: What would he do?
A: He would unzip.
Q: He wouldn't drop his pants?
A: No, just unzip.
Q: What about when intercourse occurred?
A: He would drop his pants but he wouldn't take them off.
Q: He would leave them on?
A: Yes.
Q: Underwear too, I presume?
A: He dropped them too.
Q: Didn't anyone ever knock at the door or try to get in?
A: No.
Q: Never? You're sure of that?
A: Yes.
Q: And all of these acts of intercourse occurred on the floor?
A: Yes.
Q: Who was on top and who was on the bottom?
A: Chaplain Jensen was on the top and I was on the bottom.
Q: How were you about disrobing? What would you do?
A: I usually had on a nurse's uniform.
Q: What part of your uniform would you take off?
A: My stockings. I had panty hose on.
Q: Did you take them completely off?
A: Not completely.

Q: Well, could you tell me just what you did do?

A: I would take them down to my ankles, take one shoe off, and take one leg of the stockings off to free one foot.

Q: All right, now let's refer to the acts of masturbation. When the cycle was completed and ejaculation had occurred, where would the semen end up? In your hand, your mouth, or where?

A: On my clothes.

Q: How about when the acts of intercourse occurred?

A: I had my stockings down and I would pull them right up and it would have caught anything. It usually didn't come out until I stood up.

Q: Then it would come out on the stockings?

A: Yes.

Q: You never went to the ladies' restroom to clean up at all?

A: Yes, once in a while. Sometimes I didn't.

Q: All right. Now when the masturbation occurred, where did it end up?

A: Sometimes on my clothes, sometimes I had a napkin of some sort. He used to have some cotton Kleenex of some sort.

Q: Did you bring those?

A: No, they were in his office.

Q: Kleenex like these? (indicating a facial tissue)

A: No, they were celluloid. They were in a green container. They were like a heavy Scotty tissue.

Q: Did you arrange so that the semen landed in the napkin?

A: One time I did.

Q: So it always landed there or on your clothing?

A: I didn't always have a Kleenex or anything like that.

Q: You didn't have any objection to the possibility of it getting on your clothing?

A: It bothered me a little bit.

Q: You didn't really enjoy doing that, did you? You say in your statement that you did it out of pity for him, isn't that right?

A: (No response.)

Q: I gathered from what you said before that you didn't enjoy that sort of activity, you enjoyed the normal sex act. We don't have to define the normal sex act, but everything else we have talked about is considered a little bit unnatural in common parts.

A: (No response.)

Q: Do you consider masturbation by a woman upon a man to be natural?

A: I don't consider it to be natural but not so unnatural.

Q: Irrespective of that, is that something you enjoy doing?

A: No.

Q: Do you in fact, although you enjoy one act more than the other, get any enjoyment at all out of masturbating a man?

A: No, why should I?

Q: I'm asking you.

A: No, I don't.

Q: You would never do it of your own volition, except out of pity. Would that be your answer?

A: No, that wouldn't be my answer.

Q: What would your answer be?

A: I would do it out of love.

Q: But not through personal preference?

A: I don't know.

Q: Do you think you might enjoy doing it? I don't ask that to cast a personal judgment upon you. I'm asking because I need an answer if you can give me one. I think you ought to be able to tell me whether you enjoy doing this sort of thing.

A: I enjoy—what you're terming as sex I am terming as a whole love-making session, and what we term the work-up or what may be termed masturbation, to me this is something that's beautiful and something that should be beautiful. Just plain masturbating to climax, no.

Q: So, you in fact would never, just out of personal prefence, masturbate a man and nothing else, is that correct?

A: If it got to my sympathy I might.

I am well aware that the foregoing testimony—and its elicitation—is something less than attractive. I opposed it and, as mentioned, was upset by it, I think more for Kathleen than myself. Without presuming to appear more generous than I humanly felt, I also was upset to hear it being drawn even from somebody such as Mary Ann, who had conspired to bring against me these destructive charges. I was not, I honestly feel, insensitive to the humiliation for her and her husband. At the same time, I cannot reasonably overly apologize for going along with efforts to salvage my career and family life.

Further, there is no reason to overlook the dissembling attempt of Mary Ann in her Article 32 testimony to make me look as bad as possible and herself as decent and naïve as a woman in love could possibly be. In her N.I.S. affidavit she said she had performed certain acts upon me because she felt sorry for me and my needs. In the pretrial testimony just presented, it had changed to an act of love by a woman in love, unable to deny her lover anything he might wish—a victim of her honest passion. Andrew Jensen had changed from victim to Svengali-like love object; Mary Ann from rather detached purveyor to victim-in-love. A nice refurbishing for her, a clear effort at placing responsibility on me as an amoral sybarite who diluted and beclouded her good moral attitudes, helpless before her romantic love-justifying-all emotions toward me.

The suggestion, then, is that without attempting to sit in judgment, we had reason to be somewhat skeptical of Mary Ann's protestations of high morality and partaking in sexual acts only when deeply in love, and with this in mind her testimony given below, as elicited by Chuck Pope, becomes somewhat deceptively simple and self-serving. And this is significant in demonstrating the fact that she did willfully connive and conspire to destroy me, and perhaps more importantly she did so with the active collaboration of the command—both for their reasons as mentioned before, and her own special ones, including her strong fear of and anger at the possibility of my revealing her stated lesbian predelictions. Mary Ann, by the time of the hearing, was intended to appear sweetly reasonable, helplessly in love, and modern without being extreme. Such is indicated in the following exchanges. I suggest they are rather difficult to accept as coming from Mary Ann without outside help and are self-effacing for the sake of face-saving rather than genuinely her own.

> Q: I supposed the time has come to ask you some other questions and believe me these are asked for no other purpose than to establish the full picture for higher authorities here and also to give us the information I think we need. I would like to move into your attitude on sex. . . . Do you believe in all of the doctrines which you think the Catholic Church prescribes?
>
> A: No.
>
> Q: Which ones don't you believe?
>
> A: I believe in general absolution, God forgives. I don't

believe in the birth control that the Catholic Church teaches.

Q: Do you believe in the institution of marriage?

A: Very much.

Q: Do you believe in divorce?

A: Yes.

Q: Do you believe in remarriage after divorce?

A: Yes.

Q: Do you think that adultery is a sin?

A: Yes, I do.

Q: Do you think fornication is a sin? Let's understand what we mean by fornication; fornication is sexual intercourse between two unmarried consenting adults, right?

A: Yes.

Q: Neither of whom is married to anyone else.

A: Yes.

Q: Do you believe in Hell?

A: Yes.

Q: Do you believe that a person who had committed adultery has committed a sin for which they can go to Hell?

A: No.

Q: Do you think, in view of what you have said, that there is any place in life for adultery between two consenting adults? . . . Do you believe, in view of what you have said, that there is any permissible area where there can be adultery between two consenting adults? You said that you believe that adultery is a sin, but that it isn't a serious enough sin to go to Hell. Is that correct?

A: Yes. I believe that maybe my viewpoint has changed in the last few months. Let me give you my viewpoint. My viewpoint at the time this affair started a year ago was that if you loved someone and there was love it wasn't adultery and I felt that by leaving my husband then I was not committing adultery because I was going on with the divorce. I believed Chaplain Jensen would leave his wife, and that it wouldn't be a sin. It wouldn't be a condemning fact, but I had a lot of guilt from it, a lot of guilt that I couldn't rationalize. Now, what do I feel adultery is? I probably can't let myself think that it's absolutely wrong, because if I did I couldn't cope with it.

Q: Cope with what ?

A: Cope with what I did.

Q: All right. So I take from what you said then that we can imply that there are occasions when in your opinion it isn't a sin to commit adultery, whether it's a little sin or a big sin, is that correct?

A: I'm saying that it's wrong. It's against the standards, the norms that society sets up, so therefore there's got to be a reason for it.

Q: Okay, now let's get into the way one performs the sex act. Now, I don't think we need to isolate this either to the marriage or the adultery aspects. Let's just say when two consenting adults are having sexual relations with each other, do you think it's wrong for the woman to commit a sodomy which essentially is involved when we mention oral copulation, isn't that correct?

A: Yes.

Q: That's the old term for it. Sodomy is the case of Sodom and Gomorrah. Now, what is your view on that?

A: I'm not really that . . . to be honest with you, I don't know. What do I think? Well, sometimes I do things like what you are talking about, sodomy, being a girl, stimulation, out of love and I condone it and I say it's right. I don't think in my background that I accepted it as being right, but that's just something I just can't answer honestly. I don't know my true feelings about it.

Q: You don't know then, whether . . . or did you ever know for sure that committing an act of sodomy either by a man or a woman is something which you would consider wrong or immoral?

A: I never knew until somebody pulled it out of a legal book that it was against the law. Now, maybe that's stupidity on my part, but . . .

Q: All right, I'm not holding you to any knowledge of the law. All I'm asking from you . . .

A: You're asking for an opinion and all I know is that it's against the law.

Q: How do you feel about it now? Can it be against the law and still be within your ideas of correct moral conduct?

A: Well, I believe that just like the legal books, just like the Bible was written a long time ago, and so were the legal books, and they might have held a different connotation, maybe sanitary conditions weren't the same then, I'm not quite sure. So, I don't know how I feel about it really, but I can't say anything about it because I don't know.

Q: So, you don't know if it's right or wrong, isn't that what you're saying?

A: Yes, that's what I'm saying.

Q: Okay, now what about masturbation where the seed comes out somewhere other than the place within the female genital area?

A: I can't say that I think that's wrong. I don't.

Q: And is your answer irrespective of whether the man does it upon himself or the woman does it for him?

A: I don't believe masturbation is wrong by the man himself, upon himself, or by a woman herself.

Q: How about when a woman does it to a man, do you think that's wrong?

A: No.

Q: Do you think the way a woman does it necessarily makes it wrong? In other words take a woman doing it with her hand and a woman doing it with her mouth. Is there anything . . .

A: There you're getting back to sodomy and I really don't know.

Q: Well, sodomy can be committed without masturbation because sodomy can be committed in the first instance and the seed can be deposited in the female organ, isn't that correct? You can have sodomy and then finish it without masturbation.

A: In other words you're saying that the climax?

Q: Well, is there any difference in your moral judgment?

A: Yes.

Q: What is that difference?

A: I did both, so what do you want me to say?

Q: Do you think either one is immoral?

A: Immoral? No, I don't think that anything that someone thinks is right in sex when they love somebody is wrong.

Mary Ann was not, as suggested above, doing so badly here in her efforts to seem rather helpless and confused—a woman confounded by honest feelings of love. Chuck Pope reasonably changed the direction of his questioning.

Q: Now, getting back to the office where the six or seven acts occurred, was there any difference in time so far as the masturbation was concerned, against when the sexual intercourse occurred?

A: Could you explain that a little bit?

Q: Well, did the masturbation occur always earlier in the day, or did the sexual intercourse always occur earlier in the day? Was there any relation in the time of the day?

A: There wasn't any relation, in other words it could have happened either late or early.

Q: Now, during the time you were having intercourse with Chaplain Jensen, did you also have intercourse with your husband? I'm not referring to the time you were separated from your husband, but from December . . .

A: Do you mean the same day or the same night?

Q: All right, let me rephrase the question. You were with your husband from December through June, is that correct?

A: Yes.

Q: You were also having intercourse with Chaplain Jensen during that period. Now, leaving aside the question of whether it occurred on the same day or not, did you also have any intercourse at all with your husband?

A: During that whole time?

Q: Yes.

A: Yes, I did.

Q: Do you recall about how often?

A: Not very often.

Q: Could you give us any kind of answer?

A: No, because it wasn't very often. If I had sex with Chaplain Jensen I did not have it with my husband. . . .

Mary Ann's period of testimony extended over most of four days and when it ended, Chuck, Lyman, and I tried to assess the results. Clever as some of it perhaps was, we felt no impartial judge or jury would accept her as a credible person. Her inconsistencies, contradictions, mixed-up and erratic statements, and vagueness on details which she should have known for certain surely gave her away. In recapping the sexual content of her testimony, Chuck made this point:

"She was totally unable to describe her alleged lover's organ, except from the standpoint of width. She couldn't tell us anything about the length in the erect state but only stated that in the flaccid condition her lover's organ was not as large as her husband's. It's astounding that a woman who claims to have slept with a man on ninety-five different occasions would have as little recall about such a central element in a sex act as she did. And remember, she said that on a number of occasions the sex act was performed in broad daylight."

Mary Ann's credibility gap seemed clearly unbreachable. Even more important from the legal standpoint was that we could fix direct lies on her. In her testimony (as well as her sworn statement), she had described me as a heavy drinker and had identified the flask found in my desk as one she had brought to me so I could pour whiskey from little bottles into it. But two chaplains had been with me when I found that flask out on the chapel grounds, and they could so testify.

Mary Ann had finally made reference to her affair with a man in Beeville, Texas, to explain why she and her husband had first come to me for counseling. She had been in love with this man, too, she testified, which explained and made right her spending a night in a motel with him. She had been specific on the stand in limiting her relations with him to one act—whereas in counseling she had said that she had been intimate with him on other nights as well. She also testified that she had had an affair with only one man—myself—since coming to Cecil Field. When she was asked about Dr. Blanc from the nursing home, she had asserted that she knew him only as a friend —there had been no sex with him or with the salesmen or with other men she knew socially. Yet I knew from what she had told me very specifically about Dr. Blanc that this was also a lie. If I could find documentary evidence at the motels where she had stayed with the man from Beeville and with Dr. Blanc, I could prove her to be a blatant perjurer. And how could any prosecuting authority reasonably proceed to trial with a star witness who had already been proved a liar? Who would believe her?

Logic tends to be exalted by hope and wishful thinking. Of these I *was* guilty.

CHAPTER 14

Mary Ann Curran seemed a somewhat light-headed witness. Lora Gudbranson did not. As the apparently more dominant and intelligent of the two, she seemed determined to put the defendant, defense lawyers, and indeed the investigating officer in their places. She would brook no nonsense about anyone trying to upset her testimony. While Mary Ann, when confronted with her errors and contradictions, would rather casually explain them away as memory lapses, Lora belligerently contested any insinuation that she was telling something less than the complete truth. Chuck Pope's probing angered her greatly and it was soon apparent she regarded him as her mortal enemy. In appearance she seemed more severely dressed than ever before, and her strident tone and demeanor tended to match the appearance.

Lora had her reasons for anger. She had expected to be called as the principal witness on the first day of the hearing; instead she wasn't called until the ninth day and she bitterly complained about "all the days I just sat around and waited." (Lora and Mary Ann might be colleagues in conspiracy, but Lora clearly considered herself—as in other matters generally—the senior and dominant partner.) The delay was caused by the long interrogation of Mary Ann Curran, the fact that her husband and some of the N.I.S. agents were called next and the investigating officer's habit of moving the hearing around to different conference rooms in different buildings. Sometimes we would be obliged to wait hours before getting started on a particular day's proceedings. I felt the delay in my pocketbook because I had agreed to pay Lyman Fletcher at the rate of thirty dollars for each hour spent on my case; on such occasions the money was spent on waiting time.

Lora's ire was also aroused when an enlisted man and fellow-member of our Protestant planning board called her shortly before her date for testimony to ask if she intended to continue working on the chapel's mission project. During their conversation the subject of my Article 32 investigation came up and he told her he was supporting me. She immediately told him she would report him to the command, that he'd soon change his tune when a "surprise witness" appeared against the chaplain.

When Kathleen and I learned of this we worried that a "surprise witness" might mean a feared "somebody" who would give perjured testimony. The command with the N.I.S. had behaved in such a manner from the start that I had had to consider the possibility they might go to the extreme of pressuring witnesses into testifying who would in turn make false statements. The possibility was upsetting enough to give Kathleen another attack of respiratory spasms and Joy Oneth and Betty McKean were kind enough to help nurse her and take care of our kids while I was occupied with the hearing.

It developed in this instance that Lora's "surprise witness" was Lora herself. Apparently she felt she would be so effective that her impact would have the disruptive impact on the defense of a surprise witness.

Obviously she had been told that Mary Ann's credibility had been damaged by inaccuracies and contradictions; by contrast, she came prepared to be as explicit as possible and to defy all efforts to undo her. She brought a date book with her to the witness stand and with Lt. Duncan's permission, consulted it to make certain she had her dates right. There was, of course, no way we could tell when and under what circumstances she had written these items in her book.

Her first display of supposed fact came when she reviewed her relationship with me and described our first alleged kissing episode following the Parent Teachers Association meeting. In her N.I.S. statement she said we had "kissed and embraced" in my car following the February and March, 1971, P.T.A. meetings at the Whitehouse Elementary School. But at the hearing she testified, "Since then I have found a calendar that had a party on it that I went to before this P.T.A. meeting, so I know that this P.T.A. meeting was probably the January one. When I saw him [Chaplain Jensen] at the P.T.A. meeting, we met in the hallway and he said, 'I was thinking of taking you out for some coffee after the meeting is over.' I said, 'I can't think of any place where we might get coffee around here,' and he said, 'Well, we'll find some place.' So he told me where to watch for him after we had visited all of the teachers' rooms and when our visits were over with the teachers we went for a drive, and that was the first time there was any physical contact."

She testified that we got into our individual cars, drove a short distance to the grocery store, where she left her car and got into mine. "Then we drove for a short time—perhaps half an hour—stopping periodically for some kissing, caressing, that sort of thing . . ."

When the investigating officer asked her to be more specific about the January date, she consulted her date book and fixed the date as "January 21." She looked quite pleased as she said it; she was no mixed-up Mary Ann Curran.

She was as deliberately precise in detailing our alleged sexual adventures. Our first intimacy, she said, occured at the Howard Johnson's motel on Golfair Boulevard near the Methodist Hospital. She knew by consulting her date book that it was May 18. "I don't have any listing in my book of 'This is the day I had sexual intercourse with Chaplain Jensen,' she said with amusement when Chuck Pope questioned her about the accuracy of her listing. She did have, she explained, notations about other activities that occurred the day before or the same day and which enabled her to fix some important personal event that also happened at that particular time. She had a meeting of the Protestant Planning Board the day before, she said, and that was the day the chaplain suggested the motel rendezvous. Her date book showed she was hostess at a luncheon on the next day, May 19th, and she was able to get away from there and over to the motel at 2 P.M.

Love-making, complete with heavy consumption of vodka by the chaplain, went on until five o'clock, she further testified. She was not the kind of woman, she pointed out later, who would casually share a bed with a man no matter how much he attracted her. She required the proper kind and degree of romantic preliminary, and she went to some lengths to distinguish herself in this matter from Mary Ann Curran. One might not unreasonably get the impression that she was showing some competitive jealousy and resentment toward her partner in this accusation.

"My relationship was quite different from Mrs. Curran's relationship with him," she said. "He understood from the beginning that I was not interested, even though he aroused me, that I was not interested in playing the teen-ager in the car or flailing around on the floor of the chapel. It just seemed a little bit below my dignity. I think he knew me well enough to realize that I wasn't going to leap into a motel for half an hour, that that also was not the kind of expression of love I had in mind. When we went to a motel, it was for two or two-and-a-half hours. That experience was not exactly fulfilling because he was nervous and afraid of being caught or seen. When we were in his home, there was a relaxed atmosphere. It was late at night, there was very little chance of being caught or being seen, there was no rush of time, there was no place either one of us had to be and my only concern was that I might fall asleep and wake up with the sun shining and have to try to get back to my house in broad daylight."

Continuing in this self-assured manner, Lora went on to the July 8th episode. She could pinpoint the date of Thursday, July 8th, she said, because she had visited a friend in the hospital on the same day she had her rendezvous with me and she had recently checked out the date of her hospital visit. "I was in his office on Tuesday or Wednesday of that week, and he said he was very interested in meeting me again. He said that my just walking into the office was enough to arouse him. He said that he didn't know where we would go and he asked me if I had any ideas. I said, 'No, I don't.' He said not too long ago he had been out driving and had seen quite a few motels in the Starke area."

She testified that we agreed to meet at a shopping center not far from the hospital at 2 P.M. and that we finally hit on the Gator Lodge on Phillips Highway as the site for our rendezvous. She provided one precise detail after another: the chaplain had told her on the phone that he was in uniform that day and didn't want to register at the motel in uniform. She therefore bought a sports shirt "with orange and green in it" at the Pic 'N Save store in the shopping center and the chaplain took off his khaki uniform shirt and put this sports shirt on. The chaplain then put his Navy hat in the back seat of the car, and she covered it with the uniform shirt so it would not attract attention. Arriving at the Gator Lodge, the chaplain was careful not to park directly in front and instead parked away from the entrance. She then joined him in a unit near the motel swimming pool for refreshment (sherry, not vodka, this time) and sexual intercourse. The meeting lasted from two-and-a-half to three hours. She also recalled a phone call she made for the chaplain which he was unable to make himself due to his inebriated condition.

"By the time we began thinking about leaving the motel, he seemed to me to have had too much to drink and I was concerned about his ability to drive, especially since we had to go on a major highway to get home. At approximately five o'clock or thereabouts, I suggested to him that it might be a good idea to take a cold shower. He obviously had had quite a lot to drink and he was acting silly and giddy and a way I had never seen him act before, and I thought a cold shower might prepare him for the drive. He had asked me to make a phone call for him and when I went to do that he went in to take a cold shower.

"The phone call was to the Baptist Book Store. He told me that they closed at five o'clock and he was supposed to order some books for the chapel, so I called the Baptist Book Store for him and put in the order."

The books, she said, included a Bible and three copies of a book titled *Reach out,* used by young people in the chapel. When asked for the name of the purchaser, she said, "I'm calling for Chaplain Jensen and he authorizes this purchase." She said she told the store to charge the purchase to the chapel.

She could be exact about the meetings in the chaplain's home on July 16th and 17th, she said, because her husband left for Whidbey Island on July 14th and was gone until Sunday, July 18th. And the chaplain had told her his wife and children would be leaving for Philadelphia on Friday morning, July 16th, and invited her to come over the same night. "The children were watching television and I went out for a walk," she said. "It was around nine o'clock. I walked down the street and I checked the street over fairly thoroughly and I walked up to his front door. He had all of the lights off and he was waiting for me. He suggested we have a drink. He had some, I believe, and I can't swear to this, but I believe it was some Seagram's in a . . . I don't know what size bottle . . . but it's a fairly short bottle and it's square."

The sequence thereafter, she said, went in this fashion: Heavy petting and kissing as warm-up. The chaplain kept making sure it was completely dark with all the shades pulled down so that nobody could see her shadow and his. They broke off love-making to allow her time to go home and put her children to bed, but she returned at 11 o'clock, this time through the back door. There followed the pattern established in motel sessions of heavy drinking and sexual intercourse. She returned home at 3:30 in the morning. The chaplain called her several hours later, complaining of a bad hangover but inviting her nonetheless for another night of pleasure. She obliged by coming again the next night at 11:30 P.M. and staying until 2:30 A.M. On both nights she had to pass by the back of Quarters F, the house next door to the chaplain's, occupied by Commander Henry Chase and his wife Faye, but it was dark out and she insisted nobody saw her.

She continued as the very careful witness when Chuck Pope pressed her for physical details about me that she would have reasonably noted during periods of intimacy. She countered by saying she was the sort of person who wasn't especially observant, particularly during relations conducted in semidarkness. She thereby sought to avoid the credibility damage suffered by Mary Ann who reported so exuberantly on the details of her relations with the chaplain and then became so confused and forgetful when asked for certain specifics of her loved one's sexual equipment. Lora even testified she was unsure whether the chaplain was circumcized, even though we already knew she had been told he was not. This portion of her testimony went as follows:

> Q: I have to ask you some questions which are unpleasant ones for me to ask but I think you can see why I am interested in asking them. I suppose we may as well start at the beginning and work down chronologically, but before we begin, let me ask you some general questions. Are you aware, as a result of your alleged sexual intercourse with Chaplain Jensen, about any of the personal details, markings, or configurations of his body?
>
> A: No.
>
> Q: You're not?
>
> A: No.
>
> Q: Was he circumcized or uncircumcized?
>
> A: I don't know.
>
> Q: When you committed these acts, were there any lights where you could see anything or observe anything?
>
> A: In the motel, since it was during the day, it was impossible for it to be totally dark; the blinds were pulled but it was light.
>
> Q: You then were in a position to see something?
>
> A: No, not necessarily, I wasn't examining each part of him in minute detail.
>
> Q: Were you fully disrobed at all times?
>
> A: I was, yes.

Q: Was he?

A: No.

Q: In what state of disrobement was he in?

A: In the motels, he kept his T-shirt and his underwear on.

Q: The bottom part of his underwear?

A: Yes, until intercourse took place, then he pulled that down.

Q: Completely?

A: No, not all the way.

Q: What was the reason for that?

A: Why did he pull them down?

Q: No, why did he keep them on?

A: I don't know. I assumed at that time that he was shy.

Q: What about at the quarters, was he fully disrobed at the quarters?

A: Yes, but it was completely dark except for a small light showing through the bathroom.

Q: I guess the next question is, on all of these occasions, was there what you consider . . . was there anything unusual . . . I guess I'd better explain what I'm getting at. Let's explain normal sexual activity as activity whereby neither party . . . Let me tell you what Mrs. Curran said . . .

WIT: Do you think it's really relevant to hear something Mrs. Curran said?

INVESTIGATING OFFICER: I think we can inquire more directly into the matter of normal sexual activity.

WIT: Would you like for me to explain normal sexual activity since you are having such a problem?

DC: Well, I dont want to pass the buck to you, but if . . .

WIT: I believe what took place is what I would consider normal sexual activity. If you consider that to mean that the male penis entered the female vagina, there were certain spasms which took place resulting in an orgasm. The only thing unnormal about it is that the chaplain didn't completely undress. Under the circumstances, with the kind of person I felt him to be that didn't really strike me as being odd. I just thought he was shy.

Q: Prior to the completion of any actual sexual intercourse was there any oral genital stimulation by either you or Chaplain Jensen?

A: No.

Q: Was any such thing suggested in any way [. . .]?

A: At the Gator Lodge, it was suggested.

Q: And what did you reply?

A: He didn't ask me, [. . .]. It did not arouse me and he sensed this [. . .].

Q: And you yourself never did anything on your part towards that type of activity . . . Either by yourself or suggestion?

A: Do you mean by that, putting his organ in my mouth?

Q: Yes.

A: No, I did not do that.

Q: Did you ever hold it in your hand?

A: Yes.

Q: Because of that would you be able to say, if you were thinking about it, whether or not the organ was circumcized or not?

A: I don't believe I'd know how to tell, as a matter of fact, I wasn't thinking about it.

Q: Are you familiar with what an uncircumcized organ looks like?

A: More or less.

Q: There is a substantial difference between the two, isn't there?

A: I suppose so.

Q: How many acts of intercourse occurred altogether? You can give us your best recollection or if you remember, the total number.

A: I believe there was two at Howard Johnson's, I believe it was two at the Gator Lodge, I believe it was two on the night of the 16th at his house, and at least two, possibly three, on the night of the 17th at his house.

Q: Are you able in any way to describe the relative size or actual size of the male organ?

A: Do you mean Chaplain Jensen's?

Q: Yes.

A: Do you mean in inches?

Q: Yes.

A: That's an interesting question, I don't believe I can answer that.

Q: Well, would this be a fair statement, Mrs. Gudbranson,

that there is nothing of any personal nature about Chaplain Jensen that you're able to tell us which in fact you didn't receive from his wife, is that correct? If it isn't, please tell us one thing about the intimate details of Chaplain Jensen's private person that you are aware of that couldn't or didn't in fact come from his wife. I'm referring now to scars, marks on his body, anything.

A: No, I don't know any.

Q: The Gator Lodge was on the 8th of July, is that right?

A: Yes, that's right.

Q: And you didn't notice any marks from his skin condition at that time?

A: No, I didn't notice any.

Q: Of course you said you didn't notice anything at all . . .

A: My knowledge of circumcized and noncircumcized males is fairly limited. But since my husband is circumcized and there is some difference between him and Chaplain Jensen, I would say, and this is without background of what the difference is, I would say that Chaplain Jensen is probably not circumcized.

Q: But you're not sure?

A: Not really. Nobody has ever given me pictures of male organs and shown me what they look like one way or the other, but judging from the difference in the two, I would say that he probably is not.

Q: What would you base that on? Why do you now say that when before you said you didn't know? There must be some reason since you've now changed your story.

A: Well, because as I think about it, the foreskin on the penis extends farther toward the end and I assume that means . . . that's the difference between his organ and my husband's. Since there is that difference I would have to say that perhaps that means a lack of circumcision.

Q: Can you give us any comparison in any way to Chaplain Jensen's male organ in relation to your husband's?

A: Well, I would say that perhaps my husband's is a little shorter and bigger around.

Q: How about in the flaccid state, that is, nonerect, can you compare your husband's to Chaplain Jensen's?

A: Yes, they are fairly similar.

Q: Did you notice any scars on Chaplain Jensen, on the upper part of his body, arms for example?

A: No.

Q: On his legs?

A: When we were in the motel, he kept his T-shirt on. In the house, we were in the dark.

Q: Anything on his legs at all?

A: No.

Chuck Pope did manage to secure from Lora an admission to what we already suspected—that a principal reason the command had ordered me to take a physical examination was to determine whether or not I was circumcized. She said she was told this by her husband, but was never told what the outcome of the examination was. This seemed most unlikely to us, and judging by the expression on Lt. Duncan's face, he apparently felt the same way.

Lora also talked of other "intimacies" between us in the chapel office following our being together in the car on the cited P.T.A. nights, but could not explain why there was no mention of them in the sworn N.I.S. statement. These "intimacies," she quickly explained, did not involve intercourse because she didn't believe in the "undignified business of making love on the floor of an office"—again distinguishing herself from Mary Ann—but she insisted, nonetheless, that she had readily told the N.I.S. all about them (presumably a not undignified performance). She was also insistent, as was Mary Ann, that she would never have had relations with me if she had not been in love and added that she had only "fallen out of love" in the last couple of weeks. Also, like Mary Ann, she had neglected to say anything about love in her statement to N.I.S. This is how she responded to the questioning:

Q: Do you require an emotional buildup, Mrs. Gudbranson, before you engage in intimate relations with a man? Let me explain what I mean. It is generally understood and I invite your attention to your statement about women being different from men. I certainly agree with that, but it is generally understood and I think agreed to that a woman, before she can become intimate with a man, requires much more personal attention than a man might require. For example, she likes to be taken to dinner, dancing, and I take it you would agree that most men are pretty hasty about sex . . . would you say that's true about men?

A: From all the books I've read.

Q: Would you also agree, and tell me if you don't, that a woman requires more attention and more time than a man, would you agree to that?

A: Well, I can only speak for myself. I've only had relations with two men in my life, both men I was in love with.

Q: When did you fall out of love with Chaplain Jensen?

A: Within the last two to three weeks.

Q: On the occasions of your intimacies with him, did you receive what you consider sufficient emotional buildup to satisfy you, from him?

A: He did not satisfy me the first two times . . . sexually, are you talking about?

Q: Yes.

A: But the other two times he did.

Q: In what respect did the two occasions differ, can you give us any kind of description? I don't want you to go into the raw intimate details.

A: On the first two occasions, he was very nervous and he didn't reach a full erection. He said that he was satisfied, that he was sorry that I was not, but I told him it didn't matter.

Q: And you felt on those occasions you were in love?

A: Yes.

Q: You say he didn't reach a full erection, could you be a little more specific on that?

A: Do you know what a full erection is?

Q: Yes.

A: That's what he didn't reach.

Q: Now did this prevent penetration?

A: No.

Q: It didn't prevent climax on his part?

A: It didn't.

Q: So in what respect did the first two occasions differ from the last two insofar as what he did to arouse you emotionally in a way that would satisfy you?

A: I think we're getting mixed up between arousing emotionally and arousing sexually. Emotional buildup before an affair of this kind takes, at least for me, took months. It's not just one particular day of emotional buildup. During the time that we were together having intimacies, that was sexual buildup. In his own home, he seemed more relaxed, he was certainly more relaxed, he undressed completely and in every way he seemed at home. After all, he was.

Q: Taking the first act of intercourse, how long did it take for you to reach a climax from the time he began paying attention to you in an intimate way, from beginning to end, do you recall?

A: I don't recall and I wonder if there is any purpose in that line of questioning other than to feed Mr. Pope's sexual fantasies.

DC: Well, Mrs. Gudbranson, I have no intentions along those lines and I would like to state the purpose, Mr. Duncan. The purpose of this question is mainly as follows: We want to determine whether or not normal sexual fulfillment was involved here inasmuch as Mrs. Gudbranson states she was in love with the man and as we stated before, there is a difference between a man and a woman in emotional and sexual buildup. Taking Mrs. Gudbranson's and Mrs. Curran's testimony together will give a definite appearance of being sort of a rapid operation, to say the least, on the occasions involved. They're talking about rushing in and out of these motels, apartments, or any other place we're talking about, rather than conducting these intimate affairs in a leisurely prolonged manner, the way, as I understand, most women require in a situation like this. That's my only purpose in asking that question, Mrs. Gudbranson, and I think if I had any sexual fantasies they would have been well-fulfilled before this time just by reading the statements.

Lora Gudbranson's explanation of why she "fell out of love" was indeed strange. She could understand the fact of my turning to another woman, she said, since she had never tried to put any demands on me. If it was just a matter of my seeking and finding fulfillment with another woman, she would have remained in love with me and probably would not have said anything. If I had never so much as touched her from the time she first fell in love with me and if there was no other woman in my life except my wife, she would have remained continually in love with me. It was her realization, she said, that I had misused my position as marriage counselor and chaplain to gain the trust and confidence of women (herself and Mary Ann, most significantly?) that made her see me as a different kind of person. I had misused my office with at least two women, she insisted—and then alluded to others but never mentioned any names—and thus had to be stopped from "damaging" more.

"The man I fell in love with doesn't exist anymore. He was simply playing a role with me," she declared in a rather dramatic voice.

There was no question that Lora had made out a strong case against me. She had provided specifics and they sounded authentic enough to make an important impact on the investigating officer. Further, two depositions were introduced into the record that seemed to provide corroboration for the first time of what my two accusers had been saying about me.

The stronger one was from Patricia Franklin and it jarred Pope noticeably. The statement, sworn to before an N.I.S. agent, said that she had indeed seen me leaving Mary Ann's apartment one morning in October, 1970, with Mary Ann following me out.

The second one was from Sharon Smith, the widow of a Marine pilot who had become a friend of Mary Ann in March, 1971. She was having lunch with Mary Ann at Howard Johnson's one day, she said, when I drove up, joined them, and then insisted on driving Mary Ann to work. On another evening, she added, she had seen me walking in the back of the apartment house where Mary Ann lived, heading toward Mary Ann's back door. Some time after that Mary Ann had confided that she had had relations with me.

Such depositions did indeed seem most damaging to me. Our only hope was to disprove them—and thereby further demonstrate the extent and depth of the efforts to discredit me. *How* this might be done was totally unclear.

CHAPTER 15

The long interrogation of Lora and Mary Ann convinced Lieutenant Duncan that he should limit the number of witnesses who would appear in person at the hearing. He was under pressure from the command "not to let this thing drag on too long" and told us he would prefer depositions rather than having them testify in person. Pope, Fletcher, and myself were anxious to have former chaplain Joe Simpson testify in person because we believed he would make an effective and persuasive witness. We also knew from our conversations with him that he could offer the most revealing characterization of Lora Gudbranson.

Duncan agreed to interrupt his planned proceedings to allow Joe to appear for one day's testimony. Joe had gotten to know Lora before I came to Cecil Field. He had bowled on the same team with her and her husband in a mixed officers' bowling league, and she had engaged him in long conversations whenever she came into the chapel. He had been far more perceptive than I in recognizing early on that she had destructive tendencies and an apparent need to control and even destroy people. His testimony began with her anomalous role in our chapel activities.

> Q: Do you in your own mind have any idea why she became interested in chapel activties in light of what you feel her views toward Christianity were?
>
> A: That's a very good question, and I have a strong feeling as to what her motives were. I felt that it represented a challenge for her to exercise her denunciation of certain Christian ethics, starting right with the people who were in charge. Chaplain Jensen and I. Though she did not discuss her motives with me, I felt she made it very clear to me that she thought Chris-

tianity was nothing but a hoax and I was reluctant to recommend her to become a member of the planning board. . . .

Q: Do you know whether she ever discussed this point with anyone beside yourself?

A: I don't think she discussed it in detail with anyone she considered on an inferior intellectual level to herself. In other words, I don't think she would have talked to enlisted personnel or the wives of enlisted personnel about this. I think this was reflected in her attitude toward them. . . .

Q: . . . What did Mrs. Gudbranson believe about "free love"?

A: She made it very clear to me that her feeling about "free love" was essentially this: she felt that "free love" was the answer to any person or persons who were victims of a shallow marriage, that "free love" offered them a chance for sexual fulfillment, and she felt like anybody regardless of who they were if they were victims of a shallow marriage . . . a shallow man/woman relationship . . . that they were candidates for "free love."

Q: Now, do you think Mrs. Gudbranson might possibly have been a candidate for "free love" herself?

A: Yes, I do.

Q: Can you explain that a little further?

A: Mrs. Gudbranson made it quite clear that as far as her home life was concerned that she was lacking intellectual stimulation from her husband and that communication between her and her husband was at a very low ebb.

Q: Okay. Now, we'll get into this point later, Mr. Simpson, but right now let's pin one thing down. Did you consider it at all unusual that she would discuss this topic of "free love" with you?

A: Well, yes and no. When people come to the chapel to talk with a chaplain about a problem they spill it right out on the desk and you get used to not being embarrassed about anything you hear. In that respect, no it was not unusual. Unusual, yes, in that . . . not coming to me for counseling she would seek out an opportunity to talk to me about "free love."

Q: Did she always discuss this with you in your office or would she discuss it on the outside?

A: Well, she would discuss it . . . she discussed it primarily in my office, always when there was no one else around to interfere with the conversation.

Q: Was the door closed?

A: No. I would never permit my door to be closed.

Q: All right. Now, tell me this: Where, if you can recall, on the outside did she ever discuss the topic of "free love" with you . . . that is, outside of your office?

A: Well, maybe somewhere else in the chapel. Maybe in the fellowship hall, or I think a couple of times she made reference to it at cocktail parties or something of this sort.

Q: Okay. Now, do you recall any particular incident with Mrs. Gudbranson that would lead you to believe that she might have been interested in "free love" involving you?

A: I can.

Q: Would you tell us about this and give us as close as possible the date and the time?

A: As to the date, I know that it was only a couple of months before I left, before I was detached from Cecil Field. . . . This particular occasion was when she came to my office and she was waiting to see Chaplain Jensen to talk to him about ecology and he was tied up, so she became involved with me in this discussion about ecology, Christian ethics, and "free love." And time permitted her to talk at length about "free love." Then Mrs. Gudbranson put her hand on me, and the way she put her hand on me and the smile that she showed me made her intent very clear.

Q: Now, with Mr. Duncan's permission, I would like to have you stand up here where I'm standing now, Mr. Simpson, and if you will imagine that you're Mrs. Gudbranson and I'm you. What hand did she use?

A: We were talking . . .

Q: Just a minute, please. If you don't mind, just answer the one question for now, please. Which hand was it that she used?

A: The left hand.

Q: The left hand. All right. Now you take your left hand and stand as close to me as you think she was standing to you when this happened so that the court reporter can see it and Mr. Duncan can see it and . . .

A: This is about . . . well, will you stand right here at the end because I was standing at the end of my desk and she was standing here and she was talking to me about it and asking me if I agreed with it. [At this point the defense counsel and the witness are up before the hearing physically demonstrating the incident being discussed.]

DC: Let the record reflect that this is being observed by everyone in the room—that being Chaplain Jensen, Mr. Duncan, Mr. Schraver, and the court reporter. Am I correct in stating that everyone can clearly see this?

IO: Yes, sir.

Q: Okay. Will you go ahead now and continue and make the motions as you remember them. Was it your left hand?

A: Yes, it was her left hand.

IO: Let the record show that the witness and counsel are standing approximately eighteen inches . . .

WIT: Yes, or about this distance [moving toward defense counsel], about eighteen to twenty-four inches apart. I was kind of leaning against my desk casually talking to her and as she was talking about "free love" she asked me if I agreed with that. I told her that I thought that the Christian ethic ought to have something to say about promiscuity and that we had certain guidelines and conscience that we had to answer. But she tried to demolish these and when there was an interruption from outside and the indication that a counsellee was coming in, she reached over to me and did this to me [making the motion]. She touched me on the shoulder . . .

Q: On the left shoulder?

A: On the left shoulder with her left hand and her hand ran right down my side, down here, and she put her hand inside my belt and tugged and at the same time she ducked her head down and smiled at me and went like this with her head [nodding motion]. Then I backed away and she backed away.

DC: We had better let the record describe this, Mr. Duncan. You want me to describe it?

IO: If you would, please.

DC: I would describe the hand motion as being fairly slow and taking a total time of, let's see if I can determine that [moving his hand in actual motion as previously described by the witness]. Maybe six to seven seconds to go from the top, down to the belt. Now, how many seconds, Mr. Simpson, did the hand remain on the belt?

WIT: About half a second.

DC: About half a second. All right. So maybe a total of seven or eight seconds? Is that right?

WIT: Yes, that's right.

Q: And the hand moved from the top of the left shoulder, that is, the left hand moved from the top of your left shoulder down the body in the front to approximately the mid-section over the solar plexus? Is that right?

A: Down the shoulder over my left chest area and to the belt somewhere between the middle and the left pocket and her fingers . . . two of her fingers, I'd say, went inside my belt, and she tugged . . .

Q: Pulled you toward her?

A: Yes. When she went to my belt and touched my belt and began tugging with that look on her face, I thought it was time for me to move back.

DC: All right.

WIT: May I add some more to what I've just said?

Q: All right. Go ahead.

A: Now, this particular look that Mrs. Gudbranson gave me on that occasion was repeated in public. Sometimes she would see me and not say a word, but she would nod in the same way and she would smile the same way. So I know that this happened half a dozen times after the incident in the office.

Q: Up to the time you left?

A: Yes, before I left.

When Joe was asked directly whether Lora was "propositioning" him, he answered that he believed she was.

In a further discussion of Lora's views on free love, Joe said he felt she would be unlikely to suffer from any guilt feelings about having practiced free love in any form, and that she would also favor free love in homosexual relationships between consenting adults.

Pope pointed out to Joe Simpson that the book *The Intimate Enemy* had been cited by both Mary Ann and Lora as a motivating force behind their decision to make a joint accusation against me. He read the passage in the book that he found of significance: "A few [marital] partners go so far as to make fake confessions of infidelities in order to probe how tolerant or punitive their intimates will turn out to be." He then asked Joe whether he believed this could have influenced Lora to make her charge. Joe answered this way.

"I think Mrs. Gudbranson would consider it an intellectual challenge to implement something of this nature, to try to incense her husband to do something to make him angry in order to try to stimulate something between herself and him, whether negatively or positively." [This would tend to follow logically from Lora's complaints to me that she felt little intellectual rapport with her husband.]

Simpson was then asked about the statement Lora and Mary Ann made that they had agreed to divulge their relationships with the chaplain because he needed help and was in a position to damage too many lives. Joe Simpson smiled at this and said his knowledge of Lora Gudbranson and her way of thinking would make that a most unlikely motive.

Pursuing motivation, Lt. Duncan put this question to the witness: "If we were to work on the supposition that there was, indeed, an affair with Chaplain Jensen, do you have any thoughts about what her motivation might be for bringing this matter to light in this way? Would it be for any of the reasons she stated?"

"I don't think they would be her motives at all," Joe responded. "I think her motive would be to destroy the Cecil Field Protestant chapel community, which has loved this man, Chaplain Jensen, very dearly; which is very upset about the fact that he's been subjected to this investigation . . . It is my opinion that if she could not destroy the fellowship at Cecil Field, the Protestant fellowship, one way, then she would do it another. And if she could destroy this man or anybody else connected with the leadership responsibility of the chapel program, I believe she would be greatly satisfied for having done so, regardless of the price she had to pay to do it."

As developed earlier, I had information to indicate further and perhaps more convincing motives for Lora's action, but this one proposed by Joe Simpson was doubtless a strong one as well, and more easily presented and understood by others. And it was essential that plausible motive be established that would be likely to be believed to counter the original and no doubt still strong conviction that no woman would publicly brand herself as Lora had done unless it was true.

After testifying *why* he believed Lora's charges were made, Joe tried to reinforce the reasons why the charges against me were wholly implausible.

Physical condition: "Chaplain Jensen is a very weak person physically. Chaplain Gerlock and I invited him to work out in the gymnasium shortly after he came to Cecil Field. He tried to play basketball with us and in about three minutes, had to sit down. We thought he was going to pass out. . . . There were different times he had a tough time breathing . . . Chaplain Gerlock and I made the suggestion to him that he and his wife go to motels to get away from the office and away from the phone. I know that when he went to the dispensary to take an EKG exam the doctor advised him to quit working so hard, to get away. We had a chaplains' meeting once a week and quite often we would tell him that he had better slow down and take the doctor's advice and try to get some rest. . . . His children were often sick and there was a suggestion about a baby-sitter if he and his wife could get away together . . .

"In view of his weak physical condition, the idea of his having had all that intercourse with the two women, ninety-five to one hundred times, is a ridiculous assumption. . . . Besides, because of his deep consciousness of and his commitment to his religious views, I don't think he could possibly have had such a relationship with these women."

Lack of opportunity: "He would be at the chapel office by eight o'clock and would work all day until supper time. We would see him at lunch virtually every day. He was involved in activities at the chapel a few evenings a week . . . Also, in July, 1970, and in August, Chaplain Jensen had to stand duty every other day, or every other three or four days, in the light of my being prepared to make a transition and be detached from Cecil Field. The duty chaplain had to be on call; and there were always some calls."

Timing: "The time that the alleged affair [with Mary Ann Curran] began was a time when the N.I.S. had been conducting an investigation into my own personal affairs. . . . He was well aware that the rumors about me were quite extensive. He counseled me, when I asked him to. . . . The investigation and my departure had a strong emotional effect on him. I knew he had a very tough time sleeping. He was upset, he had a great deal of personal concern about me. While this was going on, the likelihood of him taking off at this time and involving himself in promiscuous sexual activity is just something in another world. Not this world. Not in the life of that man.

The drinking charges: "Anybody who knows Chaplain Jensen and has been with him for any length of time knows he doesn't drink at all. From my own experience and knowledge of myself and other people, I would notice physical indications on a person who might be a heavy drinker, and I never observed any signs that Chaplain Jensen was a drinker. I never detected liquor on his breath, never found drinking apparatus in his office or in the area where he worked (I had the occasion and the freedom to go into his desk drawers for materials) and I've never been with him on an occasion when he ever had anything to drink, when Chaplain Gerlock and myself did have something to drink. On one occasion at Cecil Field I was called upon at a hail and farewell party to be an M.C. and I had three drinks myself that evening. The next day Chaplain Jensen called it to my attention. He felt that in the interest of the command and my position as chaplain, maybe I should not be drinking at all. The charge [by Mary Ann Curran that Chaplain Jensen drank between a half to three-quarters of a bottle of hard liquor when he was with her on many occasions] is an absurd one. It would be impossible, in my opinion, for him to have consumed alcohol in the amount indicated without my detecting it at some time."

The use of Simpson's office: "The statement by Mary Ann Curran that on the last Friday of July, 1970—July 31—Chaplain Jensen took her into my office, kissed her, etc., is highly unlikely. My office was for the most part locked, since I had stuff lying all over the floor and everything in my office was piled up just prior to my departure. I had books stacked up in the middle of the floor, and I had all kinds of things . . . It was very cluttered there. If Chaplain Jensen had come in with her and used any of the chairs, as she said he did, he would have had to remove books and other things for them to sit down. His office had far more room than mine . . . There was no reason to go into my office . . . And on Friday, July 31, I was in and out of my office continually."

"The absence of rumors: Simpson pointed out that at a small station like Cecil Field there would have been rumors if somebody such as a senior chaplain had been involved with a woman, or women, particularly when one of them had alleged almost one hundred acts of intercourse on sixty-five different occasions. But

Simpson had learned that there were absolutely no rumors at all concerning me prior to August 12, 1971, which was when the investigation began. "I know how women talk . . . in my own matter [Simpson's affair] I was made aware that the rumors were quite extensive."

Lt. Schraver, the assigned government counsel, declined to cross-examine the witness, even though his personal record made him possibly vulnerable.

Lt. Larry Curran's attitude at the hearing was detached—perhaps studiedly—as he attached little importance to his wife's self-avowed adultery in Texas, even though this was his stated reason for himself and his wife coming to me for counseling in the first place. I wondered if he knew what Mary Ann had told me about him in counseling and what her relationship had been with some of his Navy friends. I suspect she had been selective in her confidences to him and tried to put them in a way most likely to represent herself as an exploited and helpless victim—much as she had been doing at the hearing.

He acted vaguely hurt about having to testify. His attitude seemed to be that he was just going along with the Gudbransons who wanted to press the case against me. He also tried to hold to the fiction that he and his wife had not even discussed divorce and that he was not aware she had gone to see a lawyer, yet Mary Ann had said the idea of contacting a lawyer to start divorce proceedings had come from him. In a subsequent session he remembered the visit to the divorce lawyer.

Lt. Curran's testimony was of a piece with his wife's. Both tried to deny fact and fell into contradictions. Both showed a casual, even light attitude that was incongruous with the material involving both of them so personally. Both, it seemed to me, were playing a role they hoped was most likely to be at least face-saving, to divert attention from themselves to the villainous Chaplain Jensen, who somehow was the cause of all their troubles. Given their position, it seemed a clever approach.

Gudbranson followed *his* wife's pattern; he was belligerent and outraged. He did not come to the hearing when Lora testified, and she didn't come with him when it was his turn. When he entered the hearing room, I was told to stand because he was a senior officer. In fact, his rank was the same as mine. He need a shave, his hair was unkempt.

Since Gudbranson was senior in rank to Chuck Pope and since Chuck did believe in protocol, he asked Lyman Fletcher to take on the cross-examination in this instance. I had seen Gudbranson blow up at meetings, and I told Lyman that if he pushed him hard in his questioning, he might explode right in court. He did, sooner than expected, when Lyman asked him if there was some vindictiveness in his pushing the matter against me. He became red-faced and said, "My sitting in this room with the son-of-a-bitch is bad enough."

This kind of outburst violated all courtroom decorum and the investigating officer should have referred it to the command for disciplinary action; instead, he tried to have it stricken from the court reporter's record. Lyman insisted it stay in "to show the kind of people we're dealing with here."

Gudbranson denied the reports common around the base that he and his wife drank a good deal and had violent arguments. He was evasive when asked about the threats on my life, and said he couldn't be held responsible for what he had said in his situation. He did acknowledge he had heard no rumors of any improper behavior on my part before his wife told him of our supposed relationship and that he heard that with "complete, utter amazement." His anger, though, was directed at least publicly only at me, not at his wife. One can only speculate about the possible reason for this, but it may be that he had cause to be furious with Lora that he could not bring himself to acknowledge—not even to himself, let alone a public tribunal.

Chaplains Lew Allred and Hoyt Swann were put on the stand to show the sequence of events that led to the formal charges against me. Both claimed their roles in this case were not directed against me and that they were simply carrying out assigned responsibilities. They did not explain, though, why accusations that were being made against a fellow chaplain were not taken up directly with the chaplain so he could at least have an early chance to answer them and expose them as false.

Allred said he "had the thought" of going and confronting Chaplain Jensen "to hear his side of it." But before he got around to it, he said he received a call from Mary Ann Curran that another woman was involved and this woman's husband was insisting on going to the command. Allred then wanted to contact me in New Jersey to forewarn me, he said, but he never did. Although, as mentioned, information a chaplain receives in counseling is privileged, Allred had passed on what Mary Ann had told him to both Danielson and to the Chief of the Chaplain Corps. His justification was that Mary Ann Curran had authorized him to reveal her confidences. But, true or not, I was the one who would be hurt by the disclosure of these confidences and I had never authorized any such disclosure, nor subsequently even been given a chance to tell my side of the story before it was turned into a legal proceeding.

Allred had behaved not as a minister or counselor. Without making any attempt to determine whether or not Mary Ann's account of adultery was the product of reality or imagination, he had urged her to tell her husband about it—most peculiar behavior for anybody involved in marriage counseling. His explanation was that Mary Ann "gave no indication [whatever that would be] that she was lying." Chuck Pope, however, was able to show how irresponsible Allred had been by pointing up discrepancies between what she had told him and some of her sworn testimony. She had told Allred, for instance, that she had seen a psychiatrist for help, while in her testimony she insisted she'd never been to one before coming to Jacksonville. She told Allred she was confessing her affair to him because she just had to tell *somebody*. But in her testimony she said she had told her husband about petting incidents back in March, and also had told the entire story to her friend Sharon Smith and to a counselor in a private agency.

"Isn't it possible for people to lie very convincingly?" Chuck asked in his cross-examination.

Allred conceded that "in matters like this . . . when you take somebody at their word you're taking a risk"

Swann tried to exclude from his testimony information he said he had learned from Mary Ann Curran in confidence and therefore could not reveal. He said that she insisted he tell only certain things she had told him. We argued that confidences had to be disclosed completely or not at all, and that he could not be selective according to the whim of Mary Ann or himself. He admitted he had heard no rumors of any improper involvements on my part and had no reason to suspect I was having an affair with either Mary Ann or Lora. He also said he had no reason to suspect them of concocting false stories. He explained his role in arranging for the two of them to sign statements against me and then witnessing them as simply following the wishes of the command and the Chief of Chaplains. As for not alerting me to what was going on, he excused that on the ground that he couldn't disclose privileged information.

One chaplain who did not testify was John Danielson. He had come to Chuck prior to the Article 32 hearing and urgently requested he not be called as a witness. He had only relayed information to the N.I.S., he maintained, and had no testimony that would be relevant to the charges against me. Chuck went along with this request, although I had misgivings. Danielson had, after all, been receiving privileged information from Allred and had agreed with the Chief of Chaplains to push for a command investigation rather than an ecclesiastical one. He also had been convicting me with remarks to other chaplains to the effect that "they caught Andy." I felt he would be uneasy at having to admit such behavior under oath, that this was the true reason he had begged off from testifying.

I readily confess to feeling renewed bitterness toward the chaplains who had joined against me. That feeling was accentuated by a report Kathleen and I got from a young man who was a member of our chapel and had gone to Swann's apartment one night during the hearing. The apartment was in the same complex as the Currans' and the young man found the Currans there laughing and joking with Swann. Apparently now that the Currans had been useful to Swann in his desire to take over my job, they had become good friends and allies. "The trouble with our church these days is not its principles but the people in it who don't have any," Kathleen said.

The N.I.S. agents conceded in their testimony that although they had taken my picture and Lora's and Mary Ann's with them to various motels in the Jacksonville area they had not found anybody who remembered seeing me, much less remembered seeing me with Lora or Mary Ann. They now also agreed under oath that the notation "2" on my motel registration receipts was not in my handwriting. Nevertheless, they made it plain that they still considered these registrations for double occupancy contributing proof of the charges against me.

They also made the discovery of the flask in my desk sound very important, even though they had only Mrs. Curran's word that she had brought it to me and there was no odor of alcohol from the flask, indicating it could have been there a long time. (They at least remained consistent in their position and the command's generally from the start of the entire business that when it was a matter of my word against one or both of my accusers, they would invariably take the latter's.)

As additional "evidence," Arnold Sleeper, agent in charge of the investigation, read a report from the N.I.S. files in which he charged me with "covering up" for former Chaplain Joe Simpson. This report —whose significance even if true was questionable—was based entirely on his own opinion, but Sleeper apparently wanted to get it into the Article 32 record to be of influence in the decision whether or not to court-martial me.

Sleeper refused even to let me touch the exhibits he put out on display—exhibits including the so-called "love notes" that Mary Ann had turned over to him along with the motel registration receipts. His telling explanation was that "there are times when an accused will pick up evidence and eat it."

From some things the Gudbransons had been saying about Cecil Field, Kathleen and I got the strong impression that the N.I.S. had tapped my phone in hopes of picking up damaging evidence. When Chuck Pope questioned Sleeper about this, however, he answered emphatically that there had been no use of any eavesdropping or electronic equipment.

The improper, to put it mildly, tactics of the N.I.S. became even more evident when we got into the matter of the Patricia Franklin deposition. When Pope first heard about it at the hearing, he was shaken. When I assured him that the account of my coming out of Mary Ann's apartment at seven in the morning could not possibly be true, he insisted that Mrs. Franklin appear at the hearing for cross-examination. However, when Lt. Duncan contacted Mrs. Franklin, she told him she had not seen *me* coming out of the apartment. She had seen a man in Naval uniform but didn't know who it was. Why had she signed a statement saying it was me? Well, she explained, the N.I.S. agent had insisted she sign it, and she felt compelled to do what he said.

As an ironic postscript, Mrs. Franklin came to me for counseling on domestic problems of her own *after* this alleged incident at Mary Ann's apartment. And, remarkably, she came to me on Mary Ann's recommendation. It does seem unlikely that she would have gone for this kind of help to a chaplain whom she believed to be involved with another man's wife.

Sharon Smith's deposition was in part the result of her friendship with Mary Ann and in part of her feeling of bitterness toward me. She was the widow of a Marine pilot and had become engaged to another pilot. While this pilot was away on an overseas tour of duty, she began to date another officer named John who had been introduced to her by Mary Ann. The thirteen-year-old daughter of Chief Petty Officer William Buntsinger and his wife Margaret—both active members of our chapel—frequently baby-sat for Mrs. Smith and slept at her home overnight. The girl told her parents that when she woke up in the morning she would often find John and Sharon Smith together on a daybed, or John with rumpled clothes asleep on the floor next to Mrs. Smith, who was on a couch. The Buntsingers were disturbed and we discussed making a complaint against Sharon Smith for impairing the morals of their daughter. Mrs. Smith soon became aware that the Buntsingers had been talking to me and apparently was fearful I would alert her fiancé to what had been taking place. At my suggestion, Chuck Pope also requested that Sharon Smith be brought in for cross-examination before the Article 32 hearing ended. When Lt. Duncan called her, he found she was away and later she continued to be "unavailable."

She did surface again after the Article 32 investigation was closed and said she would not be available for any personal appearance in the event of a court-martial. She agreed, though, to make another sworn deposition and be questioned on it at a private session. We objected to this arrangement, but the command approved it. At the deposition hearing she said some things that were inconsistent both with her first sworn statement and with statements she made to Lt. Duncan when he spoke to her on the telephone. And her most significant charge—that she had seen me late one afternoon heading toward the back door of Mary Ann's apartment—turned out to be another instance of apparent N.I.S.-inspired embellishment. It developed that she had merely seen me heading toward one of the buildings in the Yorktown Apartments complex where Mary Ann had an apartment—as did other personnel from Cecil Field, including, for example, Chaplain Swann. There was even serious question whether she saw *me* at all—she only recognized me from seeing the *back* of my head, she said. "You didn't actually see Chaplain Jensen's face, then, did you?" she was asked. Her answer was unequivocal: "No, I didn't."

The Buntsingers did subsequently file a formal statement with the command requesting an investigation into Sharon Smith's behavior as it related to the impairment of the morals of minors. The command and the N.I.S. both failed to act on it.

CHAPTER 16

The windup of the in-person testimony phase of the Article 32 hearing left Chuck Pope in an optimistic mood. He kept stressing that in military as well as civilian courts a prosecuting authority could not make out a valid case solely on the basis of testimony of accomplices. Mary Ann Curran and Lora Gudbranson were at least both accomplices with me in committing the crime of adultery. They had confessed to it. The open question was whether I too was guilty. Their testimony required some kind of corroboration to make a case, and Chuck maintained that "no sensible person can say that we have seen corroboration in a legal sense." The motel receipts by themselves could not be called corroboration as long as nobody had seen me at or even near the motels with either of the two women. The "love notes" could not, because none of them was addressed to Mary Ann. And the N.I.S. attempts to show corroboration in the depositions by Patricia Franklin and Sharon Smith had been frustrated.

Lyman Fletcher was more pessimistic. In civilian life, he said, presumption of innocence is generally observed in practice as well as in theory. In practice, the military proceeds on the assumption that once a man has been charged he is guilty until proved innocent. Although we had seen Mary Ann's credibility apparently unravelled during the hearing and although Joe Simpson had been effective in exposing Lora Gudbranson's character and credible motive, the command could still assert that the two had made a *prima facie* case against me. They could also insist that the receipts and the "love notes" *did* constitute corroboration, no matter what others might say.

Regardless of their differences, Chuck and Lyman agreed it was important for me to collect all the statements and evidence I could to disprove the charges against me. Even before the Article 32 hearing began I had asked through Chuck that the N.I.S. go to see members of the Cecil Field chapel who knew enough about me and my work habits to contradict what Mary Ann and Lora had said. They refused to do this. We wanted them to investigate Mary Ann's relationship with Dr. Blanc, to check out some of the drug salesmen with whom she'd been involved, and to get the facts of the relationship with the woman she had confided to me. They didn't do it. They only saw Dr. Blanc at Mary Ann's request and then to get a statement from him about phone calls supposedly from me that had annoyed her. He described his own relationship with her in the statement as purely professional. They accepted this characterization.

Chuck Pope was kept too busy on other matters to do the actual interviewing for me. I would have to do it for myself. I had always made it a practice to keep a detailed calendar of official appointments and activities as well as social and family functions, and later scribbled notes on my calendar if anything noteworthy happened at any of these functions. Kathleen also kept a calendar, as well as careful records of our correspondence, invitations, bills, and cancelled checks. I also had taken the official chapel calendar along with my appointment books and records to Lyman's office and made copies of data I felt might be pertinent to the case. Later I was forced to return these records or be arrested, but I believe the copies I made discouraged thoughts by the C.O., the Executive Officer, or Chaplain Swann of perhaps altering dates and times on the original records.

Kathleen and I were going over the calendars one night with Chuck and his wife, Nancy, when Joy Oneth dropped in. When we told Joy that Lora had fixed on the January 21st P.T.A. open house as the night I had taken her for a half-hour's so-called love-making ride, she said she remembered that after we had all gotten into our respective cars and headed for home she had seen my car directly ahead of hers virtually all the way back to Cecil Field. If Lora Gudbranson had been there with me, she would have seen her. She did not. Joy gave us a sworn statement, and we were able to get another statement the next day from Jane Bristol. After the January 21st meeting she had seen me pulling into my driveway at practically the same time she pulled into hers.

Next I needed to verify what I'd been doing on May 18, 1971, the second date listed by Lora in her account of our alleged affair. The day was Tuesday, the day off from the base that I always spent at a counseling course at Methodist Hospital in Jacksonville.

I had checked in at the Howard Johnson Motel near the hospital at about noon that day. Besides the day's program at the hospital I was due back there about midnight for special personnel interviews in connection with this course. Kathleen was to come in for dinner with me at the motel, and we would watch television a while before she went back to Cecil Field and I returned to the hospital.

My records showed I had had a special conference with Chaplain Ronal Mudd, the supervisor of the course, that afternoon, and a check of his records showed the conference lasted from 3 to 4 P.M. His records also showed that I covered for him in his office from two to nearly three because he had to attend a meeting of department heads. I left the hospital right after the conference wtih Chaplain Mudd and went to the motel room for a brief rest. Mrs. Dana Nickel, the hospital secretary, called me a few minutes after I arrived at the motel to tell me a young boy named Blair had taken a serious turn and his family wanted a chaplain to see him. Chaplain Mudd had just left so Mrs. Nickel called me. I left the motel immediately, went to the boy, and remained at the hospital until about five. Lora Gudbranson's version had me drinking and having sexual intercourse with her from two to five at the Howard Johnson motel.

Chaplain Mudd provided me with a sworn deposition covering the hours he could personally attest to. I was somewhat hesitant to explain to Mrs. Nickel why I was so anxious to see her and why I needed her help. I need not have been. She confirmed in her deposition that the Blair boy had been admitted to the hospital on May 16th and that the circumstances that obliged her to call me had occurred two days later, on Tuesday, the crucial May 18th date in Lora's testimony. To reinforce Mrs. Nickel's deposition I obtained a photostat of the hospital records showing when the Blair boy had been admitted. Chuck Pope congratulated me on my efficiency and and assured me I was doing a better investigative job than the N.I.S. He was sincere, but I took it as faint praise.

The third significant date in Lora's saga was July 8th. She had testified I was in such an alcoholic fog when with her at the motel the afternoon of that day that I had asked her to call and order books for me from the Baptist Book Store. In fact, I had gone to the bookstore myself on July 8 and found the store temporarily out of the books I wanted for the chapel. I had called the store the next day from my office and placed the order. Lora had been in my office at the time and heard me make the call. Naturally my receipt for the books showed they had been purchased on July 9th when I actually placed the order, not July 8th when Lora said she had placed the order by phone from our motel room. I went to the Baptist Book Store to get confirmation from Mrs. Betty Hale, the sales clerk, and, as with Mrs. Nickel earlier, hesitantly told her what I wanted and why. Her records checked with the records from the chapel—she had an invoice showing that the books had indeed been purchased via phone order on July 9th and were delivered later that day. And she remembered very clearly that I had come into the store a day earlier—on the critical July 8th—to ask about these books and look for them on the shelves.

One part of Lora's testimony about July 8th was accurate. I had indeed gone to a motel, not with her or for her alleged purpose but for the highly unromantic purpose of trying to get a bit of rest and relief—at Kathleen's urging—both from the pressure of telephone calls and the irritation from the chigger infection contracted on a family outing that was almost literally making me "climb the walls." Dr. Wickham, who had diagnosed the problem and prescribed medication on July 2nd, gave me a deposition confirming that the discomfort from the infection was at its worst during this time and was very bad throughout most of July, and that any activity such as Lora had accused me of would have been most unlikely, if not impossible.

I now checked with my nextdoor neighbors in an effort to gather evidence against Lora's story of intimate relations at my home the nights of July 15th and 16th. The living- and dining-room lights in the Chase house directly south of mine were on from early in the evening of Friday, July 16th, until 3 A.M. The rooms had windows—with no curtains—facing the rear of the house where Lora Gudbranson said she had passed. Lora's testimony was that all was dark in the Chase home and the area around it.

The lights were also on at the home of my other nextdoor neighbors, the Colemans. The wives of all the officers in Dick Coleman's squadron were there making posters for the anticipated fly-in of the squadron. Lora's testimony said the house was dark and quiet.

Jeannine Coleman's deposition also covered dates Mary Ann Curran had said she and I had had nightly sexual relations at motels and apartments in Jacksonville during August, 1970. During this time, when Kathleen was visiting her family in Philadelphia, Jeannine kept Kathleen's keys to our home in order to make certain the air-conditioning was running. In many homes at Cecil Field the air-conditioning would break down if it was turned off for a period and then restarted. There were also electricians doing some work in our house, and Jeannine was able to let them in. The Colemans had me over many times during the period Kathleen was away, and they saw me, as they stated, "on almost a daily basis." Jeannine had also promised my wife to check if our dog was out at night and to take him into their house if I was out late at a meeting. So Jeannine looked out every night before going to bed to see if my car was at our house. If it wasn't, she was to go out, find the dog, and take him into her home. But she never had to go out—my car was always there.

By now depositions were also coming from chapel members who described my long working hours, my attendance at evening functions, and activities at the chapel with Boy Scouts, Cub Scouts, choir groups, Bible study groups, men's open house, and ladies' planning groups—meetings nearly every night. They gave affidavits that the door to my office was almost always open when I was there at night, and on the infrequent occasions that it was closed they would feel free to walk in and often did. None had ever seen me take an alcoholic drink nor detected alcohol on my breath. They had been at our home for social occasions and I had been at theirs, but I had never once joined any of them in taking a drink. Several of the ladies added that they had had private counseling sessions with me and that my conduct was always professional.

Yeomen who worked at the chapel provided statements about my getting upset at finding whiskey bottles threwn around the chapel grounds and confirmed that I treated Mary Ann Curran and Lora Gudbranson no differently from anyone else when they came to the chapel. Yeoman William McAuley specifically pointed out that "the availability of Chaplain Jensen's office to everyone, his practice of leaving the door open when he was there, never locking it, never leaving his venetian blinds closed—plus the arrangement of his office—all made it seem very improbable if not impossible that he could have had sexual relations there."

These statements described the way my desk was often covered with papers, drafts of letters I helped write for Navy personnel or their dependents having marital problems, folders containing sympathy cards, greeting cards, and similar addenda anyone could have taken at almost any time. One witness provided a statement that she had seen Mary Ann Curran going through the folders on my desk one afternoon when I was out of the office.

Paul Gerlock, the former Catholic chaplain, submitted a deposition supporting Joe Simpson's comments about my compulsive work habits, aversion to liquor, poor physical condition, and active belief in the so-called square concepts of morality. He confirmed my finding the flask in its crumpled bag on the chapel grounds and my decision to keep it in my desk until I could find who owned it. He also confirmed my participation in a variety of night meetings and his lunching with me every day except days off, thereby making it rather clearly impossible for me to have gone off on long drives to Mary Ann's Jacksonville apartment at lunch time, as she had claimed.

Although Mary Ann's account had been vague on July dates—"almost every night" . . . "almost every afternoon"—she had been specific on at least one day, the first time we supposedly were intimate at her Shindler Drive apartment. She had said I was at the apartment with her from approximately 2 to 5 P.M. I was later able to establish that I made a pastoral call that day at the home of a parishioner whose father had passed away. Because of the death she naturally remembered the time and the date. I made my call in the late hours of the morning, she said, and returned with Kathleen for a condolence call at four in the afternoon.

Dr. David Murphy, the physician at the naval dispensary who first advised me to get away from work pressure by going to resorts, furnished medical confirmation of my physical condition that colleagues in the chaplain's unit had already described. He recalled starting to get after me about taking periods of rest as far back as June, 1970. He urged it again in August when we called together on a family whose daughter had been killed and again shortly afterwards when he asked me to counsel a young Navy wife who had attempted suicide. He also told Kathleen several times, "If Andy can't take long vacations, you've got to make him take more short breaks away from here." I've mentioned another doctor, Shetterley, who gave me the names of suitable motels in the recreational areas.

Isabell Jaquette, who taught in our Sunday school and whose husband was co-superintendent of the school, furnished a statement that fitted with Joe Simpson's comments about Lora: "Mrs. Gudbranson went to extremes to gain the attention of Chaplain Jensen at meetings [of the Protestant planning board] and following these meetings. She would constantly interrupt conversations and ignore other members and make suggestions, speaking only to Chaplain Jensen. After the meetings she would then continue to pursue Chaplain Jensen. She attended refreshment periods [following Sunday services] but seldom if ever attended with her husband. At these times she would continue to pursue Chaplain Jensen in the ways I have already described . . . I felt that Chaplain Jensen handled the situation well and did his best to avoid the advances of Mrs. Gudbranson without causing a scene. However, it was obvious that she was pursuing him in a manner which seemed to me to be most improper." After reading Mrs. Jaquette's statement, eight other people who had been active in our chapel signed a joint statement of their own endorsing what she had to say.

Mrs. Jaquette also recalled "attending a meeting early in May, 1971, of the Women of the Chapel. During the course of this meeting several suggestions were made and Chaplain Jensen asked that they be written down in order to help him remember. This occasioned Mrs. Mary Ann Curran to make a comment that writing it down wouldn't do any good because Chaplain Jensen never answered notes or phone calls. . . . She made this statement on several occasions during the meeting." Mary Ann and Dr. Blanc had claimed I had hounded her with phone calls. Actually, the only calls I made were in belated answer to her own—and, as indicated by her comments quoted by Mrs. Jaquette, were never returned fast or reliably enough to satisfy her.

Two Navy wives who had come to my office at different times with marital problems and had made overtures to me, which I diverted and never spoke of, offered to give me sworn statements about the incidents providing the Investigating Officer keep their names confidential. One of them said, "I'm a better-looking woman than Lora Gudbranson and you certainly could have had me if you were looking for that sort of thing." I doubted we could have full confidence that confidentiality would be honored if they gave signed statements and so I turned down their offers. I didn't forget their generous kindness, though.

I felt especially moved and rewarded by the attitude of the young sailor, Mike Wennersten, who'd come for counseling about his troubles with his family and fiancée and who had gotten into some trouble by experimenting with marihuana. The most important of the so-called love notes Mary Ann Curran claimed to have received from me was a scrawled one that contained such phrases as "please share your love with me forever" and "more than anyone else, I want to love you." I knew this was a draft of a letter I had prepared in counseling for a sailor who wanted to write to his wife or sweetheart and after going through my counseling notes and records, I became convinced the sailor was Wennersten. He had had a difficult childhood, had had problems in the Navy, and had come to me at a time when he was having difficulty with his fiancée. But he had since cemented relations with her, had married her, and made a successful adjustment.

Wennersten was working an odd-hours shift at one of the aircraft-maintenance hangars and although I left a couple of notes for him, he kept missing me because I was banned from the base during the day. He had an apartment off the base but the phone was unlisted. We finally got together outside the hangar one night, and he explained he'd gone to the chapel looking for me but had been told I'd been transferred. I explained why. He immediately recognized the phrases in the copy of the "love note" as having come from him.

When Mike was preparing his deposition for me and having it notarized, I told him that if my case did go to court-martial and he was called as a defense witness, the prosecution might try to use his experimentation with drugs as a means of attacking his character and hence his credibility as a witness.

"If they try it, I'll just have to take it," he said. "I feel I owe this to you, and more."

It was nice to hear.

CHAPTER 17

Things seemed to be progressing as I prepared to go to the various motels that had provided the N.I.S. with allegedly incriminating registration receipts. It was Chuck who urged me to do this even though I was very nervous about the prospect, more so than before approaching people for statements. I was sure the motel personnel had been told by the N.I.S. agents that I was some variant of sex maniac, but Pope said to "go there just the way you did when you registered—in your uniform with the chaplain's cross—and take Kathleen with you. When they see you as you are they aren't likely to confuse you with the Boston Strangler and should open up."

Kathleen and I first went over our personal calendars to jog our recollections of the motel visits which we had written down. Kathleen and the boys had left for Philadelphia the second week in August, 1970—the same day Joe Simpson had been transferred out of Cecil Field. I was very depressed over the whole Simpson episode so I drove out to the beach on Saturday morning, August 15, and spent a little time under a beach umbrella. I couldn't swim in the sun because of my skin-cancer condition so I drove in the direction of St. Augustine and noticed the Gator Lodge on Phillips Highway. When I found they had a shaded pool, I checked in. I was told they only had a few rooms available but didn't ask what kind of rooms they were and accepted what they gave me. I swam, rested, read, ate, and went back to Cecil Field about 10 P.M. I then realized I had kept the key and couldn't get it back on Sunday before check-out time so I went back on Sunday afternoon after church, used the same room, and again returned at night to my quarters at Cecil.

Kathleen was to come back to Florida the following Friday for a chapel party and TV broadcast of the chapel choir. I made reservations for us at the Holiday Inn near the Jacksonville Airport, where we'd have a mini-vacation of a day and a half. But on the day Kathleen was to fly down, our boys kicked up a fuss about being left alone with their aunt and uncle and talked Kathleen into staying with them another week. She insisted that I go out to the motel anyway, and I did, although I was held up by a wedding rehearsal and didn't get there till late at night. I had to pay for a double room since I'd already made the reservation and the motel was crowded.

The next date was January 26, 1971, one of my days at the Methodist Hospital and again a time when I was particularly weary. There was to be no afternoon class that day so we arranged that Kathleen would come to meet me at 12:30 and the kids would be left with a baby-sitter. We drove to the Ramada Inn, one of the motels that had been recommended, had lunch, and decided to check in. We planned to stay overnight and return to the base early the next morning, but by evening we missed the kids and so we drove back to Cecil after a brief stop at the hospital.

March 9th was another Tuesday—a hospital day. Kathleen and I had tickets to a Jack Benny show that night in Jacksonville. I managed some time off in the afternoon and made reservations for us at the Howard Johnson on Golfair Boulevard, just a few minutes from the hospital. But it was our son Drew's birthday, and we decided to go home to toast Drew with punch and a birthday cake, then drive back again for the Benny show.

Since our plan for March 9th had yielded to Drew's birthday, we decided to try again the following Tuesday, March 16. I made reservations for two at the Howard Johnson's on Phillips Highway this time, since it was near the Baptist Book Store and I wanted to go there to check out several books. Drew—we loved him but sometimes *he* seemed a conspiracy—had a cold this time and when I called Kathleen she said she could come only if he felt better. Significantly by hindsight, Kathleen's visitor at the house when I called was Mrs. Mary Ann Curran. I had some notes to write up so decided to do them at the motel. I then got a late call from Kathleen that Drew was feeling worse and not only was she not coming in but now she wanted me to come back home, right away, which I of course did. Again there was no overnight.

May 18th was the date I had the day-and-night session scheduled at the hospital, and July 8th I again tried for a rest at the Gator Lodge.

We decided our calls on those motels should be made in the same chronological sequence, so our first stop was at the Gator Lodge. Mrs. Feryle Jump, the desk clerk I remembered from my last visit there, was not in and we went on to the Holiday Inn near the airport. We were told the manager's name was James Snyder and he was pointed out to us in the motel restaurant. After some nervous hesitation, Kathleen and I approached him and introduced ourselves. Chuck Pope was right. His greeting was friendly and he agreed to talk with us in his private office. He confided that he had been upset by the N.I.S. tactics; they had come to the motel without a search warrant and had asked to look at registration records without mentioning a specific date—a fishing expedition. In fact, they had gone through a whole year's records, then selected what they wanted and asked for Xerox copies. Snyder felt this procedure was probably illegal but allowed his assistant to go along because the agents represented the government. As I suspected would be the case, the N.I.S. men had told him I had been accused of a "sex offense."

He had only been at this motel for a few months so knew nothing of my having stayed there and nobody on his staff recognized me. He was able to explain, however, why my registration record showed double occupancy even though my wife had been unable to come and I had stayed alone. "You reserved the room for two so the clerk marked that down on the registration card. Your wife had to cancel out but you were still given the same room and were paying the full price, so there was no reason to change anything. This often happens, it's not unusual."

He also explained how double-occupancy notations could have been made on other motel registration records even though I'd come in alone and without an advance registration for two. "Frequently the only rooms left are doubles and if you take one of those at the same rate a couple would pay, the clerk might write 2 on the card. This isn't at all uncommon in the motel business. Some guests will correct things like this when they see and pay the bill, but others won't."

I told him it could be important in my defense if I could get a sworn statement from him explaining how errors about the occupancy of a room could happen and pointing out that it often happened in his business. He obliged.

Mr. Snyder's account of N.I.S. tactics and the possibility of errors on registration records were echoed by the managers at all the motels we visited. But the woman who managed the Howard Johnson's on Golfair Boulevard had given up the originals of my registration receipts—not just copies—to the N.I.S. The manager of the other Howard Johnson had done the same. He not only had turned over a receipt showing double occupancy on March 16th but had also given N.I.S. a receipt showing I was there alone and had taken a single room on July 23rd, when Kathleen was away.

The N.I.S. had not revealed this receipt at the Article 32 hearing, and when Chuck asked about it they said they knew nothing about it (perhaps shades or foreshadows of Watergate). It seemed obvious they had pigeonholed this evidence. It definitely would have helped support my contention that I'd gone to motels alone when my wife was away up north and that I would make advance reservations for two only when she was home and I expected her to be with me.

"If you'd found evidence helpful to the prosecution and destroyed it, they'd see to it you got five years," Lyman told me, "but *they* can do almost anything they want."

Kathleen and I later found records of other single registrations I'd made at motels when she was away and also records of motel registrations near the beach where our entire family stayed. The authorities wouldn't accept these as evidence either, on the grounds they weren't pertinent to the charges against me. (Good news for the defense was inadmissible news in this bizarre affair.)

On our return trip to the Gator Lodge Mrs. Feryle Jump, the desk clerk I remembered, was there and in turn remembered me coming to the motel in July. No question of the date: her records showed it was July 8th, and her initials on the registration confirmed that she was the one who had signed me in. Mrs. Jump also had seen me park my car in *front*, had seen me come in and register *alone*, had seen me wearing my *uniform*. I had *not* parked to the side, as Lora testified, I had *not* come to the motel with her, and I was *not* wearing any kind of sports shirt that she or anyone else had bought for me. Moreover, Mrs. Jump confirmed that the room I'd rented had a telephone in it, contrary to Lora's story of having to leave the room to make a call for me. Lora's fiction of the July 8th events had already been largely undermined by the deposition of Mrs. Hale from the Baptist Book Store. Mrs. Jump's deposition now proved Lora had been dissembling in all respects.

Chuck Pope again was pleased, but he now wanted statements that would further indicate understandable motivation behind Lora's and Mary Ann's accusations. "You understand and so do some of your people," he said, "but I'd like to get statements from outside professionals."

Here are samplings.

Dr. R. L. Coberly, consulting psychologist in Jacksonville: "Short of murder, this charge [of adultery] is about the most damaging that can be levied on a man of the cloth since he is supposedly above such things. The charge would be functionally designed to 'get rid of' an unwanted party. The motives could be as diverse as revenge, to wanting to 'see a new face,' or a simple exercise in power and manipulation. . . . Two very bored and somewhat unhappy women could presumably make such charges in an effort to liven up a rather meaningless existence. Attention and excitement, even though they may be of a negative variety, seem to be more palatable than deprivation. . . . This could be a way of advertising that 'I'm available and very desirable . . . that even an experienced man of the cloth found me irresistible' [comparable to the sailor who was proud he'd shared a woman with an authority figure such as a chaplain] . . . Two women (probably one at the urging of the other, more aggressive one) would be apt to make such a charge together in the hope that numbers would give the charge more creditability. Also, they would have the mutual support that would help them to carry something like this through to fruition. . . ."

Rev. Louis B. Reed, Director of the Pastoral Counseling Center in Jacksonville and a Supervisor of Clinical Pastoral Education: "A client supposedly comes to the counselor for help in reaching some solution to his problems, yet we frequently observe that instead of responding to the counselor in a manner commensurate with this objective, the client reacts as if the counselor were a tyrannical and punitive judge . . . a hinderer, a thwarter, a frustrator who deserves the client's hostile attacks. The minister, as counselor quickly recognizes this to be one of the more substantial risks of his calling."

McCoy Gibbs, the District Superintendent of the United Methodist Church: "More than once in civilian life ministers have been falsely accused of immoral acts with no more facts than seem to be true in this case. It is not unusual for the bishop and his cabinet, of which I am a member, to have to come to the defense of one of our men because of various false allegations brought on by people who for some reason feel a desperate need to hurt someone. . . . The Chaplain [Jensen] did not ask me for an observation but as a member of the profession of the clergy I am utterly appalled at what seems to be taking place in the command of a branch of the service of the United States of America."

Richard Boyer, Protestant Chaplain at the Naval Air Technical Training Center, ten years a Navy chaplain, one year clinical training at Washington University Hospital: "It may come as a surprise, especially to the outsider, that a church, chapel, or religious group often provides a haven for the emotionally disturbed . . . The problem is not that there are neurotics in the church. They should be in church and ministered to with all the disciplined love a people of God can muster . . . [but] problems arise when use or attempted use of churches, chapels or subgroups of churches is made by neurotics for their own ends. . . . The religious neurotic is essentially an idolator. His idol is a dream, an idealistic version of self . . . any sincere or unwary critic of this idol (chaplain, fellow-members of a church board) becomes not just a critic but a dangerous enemy . . . When someone has injured neurotic pride, the question is not one of getting even. It becomes a matter of obliterating the foe . . . Pride can only be restored by subjecting real or imagined enemies to the most humiliating public fate."

In addition to former chaplains Joe Simpson and Paul Gerlock, we felt it was most important that Chaplain Robert Hubbard give a deposition. He had replaced Joe Simpson as my assistant chaplain in September, 1970, and later had gone on to Vietnam, to be replaced in turn by Hoyt Swann. Gerlock's and Simpson's comments could conceivably be challenged on the basis of their own personal histories, whereas there was no such possible issue in Hubbard's case. We wrote Hubbard in Vietnam and after some delay got back the disturbing reply that the N.I.S. had already had an agent in Saigon contact him. They apparently wanted a derogatory statement from him and believed they could get it because they'd been told—incorrectly—that I had filed an adverse fitness report on Bob before his transfer. He wrote us that he had given them a very positive statement instead and was surprised that neither myself nor my lawyer had been shown a copy of it.

Once again we requested the N.I.S. produce evidence favorable to me and which they apparently were keeping from us. And once again we failed. Just as they said they knew nothing of the Howard Johnson single-room registration receipt, so they knew nothing of a Chaplain Hubbard statement.

Subsequently Hubbard was returned to the States and assigned to the Long Beach, California, Naval Hospital. I contacted him there and he gave us a second deposition, duplicating the missing one that the N.I.S. had not produced:

SWORN STATEMENT

LT ROBERT HUBBARD, being first duly sworn on oath, deposes and states as follows:

1. I, LT Robert Hubbard, CHC, USNR, am now stationed at U.S. Naval Hospital, Long Beach, California 90801.

2. I am personally acquainted with Commander A.F. Jensen, CHC, USN, whom I will hereafter refer to as Chaplain Jensen.

3. I have been asked to give this statement by Lieutenant Commander C.E. Pope, JAGC, USN, who has identified himself as the military defense counsel for Chaplain Jensen at an Article 32 Investigation being conducted pursuant to the Uniform Code of Military Justice. LCDR Pope has assisted me in the preparation of this statement.

4. I understand that this statement is to be presented to Lieutenant E.L. Duncan, JAGC, USNR, the investigating officer to the Article 32 Investigation for possible attachment as an exhibit to the investigation and for his consideration. I have been told by LCDR Pope that LT Duncan may wish to contact me concerning questions that he may have in regard to this statement.

5. I have known Chaplain Jensen since September of 1970. I was very close to Chaplain Jensen as my Senior Chaplain, as a fellow clergyman, and a close personal friend. I had great respect for him as a clergyman, a professional Chaplain, and a Naval Officer. I felt that he had a thorough knowledge of the Navy, the Chaplain Corps, and the role of the professional clergyman in the Navy. To the best of my knowledge, other chaplains in the Jacksonville area shared this respect for him with me. Cecil Field was my first assignment in the Navy after completing Chaplain School. I found that I could learn a great deal from him about the Navy and the Chaplain Corps, since he willingly shared his knowledge and experience with those who worked with him. I found that he had a willingness to learn from other chaplains and asked me on many occasions to share with him in areas where I had particular talent, training, or experience. Though we did not always agree on how things should be done, I am very grateful for having had him as my Senior Chaplain and consider him to be an excellent example of what a Senior Chaplain should be like. To sharpen his professional expertise as a counselor, Chaplain Jensen spent his day off, Tuesday, at the Methodist Hospital taking a course in Pastoral Counseling Education. I believe that he submitted several case studies a week and read a number of books in relationship to this course. He generously shared new ideas and new insights with Chaplain Gorlock and me and encouraged us to further our own professional skills and knowledge through participation in a similar course. On a few occasions Chaplain Jensen's course work required him to remain at the hospital Tuesday evenings and, thus, miss the Men's Open House which was held on the first and third Tuesdays of each month. I remember that on several occas-

Chaplain Jensen apologized for not being present at the Open House the previous evening and stated specifically that he had been at the hospital. Chaplain Jensen was an extremely dedicated, hard-working, professional Chaplain, and the only thing that may have taken from his family life was his determination to carry out his calling as a clergyman and a Chaplain.

6. For a period of time liquor bottles, wine bottles, and beer cans were found around the Chapel grounds. I can remember two specific occasions when Chaplain Jensen found liquor bottles around the Chapel grounds and was very upset about it. He discussed both of these occurences with Chaplain Gerlock and me in order to find the ones responsible for throwing them on the grounds. He may have spoken to Security about it, for the incidents of liquor bottles being thrown around the Chapel stopped after a time. If he saved an empty bottle or container, I believe it was to discover something about who was throwing them there and not for personal use. If Chaplain Jensen had such an urge to drink that he had to keep a bottle in his office, I am sure his drinking would have shown up in his actions or we could have smelled it. There was absolutely no evidence of drinking or liquor in his office, and I was in his office frequently each day. I believe he was close enough to Chaplain Gerlock and me to confide in us about drinking if he actually did drink. We spoke very freely and openly with each other about personal matters as well as professional ones. Liquor was so easily available at Cecil Field that I can see no reason why Chaplain Jensen would have ever had to keep a bottle in his office. The BOQ and ORF Bars were just a short distance away as was his home. There was never any evidence of liquor in his office, nor do I ever recall seeing any evidence of his drinking. If a liquor bottle or container was found in his desk drawer, I believe that it was there for reasons other than to sustain a drinking habit.

7. I never saw Chaplain Jensen take a drink of liquor. The only possible exception may have been at a mess night held last Fall. Then, if he had wine in his glass, he tipped his wine glass for each toast. This was in a gesture of a toast, not to drink. If he swallowed any wine, it was very little. I remember talking with Chaplain Jensen at the conclusion of the mess night and saw no indication whatsoever that he had [illegible] anything to drink. In fact, I never at any time saw him give the appearance of having had anything to drink or to have been hung over. I never smelled liquor on his breath. I have been with him on social occasions where he could easily have had a drink and there would have been no stigma attached, but on each occasion he chose to drink nothing or to have a soft drink. As a matter of fact, I was with the Jensens at a party held at the Curran's apartment. Both Chaplain and Mrs. Jensen were present. Mixed drinks and wine were served. Neither Chaplain Jensen nor Mrs. Jensen drank either a mixed drink or wine.

8. I have absolutely no knowledge or any indication whatsoever

that Chaplain Jensen was involved with the women making the charges. I do not see how Chaplain Jensen could have found time to have been involved with the two women making the charges. He would work each weekday from 0800 until after 1700. He would often work in the evenings or attend evening meetings. On Tuesdays he went to the hospital during the day and occasionally remained there during the evening. He would call at least once a day and frequently more than once each Tuesday to check on things at the Chapel. We always knew we could reach him at the hospital if we needed him. If he ever left the Chapel for any reason, he would usually tell the secretary or yeoman where he could be reached and where he was going. It was also not unusual for him to stop by my office on his way out to let me know where he was going and when he would return.

9. Chaplain Jensen was always above question in his conduct with his parishioners and counselees. At any time he was counseling during the day in his office, either his door was open or another Chaplain, the secretary or the yeoman could enter his office by simply knocking and walking in. I believe that the Chapel activity calendar would show meetings at the Chapel every night, with few exceptions, so in the evenings as well as during the day people could easily enter Chaplain Jensen's office simply by knocking or by just walking in. It is doubtful, therefore, that any questionable moral conduct could have taken place in Chaplain Jensen's office during the day or in the evening.

10. Chaplain Jensen did not appear to be in the best physical condition. He often looked tired and pale. I believe he was bothered by an allergy or other respiratory ailment that made it difficult at times for him to breathe. In consideration of his physical condition and the long hours he worked, it is doubtful that he had either the time or the stamina to have been involved with two women.

11. I believe that if the allegations against Chaplain Jensen were true, either Chaplain Gerlock or I would have noticed something suggesting such activities or someone else would have noticed and would have brought the information to one of us. To the best of my knowledge there were absolutely no rumors about Chaplain Jensen and the two women accusing him.

12. Chaplain Jensen displayed concern for the Currans' marital and religious well being. He seemed to be very happy when they decided to go back together after a period of separation. Both Mrs. Curran and Mrs. Gudbranson were active in the Chapel and, thus, came to the Chapel to participate in the activities of which they were a part. Their presence was not for any reasons out of the ordinary. Chaplain Jensen's relationship with them was professional and was no different from that of any other parishioner.

Subscribed and sworn to before me this 24th day of November 1971
[signature] Notary Public
State of California - Principal Office, Los Angeles County.

[signature]
Robert Hubbard

[signature]
FENWICK B. WARNER, SR. - Notary Public - Cal.
COM. EXP. MAR. 24, 1975 - LOS ANGELES CO.
324 S. Wabash Ave., Glendora, Calif. 91740

CHAPTER 18

Lieutenant Bob Hubbard's deposition seemed to put the icing on my case. Friends at Cecil Field thought so. Chuck Pope thought so. There were, however, some ominous signs. Enlisted men friends at Cecil Field (my friendship with EM did not go down well with some brass) reported the talk at the Center was that young Lieutenant Levy was determined to have my case go to court-martial. There would be lots of publicity. They also told me that Staff Judge Advocate Waite was talking only in terms of a court-martial, that nothing he said indicated the Article 32 hearing would clear me. A lady from our chapel who wanted me to perform a baptism called the Jacksonville headquarters and was referred to the Admiral's chief of staff, who told her I would not be doing baptisms anywhere for a long time. Chuck suggested, "One person hears something, passes it along, and it gets exaggerated." But even he, with his stubborn belief in the basically decent qualities of superior officers, was appalled when Waite made a slur on James Johnston, an Assistant Secretary of the Navy. Waite had heard I once served and was friendly with Johnston, a black man, and said to Chuck, "He's just a token appointment."

The N.I.S. continued to look for evidence against me, even in bars and night clubs in the Jacksonville area. They persistently followed me, and Lyman cautioned me never to go out alone when asking people for depositions because the N.I.S. might try to misrepresent my efforts. I heard from enlisted men that N.I.S. agents were hinting that they were bugging my phone and closing in on "new evidence" to break open my case. I knew that such evidence didn't exist, but the fear persisted that they would go to the extreme of bringing in witnesses who might give false testimony.

With their supply of government funds, the N.I.S. men spread their activities to the north. Agents were sent to the Philadelphia area to make inquiries. Former neighbors, relatives, friends, and people active in Baptist circles in Philadelphia were told that I was being investigated and information was needed about my background and reputation. The agents came up empty but they offended most of the people they interviewed. A Jewish friend who had lived through the Hitler era in Germany told me "these men brought back memories of the Gestapo."

The Cecil Field command continued to support my accusers against me. The order that I be searched if I should ever enter the chapel remained in effect, and I was searched twice when I went there after receiving permission. The chapel yeoman was told that if he ever saw me near the chapel area without my having first secured official permission he was to call the executive officer immediately. The exec, the C.P.O. reported, expressed characteristic objectivity in telling him, "I hope you're not going to embarrass this command by testifying for Jensen."

William McAuley, one of the yeomen who had given a deposition in my support, was called in by Lieutenant Ford, the young Judge Advocate at Cecil Field, and asked whether I had ordered him to give me a statement. McAuley later told me that he felt Ford tried to make him say I'd in fact acted illegally. Chaplain Swann also told McAuley that statements were being made for the "wrong side" in the Jensen case and he wanted it stopped. When McAuley refused to retract what he'd said, he was transferred out of the chapel and, interestingly, put in supply under Commander Gudbranson. Shortly afterward, I heard he was punished.

Dale Carroll, an enlisted man who had given me a deposition, was asked by Lt. Ford what he was "going to do when we find Jensen guilty." Dennis Killingsworth, who'd worked in my office and provided a statement describing my annoyance at finding liquor bottles on the grounds and attesting to the fact that the door to my office was usually open and never locked, told me he'd gotten warnings both before and after submitting his statement. The message was clear: Chaplain Jensen was distinctly bad news.

Especially disturbing was the news that an attorney, formerly Legal Officer at Cecil Field before Lt. Ford, who had gone from active service into the reserves, was now coming back to the base for two weeks and would be working on the Article 32 investigation. He had been acting as civilian attorney to the Gudbransons. Now he was reappearing in an official capacity for two weeks of "active duty" in the legal office. It seemed obvious that even though he was going on the government payroll, he would still be working for the Gudbransons. Chuck Pope had previously cautioned me never to put anything in writing that could be critical of the command. Now we began to draw up a list of all the actions the command had taken that could be construed as prejudicing my case and thereby denying me equal rights. "We may want to use it later to present before a court," he said.

The authority invoked by the command to discourage local support for me was becoming impressive. When a group of Navy chaplains in the Jacksonville area tried to issue a formal statement in my defense calling on the Navy to abandon consideration of court-martial, Chaplain Fred Brink, the Atlantic Fleet Chaplain, was dispatched to stop them. He did a good job. Brink also called me to meet him at the Thunderbird Motel, where he had a room. I went there with Kathleen. He suggested I resign from the Navy; it seemed clear he was delivering a message from Chief of Chaplains Garrett himself. I reassured him I was innocent, and began detailing the evidence I had collected for the Article 32 hearing. Nothing I said mattered. "Those motel receipts look very bad, there's just no way you can explain them," he kept saying. I went out for a few minutes to get some soft drinks. When I came back, he continued talking about the motel registrations and shaking his head (presumably more in sorrow than anger). Finally I asked, "How do you explain that you yourself rented a room at this motel and that you were in the room just now alone with my wife?" It was an imperfect analogy but a good object lesson. He missed—or chose to miss—the point.

Chaplains Allred and Danielson also seemed fixed on the motel receipts, regardless of the documented medical reasons I'd given for such attendance. So apparently was the investigating officer, who said of them, "It's just like finding an accused man's watch at the scene of a crime."

Under the circumstances my lawyers told me that a joint statement Kathleen and I had prepared for the Article 32 record should be submitted only if the investigating officer promised not to show it to the prospective prosecutor of any subsequent court-martial. The statement attested to the fact, among other things, that Kathleen always knew where I was when I went to motels for medically prescribed rest or to Jacksonville, that she either was with me during certain of my motel visits or had to cancel out at the last moment due to some family problem. Chuck and Lyman agreed that in view of the way the command had been acting the statement might be turned over to the prospective prosecutor, and that the dates of Lora's and Mary Ann's alleged meetings with me might somehow be changed so as not to conflict with the dates when Kathleen was with me. We stipulated that the statement could be shown to the Cecil Field C.O., the Judge Advocate at N.A.S., Jacksonville and Admiral Geis, but not to any court-martial prosecutor. This wasn't especially restrictive, considering that command people might well tell the prosecutor everything that was in the statement anyway, but it was too much for Lt. Duncan. He said he would accept the statement for the record only if there were no conditions about who could see it. We would not change our position, so the statement didn't go in.

During this period my father died in California. Swann and Danielson sent condolences. Chief of Chaplains Garrett sent flowers.

My father's passing set in motion a seemingly fortuitous coincidence. Commander John Carcaba and his wife Martha had lived in quarters directly opposite me at Cecil Field before he was transferred to Lemoore, California, thirty miles from where my father's funeral was held. I decided to visit the Carcabas before flying back to Florida after the funeral. I checked with Kathleen and she remembered she had asked Martha, as well as Jeannine Coleman, to check on our dog nights during that period in August, 1970, when she and the boys were away. I felt that, regardless of my reluctance, I had to ask Martha for a supporting statement.

Fortunately Martha was able to give me a much stronger deposition than I'd expected. She customarily went to bed late and would let out her own two dogs just before retiring. She would check to see if my car were home, just as Jeannine Coleman would, with the idea of bringing my dog to her house if I were out late. She never needed to because she always saw my car in the driveway. She was also an early riser, and when she got up at 6:30 each morning she would check on my car again. The car was always there in the morning so there was no need to get my dog for feeding. She had also, she said, seen me and talked to me virtually every day, yet by Mary Ann Curran's account I was involved in day-and-night intimacies with her throughout this period.

I reviewed with Martha other dates crucial to my defense. Chaplain Mudd and Mrs. Nickel had already accounted for most of the afternoon hours of Tuesday, May 18, 1971, when I was with them at the Methodist Hospital rather than in the motel room, where Lora Gudbranson had placed me. Now Martha was able to account for another hour I had forgotten about—from 1 P.M. to 2 P.M. She'd made a hurried trip with her mother to see me at the hospital during that hour because of a family problem that had to be resolved. She was certain the date was Tuesday, May 18, because her mother had been with her only that week and because she had gone to the hospital by appointment to see me—and she knew Tuesday was my day at the hospital.

Martha's deposition encouraged me to do more hard thinking about other evidence that might help my case, such as documentary proof of the relationship between Mary Ann and Dr. Blanc. I knew from my counseling notes she said she had begun her relationship with this married doctor on August 9, 1970. I also felt she had settled on that date as the start of her alleged affair with me because she'd actually been involved with him that day. She said it had been in a motel in St. Augustine (south of Jacksonville), but which one? She had told me the name during counseling but I'd not thought about it since and had not made a record. Some concentrated effort brought forth the Ponce de Leon—a fairly easy bit of free association since St. Augustine is especially known as the site of Ponce de Leon's fountain of youth.

Mary Ann had also been specific about one other time and place in her involvement with the doctor—the Saturday night before the first Monday in October, 1970. She had come to my office early that Monday upset by guilt feelings over having been intimate with the doctor in a motel in Jacksonville on Saturday night and asking, "Why do I do these things? How can I be so awful? What if Joe finds out?" . . . It was also then that she first said in bantering fashion —which I hadn't taken seriously at the time—that she could always blame "good old Chaplain Jensen." She had told me some of the details—they had gone for a drive, they had passed a motel, he had decided they should go in so he could watch a football game on TV. They watched the game, drank, had sexual relations. He had no cash so he paid for the room with his BankAmericard. But which motel was it? I didn't have the legal power of the N.I.S. to go to various motels and check records for periods of months. I at least had to have a specific place. Finally I had it—the Quality Court.

I was most uneasy about going to these two motels because now I would be seeking information about somebody other than myself.

Still, it had to be done—this was hardly the time for any sort of self-indulgence. I went to the Quality Court first, in uniform with my chaplain's insignia. I now knew the exact date because I'd checked out my 1970 calendar—October 2nd. I saw the assistant manager, told him a Dr. Blanc had stayed at his motel on that night and that I would like to get a copy of the registration. My chaplain's insignia apparently was helpful because he said only, "Will this help somebody?" "It most *certainly* will," I told him. There was indeed a registration for John Blanc, for a party of two, supporting what Mary Ann had told me during counseling as opposed to what she'd said in testimony after bringing charges. I was given a Xerox copy and left feeling encouraged.

At the Ponce de Leon motel the assistant manager was less cooperative, but after I told him this was truly an important matter and he saw that I was a chaplain he relented. Again there was a registration record for "D. J. Blanc and Mrs." and the assistant manager reluctantly permitted me to make a copy. When I brought the two copies of the motel registrations to Chuck Pope, he was pleased and said they were further confirmation that "everything you've ever told me has turned out to be true." Chuck decided he would take this evidence right over to Waite, the Judge Advocate. I wondered if perhaps we shouldn't show it to anybody from the command in case we did go to court-martial, at which time we could surprise them with it.

"No," he argued, "I'm determined to prevent this case from going to a court-martial. Why should you be put through any more? I know I was wrong when I said the case would never get as far as it has, but when I show them these receipts they'll have to accept the fact that it's been other people doing what you are accused of. It was one thing for you to say that Mary Ann's real lover has been Dr. Blanc, but it's quite another thing to produce impartial evidence to back up your story. Officially the Article 32 hearing is still on. Duncan hasn't written up his recommendation yet. Now's the time to show this to Waite and make sure his recommendation says, 'No court-martial.' "

Once again Chuck saw his efforts frustrated by the command. After turning over the new evidence to Waite and pressing him for a speedy official reaction, the only comment he received was that "Dr. Blanc may have been with somebody in these motels but we don't have any official charges against Blanc, only against Chaplain

Jensen." We interpreted this to mean they had asked Mary Ann Curran about the motel dates, that she had denied having been in these places with Dr. Blanc and again had affirmed what she'd sworn to in her Article 32 testimony—that her only adulterous affair had been with me.

A week later, Lt. Duncan issued a report equivalent to an indictment by a civilian grand jury and recommended I be tried by court-martial. "There is sufficient evidence to establish a *prima facie* case as to each allegation [of adultery] . . ." he wrote. He conceded that the testimony of Mary Ann Curran on both direct examination and cross-examination was "somewhat confused and unclear with regard to many points." But he added that "the demeanor and bearing of the witness . . . did not indicate that she was intentionally falsifying her testimony . . . Additionally, Mrs. Curran was as hesitant and uncertain in her testimony concerning matters which appeared to be uncontroverted." His remarkable reasoning seemed to be that since she was consistently confused, she must also be consistently telling the truth—or at least not "intentionally" lying. Unintentional lying was presumably okay. Against such logic our painstakingly assembled evidence was as nothing.

He also maintained consistency in making no mention of how Lora Gudbranson was shown to be lying by the statements of many impartial witnesses. Duncan noted only that "the defense has presented a number of issues for impeachment purposes in the testimony of other witnesses and . . . sworn statements for inclusion in the record . . . However, much of the testimony [of Mary Ann and Lora] does have corroboration in varying degrees in other testimony and exhibits." By so saying he was accepting the motel receipts and the so-called love notes as appropriate corroboration and ignoring the documented explanations of the defense. Presumption of guilt carried the day—with ease and a straight face.

As required by Navy regulations, the complete Article 32 record (which Duncan presumably had been studying for weeks) went with the Investigating Officer's recommendation to the Commanding Officer of Cecil Field. Captain Coleman apparently required one weekend to approve the recommendation for general court-martial.

CHAPTER 19

Chuck Pope was a man of loyalty and real sensitivity, and it hurt him to find such loyalties apparently misplaced. He loved the Navy, even though it seemed an unrequited love. He also loved the law. He had leaned over backward to give the command the benefit of the doubt each time I brought in a complaint about harassment. Although the recommendation for court-martial still had to be approved by his own boss Commander Waite and finally by Admiral Geis, he now feared this approval would be just a formality.

Sharon Smith, Mary Ann Curran's friend, reappeared in Jacksonville and Waite gave approval to a proposal by Lt. Levy that she be allowed to give a sworn deposition for use at my court-martial. Pope objected, pointing out that Waite had not yet officially prepared his report to the admiral on the question of court-martial, and the admiral, of course, had not yet convened it. The argument given for taking of the deposition was that Mrs. Smith was only going to be in the area for a few weeks. Chuck argued that if she wanted to give a deposition, the Article 32 matter could be officially reopened and Lt. Duncan could consider it. He was overruled and Mrs. Smith was permitted to give testimony at a deposition hearing, although Chuck was allowed to be on hand. It turned out that her deposition was never used because the "damning" evidence, as noted earlier, fell apart once she admitted she only saw someone she *assumed* to be me walking toward an apartment complex where Mary Ann, along with other people from Cecil Field, lived. Of real significance was that she was called in for a private hearing to give evidence for use at a court-martial that had not yet even been finally ordered.

At Chuck's suggestion, Kathleen and I made an appointment to see Captain Coleman and make a last-ditch plea for him to change his mind about the court-martial. In view of all the command had done in his name, I thought this would be useless and Chuck himself saw slight hope in it. But he thought the C.O. might be swayed by this demonstration of Kathleen's unswerving faith in me. Still, like myself, he believed that the C.O.'s near-instant approval of the recommendation for court-martial indicated that he may not have bothered to study the voluminous pages of Article 32 testimony and wasn't aware of how the statements of my two accusers had been contradicted by other witnesses. Chuck felt there was at least a slight chance he might be willing to hear Kathleen on this point.

The only thing vindicated by our meeting was our pessimism. The C.O. was unbending.

I made a new attempt to contact the chief of chaplains in Washington but this too was wasted motion. Admiral Garrett had refused to accept any calls from me or to discuss my case with me directly ever since his initial decision that I should be investigated and tried.

I had assumed that if my case did go to court-martial that Chuck would act as my defense attorney, particularly since Navy regulations would also permit another military defense counsel to be assigned to help him. Chuck now told me, however, that I should hire an older, experienced civilian attorney to act as my "lead counsel." The men who would serve on the military court would be older officers, senior to him. Lt. Levy, the prospective prosecutor, was a junior officer, but since he would represent the government for the command, he would have the prestige of the admiral behind him. As the defendant in a trial convened by the admiral, I would be at a disadvantage and needed to try to overcome this. "I realize that hiring a civilian attorney with prestige and trial experience will probably cost you the rest of your savings, but you'd better do it," Chuck advised.

He particularly wanted an attorney with a Navy background. I consulted several attorneys who'd had experience in courts-martial but none was optimistic about my chances of being acquitted. They said, however, that the evidence of command bias was so blatant and the lack of corroboration so apparent that I could win my case on appeal. I told them it didn't matter because as a chaplain and a clergyman I would be destroyed if I were convicted. Reversal of the conviction on appeal would be a Pyrrhic victory; it could not save my career. People would assume I had committed the sins I was charged with but had gotten off through a legal technicality. Besides, I was, after all, an innocent man—why justice only on appeal?

The fact that 95 percent of all courts-martial end in convictions was one answer. The fact that the appellate system in the military is removed from the influence of a local base commander was another. Small comfort, though.

I also learned that in a court-martial my defense counsel would have to submit to the prosecuting attorney the names of all the witnesses we intended to call. Along with names, we would be obliged to tell him the substance of what each would say in my defense. The prosecutor, by claiming their testimony would "not be relevant" or would be "repetitious" could reject witnesses who might be crucial to the case. We could appeal his decision to the military judge, but if the judge were allied to the command he could back up the prosecutor.

One attorney said to me: "Look, you got a strong defense in the Article 32. You didn't get a weak junior officer who would throw the case. The Article 32 should have ended things but it didn't, so now you should be thinking in terms of a compromise—reversal on appeal, maybe a conviction on some kind of lesser charge or even resignation without prejudice."

I refused to consider the idea. I felt any kind of "deal" I might accept would constitute an admission of guilt. Without mistaking a military tribunal for a schoolboy playground, I nonetheless decided it was still necessary to stand up to the bullies and fight them if necessary. Kathleen by now felt as strongly as I did. Chuck believed much of the harassment by phone calls and other means was the attempt to break Kathleen and thereby stop further resistance by me. At least in this they had failed completely.

Although the newspapers were still not aware of my case, reports of it were circulating in legal circles and I was told that two noted civilian attorneys—F. Lee Bailey and Melvin Belli—had expressed interest in defending me. Attorneys active in the civil liberties movement also seemed interested in my case, but Chuck told me a military court would be hostile to lawyers of this type and he continued to press for one with a Navy background. Then a friend of his came up with Jack Blackmon, a prominent Texas attorney who was former mayor of Corpus Christi and, more important, a captain in the Judge Advocate Corps of the Naval Reserve. Blackmon had had considerable experience in courts-martial and was one of the few attorneys to have won several cases involving military defendants. Some of his victories had come on appeal but he had also won cases on the court-martial trial level.

I flew to Texas to meet Blackmon. He met me at the airport at Corpus Christi. He was a stocky, balding man about fifty-five years old, with a slow Texas drawl. Over a barbecue dinner at a nearby restaurant I found that there was a great deal of depth and sagacity in this Texas attorney, as he led me through a complete recitation of my case. When I had finished he said, "From what you tell me, it certainly looks as though they've been trying to railroad you." I discussed, admittedly with some bitterness, the involvement of the three chaplains—Swann, Danielson, and Allred.

I told Blackmon what other attorneys had said about the unfairness of the military justice system and that they thought the best I could hope for was a compromise. "I don't want a compromise," I said. "If you take my case, can you win?"

He smiled and said, "If I could guarantee you acquittal right now, there wouldn't be much need for us to go to court, would there?" He went on to confirm what I'd already been told: It's tough for a defendant to win a court-martial, particularly when the command has taken a strong stand against him. But he also pointed out that his own batting average in court-martial cases had been good.

Then he had a frank question to ask me: "Are there any skeletons in your closet? If there are I want you to tell me now; I don't want to be surprised later." I assured him there were not. He said he would take the Article 32 transcripts home to read that night and that we would meet again the next day in his office.

Over dessert he told me some about himself and his family background. He came from a poor family in a rural section of Texas, had won a scholarship to Southern Methodist University, and finished second in his class at law school. His wife was also an attorney—they'd met at S.M.U.—and so was his son. Ironically his son was currently serving in the judge advocate general corps of the Navy and was probably prosecuting a case that very week.

When I met with Blackmon the next day, he told me he now had no doubt that I was being unfairly treated. He was concerned, however, about the prosecution's knowledge of our evidence. By turning over all our information—including the evidence of Mary Ann Curran's meetings with her real lover, Dr. John Blanc, we could not present it as a surprise at the trial. Once the prosecution knew elements of the defense case, it would be difficult to surprise witnesses. Instead of being trapped into confessing falsehoods they could attempt to explain away contradictions by blaming them on faulty memory since clarified or on misunderstanding or misinterpretation, etc. Blackmon made it clear he was not blaming us and understood our motive was to convince the command not to order a court-martial. The trouble was we didn't succeed and so the result was we would unavoidably begin at a disadvantage.

Blackmon, like Pope, felt confident that we could win the case on an appeal level, but he would not give me any promise of victory on the trial level no matter how much I pressed him. We settled on a fee of $7,000 for his services plus expenses at trial attorney for the court-martial. He said, however, that he would arrange to see Admiral Geis and at least try at the eleventh hour to talk him out of it.

Since I was in Texas, and things looked so bleak, I decided it would be irresponsible and self-indulgent not to attempt to document further what I knew to be Mary Ann's selective description during the Article 32 hearing of her affair in Texas as having taken place only once at the motel in Beeville. She had confided to me in her counseling sessions that she had not gone directly to Jacksonville from Beeville but instead had left town with her lover and had stopped in another motel.

First, I drove from Corpus Christi to Beeville to check out the records of Drummer's Inn, Identified to me by Mary Ann as the site of several meetings with her Texas friend—not just one, as testified to. The old records of the Inn were kept in town by a bookkeeping office, and the records showed that Mary Ann and her friend—I knew the name and so could identify him—had stayed at the motel not once but on May 3, 4, 5, 6, and 7 of 1970. They were registered in separate rooms. Mary Ann was unavailable in hers, as her husband Joe Curran discovered when he tried to call her from Cecil Field during the days when he was getting settled and she was staying in the Texas motel by prearrangement between them. The presence of her friend obviously was also by prearrangement—between Mary Ann and him.

The other assignation place mentioned by Mary Ann was the Executive Inn, in Dallas, on May 8th. I was able to confirm that both were registered there on that date and to secure a copy of the registration receipt. When the secretary handed it to me, she asked, "This won't get anybody into trouble, will it?" I answered her in all honesty, "On the contrary, it may keep somebody *out* of trouble."

Once again, I turned the motel receipts over to Chuck Pope; once again he turned what he hoped would be convincing evidence over to the staff judge advocate to offset a court-martial, and once again as with Dr. Blanc the reaction was that a lover of Mary Ann was not being charged with adultery, I was, and therefore this man's behavior was irrelevant—never mind that it showed that my accuser was a perjurer. We assumed that when Waite and Levy showed the Dallas motel record to Mary Ann, she told them she hadn't really lied but merely had forgotten the whole episode—which enabled them to maintain that their witness was not dishonest, merely forgetful.

Chuck Pope resisted Waite's attempt to transfer him to legal work in the Navy's drug-treatment center and told him that no matter what happened to him in the Navy he was going to stick with my case. Even though a civilian counsel would be coming in, he was going to devote full time to helping on the case and researching all aspects of military law to help me win.

When Jack Blackmon flew in from Corpus Christi to see the admiral, he was treated with courtesy, due to his age, legal status, and reserve rank of captain. He conferred with both the admiral and with Waite, who was still maintaining a neutral posture. Since Admiral Geis had formerly served as the Navy's chief of public information, Blackmon decided to use a public-relations argument to convince him of the folly of a court-martial, saying, "The Navy can't afford the embarrassment of staging an adultery [only] trial. You know, I may be talking myself out of a good fee by coming here but I'm loyal to the Navy and I don't want to see the Navy hurt."

The admiral was noncommittal, so Blackmon added a warning: "If you order a court-martial, you may be remembered in history as the first admiral ever to court-martial a chaplain and the first admiral ever to send an adultery [only] case to court-martial. I would think you would prefer history to remember you in other ways."

The admiral assured Blackmon he would consider everything he had said and the next day he went out to play golf with Waite, the official neutral, and Levy, the prospective prosecutor. A few days later Waite presented his formal report on the Article 32 investigation to the admiral and although he refused to allow Chuck Pope to see his report—in violation of custom—we had little doubt that he was following the same route as the investigating officer and the Cecil Field C.O. in recommending the court-martial.

It came officially during Christmas week, making it the most miserable Christmas of our lives. We paid a holiday visit to Chaplain Carroll Chambliss and his wife, and it was from Carroll rather than from the command or the chief of chaplains that we were informed of the order of Admiral Geis convening a general court-martial. Carroll had heard about the order through another chaplain who in turn got it from the chief of chaplains and was greatly upset to find that I had received no direct notification and that he was the inadvertent courtier of the bad tidings. Particularly painful was the revelation that the chief of chaplains was working so closely with the command structure that he was among the first to know I was going to be put on public trial.

Even though by this time we'd been expecting the bad news, the awful reality of it almost made us turn our backs to the wall. Almost . . .

CHAPTER 20

We were told that Admiral Geis' decision for the court-martial was made known to the Chief of the Bureau of Naval Personnel, the Chief of Naval Operations, and the then Secretaries of the Navy, John Chafee, and of Defense, Melvin Laird. None of these high officials apparently had made an independent inquiry into the specifics of the case, including a check on the credibility of my accusers. The commanding officer of a Naval station wanted a court-martial. His recommendation was approved and no one would interfere.

From the top of the bureaucracy's point of view you went with your people, and your people were the ones who shared and enforced your authority. Anybody who seemed out of step or somehow a troublemaker, right or wrong, tended to be a threat and had to be dealt with. Those who had initiated and supported the actions against me may have expected that I would be sufficiently intimidated by the accusations to resign and there would then be no need to prove any case against me. When I failed to cooperate, the momentum of the investigation almost inevitably led to the incredible extreme of court-martial. Once it had started, they could stop only on pain of admission of the falsity of the charges and of the personal and social conditions at the base that had prompted them in the first place. All this tended to come clear in the perspective of time and reflection. At the moment, in the heat of the situation, it hardly was evident to me or those closest to me. Our reaction was dismay, disbelief, and anger.

The announcement of the court-martial came at about the same time as the disclosure that promotions had been approved for Commander Gudbranson and Lieutenant Curran. Cases of virtue rewarded. For the record I inquired about my recommendation for promotion. The answer came back: "What recommendation? Nobody knows anything about it."

It was decided that the time had come to take off the gloves with the command. An appointment was arranged with Admiral Geis. Betty McKean, Margaret Huntsinger, and Kathleen went to the meeting along with Jane Center and Janet Rodgers, two other members of our chapel family. There had been two recent accidents involving planes that nearly crashed into a school near Cecil Field, and the admiral may have believed the appointment had been made to discuss this problem, and so he greeted the women with marked cordiality. His expansive manner disappeared when he found they were calling about the Jensen case.

They first presented a written statement saying they were convinced of my innocence and felt that a public court-martial would hurt the Navy. The admiral's answer was that Mr. Blackmon had already brought this to his attention but that he was obliged to convene a court-martial because the C.O. of Cecil Field had recommended it.

The ladies countered that since the C.O., Captain Coleman, was so anxious to stage public trials on charges involving adultery and immorality, similar charges should be investigated against the C.O. himself. They offered statements that the captain had been intimately involved with a woman who was not his wife for several months and that it was well known around the base that she had spent time on weekends with him at his quarters before his divorce. The statements charged that the captain's behavior had a damaging effect on the families of personnel at the field. Betty and Kathleen stated that they were among the wives present at a dinner at the captain's quarters the night he had said, "I may be too old to fly, but I'm not too old to R.O.N."

The admiral hurriedly terminated the meeting by saying such charges should be taken up with Staff Judge Advocate Waite. Waite told them that Captain Coleman could sue them if the charges were shown to be false. They stood their ground, so Waite told them he would make a personal investigation of their allegations. The result of his investigation: no substance to the charges.

The news of the impending court-martial was broken in the Jacksonville *Times-Union* on January 7, 1972, by a reporter, Otis Perkins. Although I was identified as the chaplain charged with adultery, the names of Mary Ann and Lora were not revealed. The article contained no statement from me, but Lyman Fletcher, who was asked for comment, pointed out that I had held to my claim of innocence from the outset.

I received calls from people active in Jacksonville who had worked with me on various civic projects and who now pledged whatever support they could give. Many protested to the admiral. Congressman Bennett, representing the Jacksonville area, was asked to investigate. Bennett had always been close to Navy officialdom and military personnel. He was not disposed to act on the protests. My friends were disappointed when he was not disposed to act on the protests.

Perhaps most difficult of all was telling our children what I was to face. We had earlier told Drew he no longer could go to the Gudbransons' quarters to play with their boy because of a "disagreement" I had had with the boy's parents. Now Kathleen gave both our boys a more forthright explanation of what had happened. She said that Mrs. Gudbranson and another woman had told lies about their father and that as a consequence I probably would have to go into court to prove that what they had said was not true. She told them there might be many stories in the papers that friends in school would see or hear about. These friends might ask questions about me, and they should always remember that I was telling the truth and that most of the families at Cecil Field believed me.

"Is that why so many people keep coming to our house?" David asked. "Yes," Kathleen told him. David didn't ask any more questions but Drew, nearly eleven, later asked Kathleen why Mrs. Gudbranson would tell lies about people who were friends of hers and what kind of lies she had told. Kathleen told him it's hard to understand why people lie but sometimes it's because they're unhappy and "mixed up." I don't think he was clear about what adultery meant but he knew the charge was serious because it meant breaking one of the Ten Commandments. He was worried about what we had told him, but the fact that so many of the people he knew and liked at the base kept coming over seemed to help some. It had its toll, though—no question.

Although the *Times-Union* story did not name the two women who had accused me, their names soon became public knowledge and I received a number of calls from people in Jacksonville about them. Most concerned Mary Ann Curran, whose behavior was apparently known to several people. Substantive information came from Phyllis Villapande, a bartender at the officers' club in Jacksonville, who told us that an officer had told her that a friend of his frequently had relations with Mary Ann when Joe Curran was out of town. She believed this friend would be willing to testify in my defense. She said she was willing to be a defense witness herself to testify about the comments she had heard concerning Mary Ann's character.

My lawyers also decided it was time to approach Dr. John Blanc. The command had insisted it was going ahead with the court-martial despite the evidence I had produced to substantiate the relationship between the doctor and Mary Ann, but we thought we should try to persuade the doctor to appear at the trial and tell the truth. Chuck said he would go to see Blanc, but he wanted somebody else to come along. We knew (from his calls to my home) the doctor would likely be unreceptive, and felt the presence of a third party at the meeting could serve as a restraining influence as well as a witness. Joe Simpson was back and volunteered to go with Chuck.

When the two men told Blanc they knew about his relationship with Mary Ann, he became angry and said he'd have Chuck disbarred. He confirmed that he had indeed threatened me over the telephone and said that I must be guilty or I would have sued him (his logic was also in line with the whole presumption of guilt by accusation). He ordered Joe out of the room and said he wanted to talk to Chuck alone. Chuck reported that he then said that Mary

Ann was a "lying little son-of-a-bitch who can't be trusted." This was rather substantially in contrast to the favorable remarks he had made about her in his original statements to the N.I.S.

He was stunned when Chuck told him we had the motel receipts to prove his liaison with Mary Ann, but when Chuck insisted he testify voluntarily or face a subpoena, he threatened to "destroy" Chuck. We subsequently learned that he had called Mary Ann, asked her that his name be kept out of the trial and demanded that she take back everything she had said. It was never entirely clear what he meant by "everything," but in any case Mary Ann took nothing back. Apparently concerned about his conversation with her, she prepared an affidavit for the government saying that the doctor had made threats against her. We decided we would have no alternative but to subpoena Dr. Blanc as a witness and force him to tell about Mary Ann by confronting him with the motel records.

The command was unswayed by what it had already been told about Mary Ann's background. In fact, they insisted on starting the trial on January 19th on the grounds that Lora and Mary Ann were becoming nervous and shouldn't be obliged to wait any longer. Chuck Pope submitted a vehement statement of protest, pointing out that my civilian counsel had only recently come into the case, had not had time to prepare the defense, and was still tied up on some legal business in Corpus Christi. Nonetheless, Levy was so anxious to go forward that he would have held us to that January date if it had not been for the unexpected death of the father of Lt. Tieman Dippel, the Navy lawyer who had been Chuck's assistant military counsel. Lt. Dippel received a hardship discharge from the service, and we were told he would be replaced by another young lieutenant. This did give us a postponement until March.

The entry of my religious denomination into the case also had minimal effect on the command's determination to prosecute. Chaplain Charles F. Willis, head of our chaplain unit in the American Baptist Convention, had briefly visited me before the Article 32 hearing to assure me the charges would be dismissed. Announcement of the court-martial came as a shock to him and to the denomination, and his chief assistant, Chaplain Herman Benner, a retired colonel and army chaplain, was asked to go down to Jacksonville and examine the evidence in my case.

Chaplain Benner did examine the evidence, then spoke to Kathleen, Chuck Pope, and myself, and reported back to the denomination that "they have no case against Chaplain Jensen—there is no justification for a court-martial." He also reported the pattern of harassment against me and that the chief of chaplains had asked the military command to investigate and prosecute me instead of taking the matter up with the Baptist Convention. The Convention voted to support me and raise funds. Chaplain Willis then wrote Admiral Garrett to advise him that I continued to be a minister in good standing in the American Baptist Convention. He added these comments:

"American Baptists await the outcome of this court-martial with considerable interest. We are concerned with Andrew Jensen. If he has been unjustly charged and if, as he alleges, he has been harassed during the pretrial investigation, this denomination will insist that he receive justice. We are also concerned with the good name of American Baptists. Our prestige will be affected by the fact that an American Baptist chaplain has been tried for this particular offense. When I recall the number of servicemen I have known over the years who not only admitted their sexual conquests but boasted of them, I am appalled that the Navy has chosen a chaplain, an American Baptist chaplain who is spending his children's educational funds and mortgaging his home to defend his innocence, for trial on specifications of adultery. The entire country is entitled to ask when the trials of the admittedly guilty personnel will begin.

"American Baptists endorse their chaplains to the Armed Forces in full knowledge that they are subject to the Uniform Code of Military Justice. We have not sought and do not seek any exemption for them from the discipline of the Service whose uniform they wear. We do expect that they will be treated justly. The charges made against Andrew Jensen and his report of the investigation process as implemented in his case raise some serious questions. I express our concern to you as administrative head of the Chaplain Corps, United States Navy, and take this means of advising you that the American Baptist Convention stands back of Andrew Jensen."

What came back from Admiral Garrett were comments to the effect that the court-martial would be a fair one and that he accepted Chaplain John Danielson's representation of Mary Ann and Lora as "two lovely housewives."

Danielson's assurance was repeated to Chaplain Benner when he came back to act as an observer for the denomination at the trial. He also suggested to Chaplain Benner that taking special courses in counseling troubled persons as I had at the Menninger Clinic would cause the ruination of chaplains. He also said that the N.I.S. had been suspicious of me and had been following me for months *before* thet two officers' wives had made their charges against me.

When Chaplain Benner reported this, I immediately presented the transcript of the Article 32 hearing and showed him the sworn testimony of the N.I.S. men that they began investigating me for the first time on August 12, 1971, following the filing of charges by the two.

Benner told Admiral Geis that a court-martial could not possibly be justified. "Show me some real evidence and I'll see to it that Jensen resigns and gets out of the service," he told the admiral. He reported that the admiral said, "Thank you for coming in," and dismissed him.

When we finally did get our hands on the pretrial advice that Staff Judge Advocate Waite had sent to the admiral in recommending the court-martial, we found it was misleading and prejudiced and therefore *could* have convinced an unsympathetic C.O. who dug no further into the facts. Waite's report also included a personal attack on Chuck Pope, which was probably why he withheld it from the defense for fifty-one days, in violation of military custom. We finally got a copy of the report on February 16, 1972, only after Chuck had submitted a formal motion in military court demanding it.

The essence of the attack was that portions of Chuck's cross-examinations of Lora and Mary Ann at the Article 32 hearing were "inappropriate, irrelevant, unnecessarily humiliating . . ."

We assumed he meant the questions on sexual behavior that Mary Ann had answered with alacrity. Still, as Jack Blackmon and other attorneys later agreed, Chuck was right to pursue this admittedly painful line of questioning inasmuch as the matter being investigated was illicit sexual behavior. Specific details were essential to develop in such a case. We felt what really bothered Waite was that Chuck's questions had presented Mary Ann in a number of damaging contradictions (later we were to find she had been shown to be more than contradictory). I also felt that Waite was hitting back at Chuck for not acting like a "team man" in insisting on providing me with a strong defense.

In summarizing the evidence brought out at the Article 32 hearing, Waite echoed almost literally the report of the Investigating Officer—reinforcing our belief that the I.O.'s report was virtually dictated by Waite. All Waite said, in a very general way, was that both women gave sworn testimony, that Mrs. Curran was a bit unsure of dates and places, and that there were sworn defense statements. He omitted mention of the fact that both had admitted there was nothing they knew about me that they could not or did not in fact receive from association with my wife; that there had been no previous rumors of any involvement of myself with them; that there were no eyewitnesses who could give evidence of any illicit association with either of them, even though I had worn Navy uniform and chaplain's cross when going to motels in the recreational areas and so was highly identifiable; that Mary Ann Curran's testimony showed her to be so evasive and contradictory (she even claimed to have forgotten where she had her first tryst with her lover) as to make every word she said suspect; and, most important, that a succession of impartial witnesses had given the direct lie to much of the testimony Mary Ann and Lora Gudbranson had given about me.

Admiral Geis' spirited answer, as mentioned, was to go along with what the C.O. at Cecil Field and his own staff people felt appropriate. And it was to go up the line—from Geis to Garrett to Secretary of the Navy Chafee to Secretary of Defense Laird and perhaps to President Nixon himself.

Admiral Geis may also have been motivated by some of the same kind of unease apparently at work on Captain Coleman at Cecil Field —concern that "Square Andy" was about to blow the whistle on the immoral practices going on around at Cecil Field and in the Jacksonville area and therefore under the admiral's jurisdiction.

Kathleen and I both had supported Richard Nixon in the 1968 election. We approved his statements about the work ethic and his emphasis on high moral standards and law and order. Kathleen at this point still believed that if the President could get the full picture of what had happened he would take action to make things right. So she wrote a long letter to Mr. Nixon, setting down all the facts. She was not so naïve as to believe that the President read every letter sent to him but she did feel the circumstances of my case were unique and that his chief aides would bring her letter to his personal attention. In fact, the letter was referred to Robert A. Frosch, Mr. Chafee's Assistant Secretary of the Navy, who wrote back on behalf of the President that he could not interfere with the judicial process and that I would have ample opportunity during the general court-martial to present all evidence in my behalf.

Kathleen's two sisters, Jeannette Serabian and Margaret LaMania, also wrote to the President, to the Secretary of Defense, and the Secretary of the Navy. So did many of our supporters—including Navy wives and civilians. All got back the same kind of response from Mr. Frosch. Kathleen again wrote to the President, to the Secretary of the Navy, and the Judge Advocate General of the Navy. In her letter to Secretary Chafee she set down the specific instances in which we felt my rights had been denied and asked for his intervention. "At one time, I would have hoped that a letter such as this would have the effect of preventing a trial so humiliating as that involved in this case," she wrote. "Both my husband and I have no fear of a trial, especially if this is the only way to establish his innocence . . . However, if there is a sincere interest in justice this whole matter should be investigated. Will the trial be fair or will it reflect past attitudes and action?"

Neither Kathleen nor I expected that the top government officials would automatically accept her word, or the words of my lawyers, but we felt they would at least be moved to order an independent investigation. None happened. The only response was more letters assuring that "Chaplain Jensen will be afforded every right guaranteed him under the law . . ." and "The Uniform Code of Military Justice was enacted by Congrees to protect the rights of all members of the armed forces . . ."

My son Drew became aware of the letters written in my defense and decided that he wanted to write to the President too, being sure the President would know that he wouldn't lie about his father. Back came the by now form letter from Mr. Frosch on behalf of President Nixon: "Your father and his attorney will have the opportunity to present evidence in your father's behalf at the court-martial in early March."

This heartrending second-hand response from his President was, not surprisingly, disillusioning to an eleven-year-old boy, aware now that the Navy his father served had taken sides against his father. He had already been frightened by the tactics of the N.I.S. men who had investigated and kept me under surveillance. How could the high officials of his government promise his father a fair trial if they had allowed all this to go on? He was now not only worried about what was happening in his family but upset because so many of the things he had been taught in school were turning out not to be so. One day he broke into tears and said, "I wish I was old enough to vote against that man in the White House!"

I realized that my case would soon be getting national publicity and that I could no longer keep it from my sister Mildred in Washington and my brother Christen in California. Once we'd told them, Kathleen asked them to contact congressmen in their local area or other officials they knew who might be willing to help.

Mildred and her husband, a civilian engineer with the Navy, had been active supporters of the southern Baptist Church, and they were particularly angered by the way southern Baptist chaplains had not supported me. They asked the leaders of the southern Baptist denomination to support me as the northern Baptists—that is, the American Baptists—had done. They also asked the help of Admiral James Kelly, a southern Baptist who had preceded Admiral Garrett—a southern Methodist—as Chief of the Navy Chaplain Corps. But neither the southern denomination nor Admiral Kelly would lift a finger for me, which led my sister and her husband to break with the southern Baptist Church.

Christen's wife, Emma, had been active in community affairs in our home town of Selma, California, and was then running for election to the city council. She had my lawyers send her a complete dossier on my case and contacted, among others, Congressman Bernie F. Sisk, a dedicated and energetic official who represented our home area in Washington. On the basis of this dossier, Congressman Sisk asked the Secretary of the Navy to order an investigation into the way the case was being handled.

To rally more local support and help with legal expenses, a "Chaplain Jensen Defense Fund" was started at Cecil Field with the help of Lyman Fletcher, who suggested that Navy husbands stay out of it to avoid reprisals by the command. Even though the members of the fund were civilians, an attempt was soon made to intimidate them. At one of the meetings at Margaret Huntsinger's house attended by the wives of enlisted men in the Jacksonville area, sailors were noticed outside taking down the license plate numbers of the cars. When the ladies demanded an explanation from the sailors, the answer was that they were simply following orders to get the license numbers and turn them in. The wives made an official request to Captain Coleman for permission to collect funds on the base, and after this incident he issued an order barring them from any fund-raising on the base. Still, they did manage to collect $2,800 toward my legal and investigative costs which eventually came to over $18,000.

Officials of my denomination continued to have meetings about my case, and when they saw they were to get no help from the chief of chaplains, they decided to take stronger measures. In protest against the Navy's handling of the charges against me, Chaplain Willis at a press conference announced that the denomination would no longer supply its clergymen to serve as chaplains in the Navy. This was unprecedented—no religious faith had ever done such a thing before. Chaplain Willis also announced that the denomination had asked the General Commission on Chaplains and Armed Forces Personnel to join the American Baptists in withholding endorsement of chaplains.

"We have reason to believe that Chaplain Jensen is being deprived of his constitutional rights in his defense against the charge alleged," Rev. Willis said. "All our contacts have led us to believe he is innocent. We believe he is being defamed."

The action by the denomination caused the first wave of national publicity about my case. Newspapers carried the story on the front pages and it was featured on all network radio and TV newscasts. The story became even more important with the disclosure that the General Commission on Chaplains and Armed Forces Personnel had set up a special committee to hear the complaint of the American Baptist Convention.

There were incessant reminders in the press, and on radio and TV, that "Chaplain Andrew Jensen has been charged with adultery . . . he will be the first chaplain in American history to face a court-martial . . ." and we were concerned about the tendency of many people to believe the worst about a person who is the subject of lurid headlines. But the letters that poured in to us from all over the country, and from overseas, were overwhelmingly favorable. Jack Blackmon and Chuck Pope were pleased with the attention, saying it was important that a religious denomination had given public support to my position. They also felt that if the media covered what was happening to me, it would be more difficult for the local command to conduct an unfair court-martial.

Chuck and his new military assistant, Lt. Joe Durham, had found in their legal research that the record of command influence against me offered a strong basis for winning at the Article 39A hearing prior to the main court-martial. The 39A hearing would be held before the military judge assigned to the court-martial and would be restricted to legal arguments on why the charges against me should either be dropped or referred back to another Article 32 investigation. They felt it was important that the spotlight remain on the case in order to keep the Article 39A proceedings unprejudiced.

Was the unthinkable to be avoided after all?

CHAPTER 21

It was the day before the Article 39A hearing was to open and Kathleen and I had gone to the Jacksonville Airport to meet Jack Blackmon coming in from Texas. Unexpectedly Nancy Pope, Chuck's wife, drove up, looking very agitated.

She explained that in order to prepare Phyllis Villapanda, who worked at the officers' club, for her testimony at the trial and to give her a better understanding of my case, Chuck had given her a copy of the Article 32 hearing record, which contained Mary Ann's sworn testimony. He had given it to her openly at the officers' club, since it was perfectly legal and proper for her to read it. Apparently someone saw and reported it. A bit later, N.I.S. agents came to the club, took Mrs. Villapanda aside and told her that if she didn't surrender the copy she would be in trouble. They asked her questions about her job, background, children, and male friends. They also told her that "Lt. Commander Pope is going to be in very bad trouble because he gave you this."

Mrs. Villapanda didn't know whether to believe them or not, but she was understandably terrified and surrendered the material. As soon as the N.I.S. men left, she hurried to the phone and notified Chuck. The next day she called Chuck again to say that the N.I.S. men had gone to the nursery where she kept her children during her working hours and had questioned the personnel there about her background and particularly about her "boyfriends."

Chuck had registered a vigorous protest against this behavior and sent Nancy to the airport so that Jack Blackmon could be advised as soon as he arrived. Jack's reaction was, "This is the worst thing

I've heard of in all my years of practice in military courts." He felt the N.I.S. must have acted on its own—this was improper interference with a defense witness and he couldn't imagine that the Staff Judge Advocate had sanctioned it.

Next day we learned that the Staff Judge Advocate had indeed sanctioned it. We were told the N.I.S. had gone to Mrs. Villapanda and threatened her on Waite's authority and direction. Mrs. Villapanda promised she would still be a witness for the defense, but she was clearly shaken by her ordeal and fearful of losing her job and I was reluctant to have her appear. Chuck, however, said that he needed her to testify before the military judge at the Article 39A hearing about what the N.I.S. had done to her. He was furious at the intimidation of a witness at the direction of the Staff Judge Advocate and was especially incensed at the statement that he was "going to be in trouble" for giving her the Article 32 hearing material to study. Still, the judge who had been assigned to the 39A hearing, Captain Ben Cole, had come up from the military district rather than Admiral Geis' immediate jurisdiction, so there was some optimism that he would exercise independent judgment.

Chuck Pope and his associate Joe Durham had prepared an impressive (if at times annoyingly technical) set of briefs in cooperation with Jack Blackmon for the legal arguments at the 39A hearing. They also arranged for a large number of witnesses to appear to buttress the legal points and asked for the subpoena of other witnesses who would be hostile to me but would be compelled to give testimony to substantiate my case. These were the principal legal arguments to be offered:

The offense charged against me was not service-connected. This went back to the original contention by Chuck Pope and the navy attorney I had consulted informally in Philadelphia that the ruling by the U.S. Supreme Court in the O'Callahan case barred prosecution in a military court for offences not service-connected. My lawyers contended that adultery by its nature was a general, not specifically military, offense and therefore had never been the subject of a military court-martial. The persons making the charge were not under military jurisdiction—they may have been officers' wives but they were legally civilians.

Lt. Levy had prepared a brief in opposition asserting that Mary Ann had gone to me, as a Navy chaplain, for counseling, and that our relationship developed from the counseling situation. But I already had a statement from Hazel Young, manager of the family consultation service in Jacksonville, that I had referred Mary Ann and her husband to that Service in August, 1970. They had opened a case file on the Currans on August 18th, but the referral had been made at least two weeks earlier. So I no longer had an official counseling relationship with Mary Ann on August 9th, the date on which she claimed we had our first meeting. That alleged meeting was off-base, in any case—the activity she testified as occurring in the chapel office came at a much later date.

Levy also maintained that the relationship between Lora Gudbranson and myself had developed from our contacts through the chapel and as neighbors in the officers' quarters. But since Lora had specifically pointed out that she'd never had a professional association with me or come to me for counseling, the "service-connection" was nonexistent.

The article under which I was being charged was vague and unconstitutional. The original charges against me were based on Article 134: "Conduct prejudicial to the service, etc." Subsequently, charges under Article 133—"Conduct Unbecoming an Officer and a Gentleman"—were added. The charges were always based on the specifications of adultery. Waite, in his pretrial advice, combined the charges into the Article 133 violation, again with the specifications of adultery. He apparently felt that the Article 133 violation sounded stronger because officers are supposed to have higher standards (moral and otherwise) than mere mortals such as enlisted personnel (the irony of *that* is pretty staggering). The order convening the court-martial was based on Waite's advice. We argued that the Article 133 had been used as a catch-all in the military courts and that whenever there was doubt on how an officer could be charged, Article 133 was used.

Further, I was being denied equal protection under the law because I was a chaplain. We would cite statements made by individuals connected with the command that I never would have been charged if I had not been a chaplain. All naval officers were entitled to equal protection and equal treatment under the law; there was no provision for offenses under military law to be applied solely to chaplains.

We also argued that the "equal protection" doctrine was being violated by the failure to act on the complaints against Captain Coleman's behavior. If I was being charged, why wasn't he?

There was a failure to corroborate charges by accomplices—the two who had accused me were admitted accomplices, and according to military law there could be no case without corroboration of accomplices' charges. We argued that the so-called "love notes" and the motel receipts, unaccompanied by any evidence that either Mary Ann or Lora were ever with me at the motels, could not be considered corroboration.

Command influence, command prejudgment and command failure to exercise independent judgment—our presentation on these issues included the entire chain of disgraceful events that flowed from the command's initial prejudgment of me. First, I was accused while away on leave and ordered to stay off the base when I refused to resign. No attempt was made to restrain Commander Gudbranson when he threatened my life, command officers met socially with my accusers and their husbands and favored them while I was treated as a pariah, along with my family, and I was even forbidden to perform religious services for my parishioners.

Next there was the premature assignment of "prospective trial prosecutors" before the preliminary inquiry even began; the orders that I submit to an examination at the hospital on pain of being placed under lock and key; the disclosure to Gudbranson that the examination concerned circumcision; the order that I be searched like a criminal if I came into the chapel; the assignment of the civilian attorney for the Gudbransons to the Cecil Field legal office for two weeks; the promotion of Chaplain Swann into my job after he had served as witness to the accusations against me and had counseled Mary Ann and Lora; the whole range of improper N.I.S. activities, including the hiding of evidence favorable to the defense, the attempt to secure false statements from people such as Patricia Franklin and the intimidation of Phyllis Villapanda; the attempts by key members of the Cecil Field command to coerce various defense witnesses not to assist me and the continuing statements by members of the command about my presumed guilt; the prejudicial manner in which the Sharon Smith deposition was handled; the refusal to allow my supporters to solicit defense funds on the base; the assignment of my house to somebody else before the court-martial was even convened; the order that I was not to receive pastoral counseling; the attempt by the prosecutors to set a trial date only sixteen days after the formal decision to convene a general court-martial; and the deceptive summary of the Article 32 investigation by the staff judge advocate, which along with his inflammatory attack on my military defense counsel doubtless helped convince the admiral to issue the order for the court-martial.

Jack Blackmon said evidence of command influence and prejudgment was overwhelming. Lyman Fletcher, still the persistent critic of the military-justice system, was convinced that no matter how strong a legal case we made at the Article 39A hearing, we were certain to fail.

He turned out to be right. Almost from the moment that the military judge, Judge Cole, took his place on the bench and ruled on the first of our legal motions for dismissal, we felt we were dealing with a partisan. He denied each motion almost as soon as it was made. He quickly disposed of our claim that there was no service connection to the adultery charge by ruling that I was not being charged with any sexual offense, but rather with "misuse of office." I barely restrained myself. The charges by Mary Ann and Lora, the entire scope of their testimony and all the efforts by the N.I.S. investigators were based on proving I had entered into adulterous relationships. Neither the charges on which the Article 32 investigation was based nor Waite's pretrial advice that resulted in the convening of the court-martial had made any mention of "misuse of office." The specifications against me plainly stated adultery. Now here was a judge suddenly taking it upon himself to change the specifications when it looked as though they might not be made to stick. We had heard some talk around the Jacksonville law center a few days before the Article 39A hearing about me "misusing" my office, and now it seemed the prosecution had come up with this device to circumvent our argument about failure to show service connection. Our claim that Article 133 was unconstitutional because of its vagueness was also rejected. The judge accepted Lt. Levy's position that "there is no question about the constitutionality of this article, even when it is applied to conduct not within the accused's official duties and capacity." (Ironically, some months after my court-martial the federal courts ruled that Article 133 was indeed unconstitutional because of its vagueness. The decision was made on the appeal of a military conviction of a Lt. Levy—no kin to my prosecutor but rather an army doctor who refused to give training in dermatology to GIs heading for Vietnam. Article 134 concerning conduct prejudicial to the service was also ruled unconstitutional by the federal courts in an appeal on another case.)

To support our position on command influence and prejudgment we had requested the appearance of over fifty witnesses. As mentioned, under the military system the prosecutor has the right to approve or reject witnesses called for by the defense. In this case Lt. Levy rejected all but twelve. We appealed to the military judge to overrule him but he denied almost all of our motions on witnesses. Chief Petty Officer Huntsinger was allowed to take the stand, but when he began to give testimony about the way the exec John Shute had criticized me, the judge cut him off, saying his testimony was irrelevant. So we ended up with no witnesses and could only read into the record what our witnesses would have said had they been permitted to take the stand—which primarily was to establish a basis for appeal.

Kathleen and I went to the Popes' house to discuss our situation with our defense team. Jack Blackmon and Chaplain Herman Benner were there, along with Joe Durham, his wife, and Chuck and Nancy. It was now obvious that all hope of winning the case through pre-court-martial dismissal was gone. Our only consolation—as Jack and the Durhams and finally Chuck too pointed out—was that Judge Cole had allowed reversible error into the proceedings and that a guilty verdict would likely be overturned in a court of military review and appeals. Meanwhile, of course, the ordeal of trial and its personal and professional consequences could go on.

The next day Judge Cole continued to shoot down motion after motion, punctuating his rulings with scornful asides. We had Mrs. Villapanda waiting out in the hall while Chuck explained the importance of having her testify and pointing out how the N.I.S. intimidation had frightened away important defense witnesses. The prosecution insisted there was nothing out of order in the way she had been treated. The judge would not allow Mrs. Villapanda or anyone else to testify in our behalf.

We had prepared a list of sixty-five people we wanted as defense witnesses at the court-martial itself. I had written to fellow chaplains and superior officers I had served under, asking if they would testify as character witnesses. Not one begged off, despite the nature of the charges against me. Our list also included the witnesses who had contradicted Mary Ann and Lora in their Article 32 affidavits, along with five witnesses who would give expert testimony on why certain women tend to make false charges about sexual relations. Lt. Levy promptly exercised his veto under the military justice system and turned down two-thirds of our witnesses, including Assistant Secretary of the Navy James Johnston, who had agreed to be a character witness. The military judge refused to overrule Levy in almost all instances.

The Judge also refused to allow us to subpoena a woman Mary Ann had described to me as a close companion. He also refused to allow us to subpoena motel records to show Mary Ann had stayed overnight with this woman. The basis of his refusal was that the mere fact they had been together at the motels would not be proof of a relationship. Yet he was allowing the prosecution to present records that I had stayed alone at motels as a means of proving that I had improper relationships—they could not establish even that Mary Ann or Lora had been at such motels with me. Just that I had been there—and I explained the medical reasons—and they falsely claimed they'd been there as well.

The prosecutor, in turning down each witness, stated that in his opinion the testimony of this witness or that would be "irrelevant" or "not material," or "repetitious" of other testimony. Lt. Levy barred Joy Oneth and Jane Bristol from testifying how Lora Gudbranson lied about the so-called petting incident following the PTA meeting. This was the incident that supposedly launched Lora and myself on our illicit liaison. Levy said he was not going to question Lora on this in his direct examination and therefore we had no reason to put on witnesses to contradict her.

"There's just no rule of law to support this position," Jack Blackmon said when he read Levy's argument. When he brought up the issue to Judge Cole, he pointed out that the most important way to impeach a witness—particularly an accomplice witness—was to show the witness had lied. Lora had given sworn testimony about the incident in the Article 32 hearing; it was improper to forbid testimony showing she had lied merely because the prosecution now wanted to forget the whole thing. But the judge persisted in support of Levy.

The witnesses we had lined up to contradict the stories of my drinking habits were also ruled out of bounds because there would be no direct testimony about any drinking. Apparently the prosecution witnesses would now eliminate those charges that already had been shown to be false. We could not put on witnesses to counter Mary Ann's tale about the way the drinking flask got to my desk because Mary Ann was now going to skip any testimony about this.

The prosecutor opposed our using expert witnesses on the grounds of "irrelevancy" and the judge agreed that this was not a matter for experts but for common experience. Jack Blackmon tried to explain that the heaviest burden on the defense was to show *why* two women would falsely accuse a minister of adulterous conduct, since presumably they would also hurt themselves by doing so. Experts in psychology and counseling would, he contended, help demonstrate how a desire for revenge, anger over refusal to accept their advances, a need for exhibitionism or for manipulation of those in authority could be plausible motives for such women. The judge denied the motion.

Our defense forces regrouped again in Jack Blackmon's room at the Holiday Inn. My lawyers agreed that having to ask the other side for permission to put on our witnesses was of doubtful constitutionality. The Sixth Amendment guarantees the right of anybody accused of a crime to compel the attendance of witnesses, Jack pointed out, and that right should belong to members of the military as well as civilians. Levy had offered to let us present testimony of material witnesses (such as Mrs. Jump and Mrs. Hale) only by way of depositions, and Jack said that this too went against constitutional guarantees.

Could we move our legal base of operations? Lyman Fletcher had been researching the idea of my going into federal court and had prepared a paper strongly favoring this course. The request for the federal court to hear my case would be based on the charge that Article 133 was unconstitutional—the same charge Judge Cole had summarily rejected. We would also ask the federal court to enjoin the military authorities from prosecuting me for alleged off-base improprieties. This would eliminate the main thrust of the military case against me in court-martial. Lyman's brief also cited the record to charge that my rights had been violated and that the military judge's seemingly one-sided rulings and scornful demeanor had, in our view, made a mockery of justice.

If the federal court were willing to hear my case, that would automatically postpone the court-martial and might well cause it to be shelved entirely. The attempt, though, would be a gamble. I was told that federal courts refuse far more cases than they accept and they might well refuse to hear my case on the grounds that I should first go through the Navy court-martial and exhaust all military appeals before attempting legal remedy in civilian courts. If we made the attempt and failed, we would likely antagonize the members of the military court who would decide my fate at court-martial. If we got it into federal court, and then lost, it could destroy my chances for appeal from the military courts in the event the court-martial verdict went against me.

Finally, a very practical argument against going into federal court —it would cost me another $10,000. I didn't have the money and I was frightened by the prospect of having to go further into debt to raise it.

Financial considerations aside, Jack Blackmon favored the idea of my taking my chances at the court-martial. Like Chuck Pope, he was committed to proving me innocent on the command's own turf. He could understand and appreciate Lyman's strong desire that I seek legal relief in the civilian courts, in view of the way the military command had behaved thus far. He knew too that it was urgent for me, as a pastor, to win my case on the trial level and not on the technicalities of appeal. And he felt that I *could* win in the military trial. Even though I had been denied use of key witnesses, my case, he felt, was still strong. I would still have some witnesses to contradict my two accusers on their claims of adultery and he was confident Kathleen and I would make effective witnesses.

But what of the members of the military court? What if they turned out to be like the military judge?

"The one thing I have found in my experience is that it is very hard to tamper with the conscience of the Navy officers who are called on to serve on a military court," Jack said. He said it was possible for a command to tamper with nearly every step in the judicial process, but Navy honor and tradition still meant a good deal to members of military courts and, in his view, they would resist any direct attempts to pressure them. He also repeated his belief that our case was strong enough to warrant an acquittal from men of conscience.

Although Jack had made his feelings plain, he insisted that Kathleen and I would have to make the final choice and that he would abide by it. During the few days remaining before the court-martial was scheduled to begin we were getting so many visitors, so many calls, so many letters and so much advice that it became difficult to think clearly. But finally I made the crucial decision: I would gamble on the sense of honor and conscience of a Navy court.

During the nights I had difficulty sleeping I read and reread a good deal about inquisitions and persecutions of the past. I was struck by the morbid way in which false accusations involving sex were used by certain people to purge those they felt to be a threat to their authority or position. Priests who spoke up about royal *and* ecclesiastical abuses of power were often condemned on contrived charges that they had had immoral relations with nuns. Innocent and suggestible nuns would be driven into a state during which they would be induced to conjure up fantastic remembrances of seduction by the accused priests. Having served their purpose to confirm accusations against the unwanted priests, they also were declared to be possessed of the demons and so qualified for burning at the stake. The official accusations against the condemned priests were often brought by other priests who were jealous of them or who were anxious to ingratiate themselves with the secular authorities.

Why, I wondered, had sex been such an obsession among practitioners of oppression? Wholesome sex—as an expression of the love of man and wife—is a beautiful thing, and yet tyrants have always tried to make something dirty out of it. I suspected, in at least partial explanation, that they bore such deep-seated guilt feelings about their own conduct that they would try to transfer the guilt to somebody else.

At the risk of sounding overly dramatic and a martyr-too-soon, I confess I thought of certain similarities between my own case and those who had been victims of medieval tyranny. Of course we had ended the barbaric physical tortures that were a staple of the old system, but in many ways things hadn't changed so much. Here we had two women making false charges about immoral sexual behavior, and an innocent man was going to have to stand in the dock to answer these charges. Officials of government perhaps wanting to avoid responsibility for sanctioning immoral behavior had been subjecting me, in effect, to an inquisition based on false charges.

I saw similarities, too, between my situation and the various stages a dying patient goes through as outlined by Dr. Elisabeth Kuebler-Ross in her book, *On Death and Dying*. She listed five stages: (1) Denial and isolation—A stage in which you can't believe and won't accept the premise that this awful thing is happening to you. (2) Anger—why me? You want to strike out at the evil force that has chosen you as a victim. (3) Bargaining—You think about arranging a compromise, some kind of arrangement that will enable you to postpone disaster or mitigate it. (4) Depression—You give in to a mood of deep despair and a feeling of hopelessness. (5) Acceptance —You finally face up to your situation and do whatever is realistically possible to deal with it.

In my case I was threatened with death at the hands of Gudbranson and although this threat soon faded, the mortal threat to my family and reputation remained. It occurred to me that I had also been going through five stages as my ordeal moved toward its climax. When the charges were first brought against me, my reaction was to deny their reality. I had always believed in the system, in working within it, and it was traumatic for me to accept that the system could be used to oppress me. I was immobilized for a time, unable to think clearly, uncertain what I could do about all this. Kathleen and I also chose isolation because of a sense of shame over the nature of the charges that had been made and an unrealistic hope that the nightmare would vanish as suddenly as it had come. We finally ended the isolation by seeking out friends like the McKeans, the Colemans, and the Oneths. Denial gave way to feelings of anger when the command intensified its campaign of harassment and humiliation and gave favored treatment to two self-proclaimed adulteresses and their husbands. The bargaining stage in my case was simply a mental exercise in which I would tell myself that I would accept reinstatement and an apology while not pressing for retribution against those who had slandered me. My mood of depression came when I saw that no matter what evidence I gathered to expose false accusations, it was disregarded by men with closed minds. Sometimes my moods would vary and shift. I would fall back into the denial stage for a day or two, then alternately go through periods of dark depression and anger.

Although I had to accept the possibility from the beginning that I might be court-martialed, I delayed the emotional acceptance of this situation for as long as I could. But when I finally entered the stage of accepting the inevitable, I did so not in a mood of despair but with a feeling of controlled anger. I maintained an outward appearance of calm and self-confidence, but inwardly I admit to boiling with rage. I was obsessed with a determination to fight with every last ounce of strength I had in me. I wanted not only to defeat but, frankly, to crush.

Anger did not come easily for me. It was an emotion that was contradictory to my basic temperament and foreign to my life's mission. But the motivating feelings of anger had another positive aspect: they prevented me from giving way to a sense of panic. I could not be sure that the "sense of honor" of a Navy court would prevail over the pressures of an apparently partisan command and judge. There was also the recurring worry in the back of my mind that at some stage the prosecution would produce a surprise "eyewitness" who would give false testimony to "corroborate" Mary Ann and Lora's accusations. And there was the persistent feeling that basically I was a powerless individual going up against unbeatable odds—something like State Teachers College going up against the Miami Dolphins or the Minnesota Vikings.

CHAPTER 22

"The accused is charged with two specifications of conduct unbecoming an officer. The first specification alleges sexual misconduct with Mrs. Mary Ann Curran. The second specification alleges sexual misconduct with Mrs. Lora Gudbranson. The government expects Mrs. Curran to testify that she went to Chaplain Jensen in May 1970, for counseling . . . that after he counseled her for two months he engaged in sexual intercourse with her. The government also expects Lora Gudbranson to testify that Chaplain Jensen engaged in sexual intercourse with her during the period from May to July 1971, the last two times at the chaplain's quarters at Naval Air Station, Cecil Field. . . . The court will also be shown exhibits of documentary evidence—motel cards and receipts that will show the chaplain registered at motels . . . The court will also be shown other exhibits—notes and cards. Mrs. Curran will testify that these notes and cards were delivered to her by Chaplain Jensen.

"We believe that we will demonstrate that Chaplain Jensen's conduct dishonored and disgraced him as an individual and seriously compromised his standing and mission as an officer in the United States Navy. . . ."

The voice belonged to the young prosecuting officer, Lt. Levy. His staccato delivery contrasted sharply with the southern drawl of the military judge who followed the government's opening statement with the terse order: "The trial will proceed."

The setting was the courtroom at the Jacksonville Law Center, a courtroom so small there was only room for some twenty-five people in the public seats. We had asked for a larger courtroom to accommodate more of my parishioners who were anxious to attend as visible evidence of their confidence in me, but we were turned down in this request as in most all our other requests and motions. Advance newspaper, radio and TV stories had understandably fanned intense public curiosity. Those who swarmed around the courtroom were aware that this was a historic first—the first court-martial ever of a chaplain, the first court-martial ever of an officer on the sole basis of adultery charges.

Levy's opening remarks made it difficult to maintain the outward expression of calm I had pledged myself to maintain throughout the trial. The six members of the court included captains and commanders—intent, serious-looking senior officers. They would present a problem for me because I worried that they would naturally identify with the commanding officer of Cecil Field, who had requested the court-martial, and Admiral Geis, who had convened it. On the other hand their seniority could make them less vulnerable to pressure from senior brass than younger officers bucking for promotion, and they would be unlikely to feel any special sympathy for two young, ambitious lieutenants handling the prosecution.

The members of the court were all attached to commands in the Jacksonville area, so all came under the jurisdiction of Admiral Geis. Two came from the supply corps and thus would tend to have some identification with Larry Gudbranson, also a supply officer in the same jurisdiction. In a civilian court they would never have been permitted to sit on a jury; they would have been peremptorily challenged and dismissed. We were permitted challenges for "cause" providing we could demonstrate bias on the part of the members of the court who would serve as the jury, but it was difficult to show cause, and failing that, we were allowed only a single peremptory challenge. We used this single challenge to excuse a senior member of the court whose answers in the *voir dire* questioning—the questioning of potential members of the court by counsel from both sides—seemed to show bias.

We also sought to challenge the admiral's deputy chief of staff but were not permitted the cause challenge and had no more peremptory challenges left. We had nothing against the deputy chief personally—he seemed to be honest and fair-minded in the *voir dire* examination. Our challenge was based only on the not-unreasonable assumption that his close official association with the admiral might influence him to follow what he thought to be the admiral's wishes.

The basis for conviction in a court-martial is the same as that required in civilian courts—guilt proved beyond a reasonable doubt. During the *voir dire* questioning Jack Blackmon received assurances from all six officers chosen as members of the court that they would indeed adhere to this basic rule of American justice.

It began with, "We call as our first witness, Mrs. Lora Gudbranson."

The events that Mary Ann Curran would talk about at the court-martial preceded in time those that Lora would cover, so we expected that Mary Ann would be called first. But Lora had been furious at her belated call as a witness at the Article 32 hearing and apparently had demanded that she be called first this time. As she walked up to the witness stand to be sworn in, her demeanor seemed even more unfeminine than before. In the small courtroom, her seat in the witness box was only about six feet from where I sat with my lawyers. From her answers to questions, she conveyed the impression that only knaves and fools would presume to contradict her. She kept referring self-importantly to her husband as "captain-select" rather than commander, to make certain the court and spectators knew he had been selected for a promotion even though it had not yet come through.

Her testimony on direct examination was surprisingly brief, amounting to little more than dates and places. She repeated the dates she had given at the Article 32 hearing, and Levy introduced the motel receipts of May 18th and July 8th as government exhibits. Following the prosecution strategy we had detected earlier, there was no testimony about the so-called petting affair following the PTA meeting that supposedly launched our romance. Nor was there any testimony about all the whiskey I was supposed to have drunk. By not having Lora repeat this portion of her Article 32 testimony, the prosecution was able to keep secret from both the court and the press the fact that impartial witnesses at the Article 32 hearing had given the direct lie to this testimony and would have been available to do so again. Jack Blackmon did try to bring up the Article 32 PTA testimony on cross-examination, but the prosecutor objected and the judge quickly cut him off. Again the judicial pattern we had seen before: Time after time Jack would try to read from the sworn testimony to show contradictions only to be cut off on grounds that it was not "relevant." He only managed, and with great difficulty, to get a few contradictions onto the court-martial record. Meanwhile Lt. Levy was freely allowed to refer to Article 32 testimony in efforts to show discrepancies in statements by defense witnesses.

During one recess following what seemed to us an especially hostile display by the military judge, Chuck went to Waite's office and found the judge in session with Waite, Lt. Levy and Lt. Schrader, the assistant prosecutor. Such a private meeting of the judge with the prosecution was improper, but as the trial went on such meetings became common occurrences.

Jack Blackmon's cross-examination of Lora confirmed in the record that she was at least a willing participant in all her alleged acts and thus an accomplice to whatever crime was being charged. Jack also led her through a repeat of more of her Article 32 testimony, including her bringing sexually oriented publications to my office and her nonbelief in Christianity that seemed incongruous with her determined efforts to be involved with chapel activities. Jack tried to get into the record the same excerpt that Chuck had quoted before from the book that supposedly triggered the decision by Lora and Mary Ann to accuse me: "A few partners go so far as to make false confessions of infidelities or other more or less tolerable behavior, in order to probe how tolerant or punitive their intimates will turn out to be." An objection stopped him, and the judge ordered the court to disregard what he had read.

Lora repeated during the cross-examination the dates, times, and details of events leading up to the alleged adultery at the motels and at my home on the base. She was as definite in her account as she had been before, and Jack made no attempt to contest her on these points. He had defense witnesses who would expose her falsehoods later; now it was essential only to get her testimony in the record with as much specific detail as possible.

Mary Ann Curran was due to take the stand the next day. That night came a most dramatic development in the case. Kathleen and I were just finishing dinner when Jack Blackmon called from his motel to tell us that he had been contacted by Dr. John Blanc with an offer: Mary Ann Curran would admit she had perjured herself in her Article 32 testimony when she denied a sexual relationship with the doctor. In return we would release the doctor from his subpoena and he would not have to testify. Mary Ann would admit to the truth of what we already could prove with the motel receipts I had gotten from the Ponce de Leon and Quality Court motels, but she would not refer to Dr. Blanc by name and we also would promise not to do so.

Blanc had already arranged for Mary Ann and the prosecution to go along with this arrangement. All he needed was the agreement of the defense. The press and public would know him only as "Mr. X" and he would be spared the kind of notoriety that I had been getting. Jack Blackmon had already given his tentative approval to the agreement and urged me to go along. Jack stressed that our all-important defense objective was to establish that Mary Ann had perjured herself the Article 32 hearing. This would carry much more weight legally than catching her up in contradictions that she would try to explain away by saying, "I forgot" or by calling the person who contradicted her a liar. Also, since she was on record that her supposed affair with me started on August 9, 1970, and since her first motel date with the doctor was also on August 9th, she would have to admit to starting affairs with two different men on the same day. That would surely be most damaging to her credibility, Jack argued. Since we would now be assured of getting this testimony, he said we should not be diverted by Dr. Blanc benefitting in the process.

I decided to defer to my lawyer's judgment. Kathleen and I decided the doctor probably convinced her that I not only had the motel receipts involving them but also witnesses who had seen them together and so denials would now be useless. He also knew by now that she had confided the details of their relationship to me in counseling and probably thought I had tapes as well. But even now, realizing her perjury would come out, we wondered why she would cooperate with him in protecting his name, in view of his refusal to get a divorce and marry her, as I knew she had hoped. Perhaps Mary Ann was a more forgiving soul than she seemed. Perhaps she was still, or once again, smitten with affection for the doctor. Perhaps, too, he had threatened her in his fashion—his temper was no secret to me. Or he may have told her he would reveal certain relationships and tendencies of hers that she wanted kept secret more than adulterous behavior. Perhaps both.

Mary Ann's general appearance the next day was a shock. The prosecutor helped her into the witness chair, indicating she was weak. There didn't seem to be anything physically wrong, but I did know she had been getting psychiatric treatment during the previous few months. I recalled how angrily she had reacted when I first suggested she see a psychiatrist, but apparently she—or her family—had finally come to see the necessity for it. At the Article 32 hearing she had seemed in a kind of near-manic state—talkative, bubbly, blandly testifying to the most intimate sexual matters. Now she appeared to be the opposite, in a depressed state. She was dull-eyed, she answered questions in a morose monotone, she volunteered no information as she had done before; her testimony sounded rehearsed. She was blonde and looked attractive in a purple-and-white outfit, and the reporters stressed this in their stories.

At the outset, Lt. Levy had her cover the same ground as in the Article 32. She and Joe Curran had been having marital problems as a result of her affair in Beeville, Texas; Joe had arranged for her to be counseled by Chaplain Jensen; the chaplain had suggested she transfer her feelings for the man in Texas to him . . . She then skipped her Article 32 testimony about my taking her into the other chaplain's office and making advances. Instead she went directly to her account of us having sexual relations at her Shindler Drive apartment between 2 and 5 P.M. on Sunday afternoon, August 9th.

Then came a surprise. At the Article 32 hearing she had testified to ninety-five acts of intercourse, though she had been vague and uncertain about dates and places. Now she testified to eighteen acts at eighteen different times. And remarkably she was now certain of nearly all the dates and places. She recited her testimony as if by rote. Lt. Levy would ask again and again, "Did you have occasion to be with Chaplain Jensen at such and such a date"? "Yes," she would answer. "What occurred between you and Chaplain Jensen on that date?" "Sexual intercourse occurred. . . ."

This testimony was not only substantially different from her previous testimony, it was also at variance with the first statement she had written out for the executive officer at Cecil Field and the sworn statement she gave to the N.I.S. a few days later. In her statement to the N.I.S., for example, she said she had relations with me nearly every day during the months of September, October, and November,

1970. At the Article 32 hearing, under cross-examination by Chuck Pope, she changed it to less than half the amount. Now, talking about eighteen times, she placed only one of these alleged occurrences in the month of October and this was one she was not certain about.

She now was able to pinpoint specific dates, she said, because she could tie them in to particular events such as my birthday, her birthday, holidays (just before Halloween, or it was on St. Valentine's Day? etc.). Other dates were linked to times her husband was on duty at the base or away, and she said she'd consulted the duty records to be sure of these dates. When she testified, "my husband had the duty that night," I gave Chuck Pope a sideways look, a silent comment on the loss we had suffered when the N.I.S. agents apparently terrified Mrs. Villapanda and scared off the officers whose conversations she had heard at the Officers' Club bar. The one officer who had said that Chaplain Jensen couldn't possibly have been with Mrs. Curran when her husband had duty—because *he* was the one who was with her then—would have been invaluable in impeaching this part of her trial testimony.

Mary Ann claimed to have remembered August 21, 1970, as one of the dates of our supposed motel assignations because she had accompanied me to a store where I bought automobile tires. Kathleen recalled she had told her about that occasion when I bought new tires to replace a couple that were badly worn, and it was apparent to me that Mary Ann had taken this information and tied it to an August 21 motel receipt the prosecution had. But I was also fairly sure that in this instance the prosecution had outmaneuvered themselves. I believed the tire purchase had actually come a bit earlier than August 21 and I made a mental note to check my records and checkbooks.

How could Mary Ann explain giving a new account of her alleged affair with the chaplain that differed from the earlier account? She said it was because she had been under so much pressure and tension before and during the Article 32 that she had gotten some things wrong, but during the following months she had found time to search her memory, to check out dates and events and at last to come up with the truth. But the command had recommended I be court-martialed on the basis of what was testified to by my accusers at the pretrial hearing. Now one of these accusers had admitted that a significant part of that testimony was erroneous—and the court-martial was proceeding right along anyway. Moreover, we were not permitted to bring out the particulars, so the members of the court never learned that Mary Ann had first sworn to approximately ninety-five acts and now had changed it to eighteen. They never learned about the first report of relations "nearly every day" in September, October, and November, 1970, and so couldn't appreciate just how substantial was the switch in testimony that now mentioned—with uncertainty—only a single act in October. Nor did they learn that she had reported more than twenty other motel visits for which receipts were never found, and that she had falsely claimed that I registered at one of the motels under the name of "Francis Smith." It was also never disclosed to them that in Mary Ann's first report she gave a date and a place for her first alleged meeting with me that was different from the information she gave in sworn testimony and therefore we could not meaningfully call to the court's attention the unlikelihood of a woman really forgetting the place and date of her first time with her new lover.

Mary Ann's recall included a remarkable recital from the witness stand of the *numbers* of the motel rooms we supposedly occupied. She said she had gone back to these motels before the trial to refresh her memory about which rooms we had stayed in and she had succeeded. Had she been previously shown the motel receipts the government was displaying as exhibits and which listed room numbers? Her answer: she had never been shown such receipts—*or*, if she had, she didn't remember it.

We believed the N.I.S. and/or the prosecutors had shown her the receipts several times to fix them in her mind. In any case, we had Article 32 testimony to contradict her. After numerous objections, Jack finally was able to cite this testimony from Article 32 on cross-examination:

> Q: Now moving on to Exhibits 15 through 20, which are the copies of the registration receipts at the motels—you know what I'm talking about, don't you?
>
> A: Yes, I do.
>
> Q: Referring to those, I ask you again, did you discuss those items (the receipts) with anyone following your initial statements to the N.I.S. agents . . . ?
>
> A: Yes, I did. I did it one time.

Q: Was it with one of the N.I.S. agents?

A: Not to my knowledge. I saw them that one time and that was it.

Q: Who was it with?

A: I don't remember. I don't even remember all those items before you showed them to me yesterday.

So she had gone over the receipts at least once prior to the Article 32 hearing and had been shown them again at the hearing itself. Now she insisted she remembered none of those questions being asked her before. She remembered being asked about going to motels but insisted she remembered nothing that was asked about motel receipts or documents.

Mary Ann did say that when she decided to end her alleged affair with me and told me she was going back to her husband I showed no rancor and made no objections (out of character for a man who presumably desired her so much, which she made no effort to explain). She also testified that I responded to her announcement by saying, "Anything to make you happy."

Mary Ann had also become specific about the so-called love notes. She no longer was vague about when or where she had received them; she now linked them to holiday dates and cited places such as my office and the chapel parking lot where she had received them. She contradicted herself on one of the places but otherwise was firm. The term "love notes" was, as we had pointed out in the Article 32 hearing, a misnomer; they were mostly bereavement notes, get-well cards, and memo scraps. None was addressed to Mary Ann, none had been mailed to her and only one was signed "Andy." Only one could be considered a "love note"—the one we knew had been written by Mike Wennersten as a draft of a letter to his fiancée. Lt. Levy began to read it: "My life has been nothing but covered by a hard shell . . . you are the only one to break through this shell . . . Please share your love with me forever. I need you! . . . Love me, please—" Suddenly Mary Ann began to tremble on the witness stand and started to cry.

This break in her rotelike recitation of testimony—whether genuine or not—created a feeling of sympathy for Mary Ann. Some thought she really was shaken. Others suspected it was carefully contrived to offset Wennersten's anticipated appearance as a defense witness.

In an apparent effort to substantiate the prosecution claim that I had been involved with both Mary Ann and Lora, Mary Ann testified that on one of the occasions when she had come over to take care of my wife, "Mrs. Jensen said she thought her husband was having an affair. She named Mrs. Gudbranson, and I sat there and knew it was me. I called him [Chaplain Jensen] later and told him not to ever call me to have me sit with her again."

"How can she lie like that?" I said to my lawyers during a recess. "I didn't call her to take care of Kathleen in the first place—she volunteered her services as a nurse. And anybody who knows Kathleen could tell the court that it would be completely out of character for her to tell Mary Ann anything like that, even if she believed it!"

Chuck told me not to worry, that Kathleen would be a much more believable witness when she got her chance to testify. Still, I was glad she wasn't in the courtroom to hear Mary Ann's lie. (She had been coming to the court-martial every day but she remained in the anteroom most of the time, rightly feeling that it would take too much out of her to sit through the prosecution side of the case.)

Jack's plan in cross-examination was to try to elicit admissions of perjury in addition to the one we were expecting to get as a result of the Dr. Blanc arrangement. The prosecution had been putting much emphasis on Mary Ann's coming to me for counseling and had her insisting in direct testimony that I had never referred her to another counseling agency. But we had the stipulation from the counseling agency that I had indeed referred both Currans to them, and we could show that the referral had been made before the date claimed by Mary Ann to be the start of our affair. Mary Ann wouldn't concede that her direct testimony had been a lie; she insisted that I had only referred her husband and would not accept the written statement that I had referred both of them.

Since we had given the prosecution our evidence that she'd met her Texas lover in Dallas as well as Beeville, she was prepared to admit to this conflict with earlier testimony, but she wouldn't admit that she was disclosing this now only because we had the evidence I had collected in the form of the registration receipt from the Executive Inn in Dallas. Nor did she concede that her failure to acknowledge the Dallas incident at the Article 32 hearing was a matter of perjury; it was only a matter of forgetfulness. The judge readily accepted her position and told Jack he saw nothing inconsistent in her testimony now and before. Jack's normally courteous manner gave way as he argued that the defense had the right to point out contradictions in testimony.

Jack did get Mary Ann to concede that she kept in contact with her Texas friend for about two months after she came to Jacksonville, thereby further indicating she could scarcely have blotted from her mind the places where she had met him. Despite her insistence that I had only referred her husband to a counseling service, she confirmed that after August 9, 1970, she did not consider that she was coming to me for counseling. So even if there was an affair as claimed, it could not be considered "misuse of office."

Jack also got in the record that there had been no rumors or gossip involving me with either Mary Ann or Lora before the formal accusations were made and that Mary Ann plausibly could have obtained all the personal information she knew about me from my wife. Mary Ann also admitted she had sent relatives and friends with marital and other personal problems to me for counseling—something, he suggested, one would be unlikely to do if the counselor had been violating his own marital obligations with an extramarital affair.

Finally, late in the day, Jack brought up the subject I had been especially waiting for and that I expected would have a most dramatic effect:

> Q: You have testified that your first extramarital affair was in Beeville, Texas . . . and you testified here concerning extramarital affairs with Commander Jensen. Correct?
>
> A: That is correct.
>
> Q: Have you had any other extramarital affairs since coming to Jacksonville?
>
> A: Yes, I have.
>
> Q: All right—with whom?
>
> A: That party is in this town . . . he does have a family. I'd prefer not to have the names mentioned. . . .

Judge Cole, who may have known of the arrangement to keep the doctor's name secret, interjected, "You don't have to answer that question." Jack nodded, said he would avoid the use of the man's name, and continued:

Q: When did this affair start?

A: On the same day—August 9—as the incident with Chaplain Jensen at my apartment on Shindler Drive. . . .

Q: As a matter of fact, you had this affair at the Ponce de Leon in St. Augustine?

A: That is correct. . . .

Q: You went to St. Augustine for the purpose of sexual intercourse?

A: Not for that purpose . . . I didn't know I was going to St. Augustine at that time.

Q: At any rate, you ended up in the motel in St. Augustine with this party . . . and you did engage in sexual intercourse with that party in that motel, didn't you?

A: Yes.

Q: You checked in at 5:30 P.M. or 6:00?

A: Approximately, yes.

Q: When did you leave the motel?

A: I rode back in the evening with the man involved. . . .

Q: What time was it?

A: Late in the evening.

Q: Before midnight?

A: Yes, before midnight. . . .

Q: You're positive you didn't stay overnight?

A: I'm positive.

Q: If the motel records would indicate that your checkout time was 6:30 A.M. the next morning, August 10th, would that mean anything to you?

A: I couldn't explain it.

Q: Now, Mrs. Curran, this is the same date you said your affair began with Commander Jensen, is it not?

A: That's correct.

Q: So if you are to be believed by this court, then you started two affairs with two different married men on the same day?

A: That is correct.

Q: Did you enter into this relationship with that other man willingly and voluntarily?

A: Yes, I did.

Q: Without any threats or fear or anything of that nature?

A: Yes.

When Jack pressed her for the date of her second meeting with the unnamed man, the judge said, "I don't see the relevance of all these details of this third-party affair . . . this third man is not a party to this trial, why do we need the minor details?"

The heart of my defense against charges that threatened to destroy me was that I was being falsely accused by a person who ascribed to me acts committed by others. Here we were bringing out crucial information to support that defense and the judge didn't see the relevance. Jack voiced my own feelings by heatedly disputing the judge and obtaining what seemed a grudging permission to continue. "This is extremely relevant," he asserted. "This witness says, incredibly, that she starts two extramarital affairs on the same day. She has been very meticulous in telling this court-martial of specific dates, times, and places that she carried on an affair with Chaplain Jensen. But at the same time, she's saying she carried on an affair with somebody else. We're entitled to get the information, the details about the occasions she carried on this other affair . . ."

Under Jack's persistent questioning Mary Ann acknowledged the second meeting with the unnamed man at the Quality Court and also to two others at her apartment. She said she ended the affair to go back to her husband (I knew, of course, from what she had told me that she went back only when she realized the doctor would not get a divorce and marry her).

It was time for Jack to get the confession of perjury into the record. "Mrs. Curran," he said, "you have testified here concerning your sexual affair with an unnamed person. Do you remember denying at the Article 32 hearing that you had any other affair besides the one in Beeville and besides the one involving Chaplain Jensen?"

"Yes, I do."

Jack looked directly at her. "That was false testimony, was it not?"

She hesitated for just a moment, then said, "Yes, it was."

Her explanation for her perjury was that her husband did not know of her involvement with this unnamed man and that she was fearful Mr. Pope would tell her husband when he took the stand. Chuck Pope immediately got up from his seat and said angrily, "I object to that," but his objection was ignored and Mary Ann went on to say that her husband now knew the entire story of her involvements and so there was no longer any reason to protect him in her testimony.

Apparently Mary Ann had not been overly concerned about her husband learning of her behavior when she carried on an affair in Texas and announced to the world—and him—her adultery with Chaplain Jensen. Yet to protect him she'd felt obliged to lie about this last affair with the unnamed man. Why lie only about this one and not the others? She never said.

During redirect testimony, Lt. Levy tried to explain how it happened that Mary Ann had begun two affairs in one day. She said she worked with the unnamed man, that she had some papers to deliver to him, that he took her out to dinner and that she had "a good bit to drink." She remembered him saying he was getting a room and then there was "sexual contact."

"What was your state of mind after you had sexual intercourse with Chaplain Jensen and he had left?" Lt. Levy asked her.

"I went to Chaplain Jensen because I felt guilty about the affair in Beeville . . . It was hard living with my husband knowing I had deceived him . . . I don't think I was in love with Chaplain Jensen . . ." She paused, became tearful, and said, "What did it really matter after there were two, whether there would be three or four?"

Jack came back to make sure there was no question of the record of perjury.

"Regardless of what your motives may have been, you have lied in the past about your affairs, have you not?" he asked.

"I have lied about one of those affairs."

He also asked, "Mrs. Curran, in spite of the fact that you had a feeling of guilt about your affair in Texas and were having trouble living with your husband with that guilt on your mind, you did start two additional affairs on the same day—if you are to be believed?"

"Yes, on the day after I left my husband."

"This was August 9th, Mrs. Curran. You said you left your husband on August 11th. So you had not left your husband at the time you started the two new affairs. Is that correct?"

"That's correct."

"And you have been a willing participant in all of the sexual activities that you have described?"

"That's correct."

The court adjourned after that. A few moments later, Lt. Levy came up to Jack Blackmon and asked if he could see him privately in his office. When Jack came out, he had a piece of paper and some astonishing information. "Can you believe this?" he said. "They didn't just find out about her perjury when the doctor got in touch with them. They knew about it over four months ago—while the Article 32 was still officially on! Levy's given me a stipulation explicitly admitting that the government knew of her sexual intercourse with the unnamed man as far back as last November."

Chuck had been confident that when he gave the command the evidence of Mary Ann's affair with the doctor they would be obliged to drop the case against me. Instead they had made light of the evidence and kept the plans for my court-martial right on course. We had assumed that when Waite, the staff judge advocate, and Lt. Levy had originally shown Mary Ann the motel receipts she had denied she had been the woman with the doctor. We now knew she had not denied her involvement, in fact had admitted it.

Had the truth about the perjury been told to Lt. Duncan, the investigating officer, who had still not written his report on the Article 32? We doubted it. Lt. Duncan, we believed, had felt his superiors wished him to prepare a report recommending a court-martial, but we did not think he would be a party to omitting evidence of perjury. Lt. Levy's disclosure to Jack came, we felt, from a concern that we had learned of this, as had this stipulation he had prepared.

We now felt it was clearer why Waite had tried to prevent Chuck Pope from seeing the official advice he had prepared for Admiral Geis. The admiral had acted on that advice to convene the court-martial—on advice that had not only omitted references to Mary Ann's series of evasions and contradictions but the fact of her perjury as well. "If the fact had been included in the advice, I don't see how they would have dared order a court-martial," Chuck told us.

Kathleen suggested we go to the newspapers about this and explore bringing charges. But Jack Blackmon cautioned us against such action. "The court-martial is on and we can't reverse that," he pointed out. "We can't talk of charging anyone while Andy is still not in the clear. Mary Ann's perjury is now on the record and will certainly weigh heavily in the minds of the members of the court. And it will help strengthen the motion I will make for dismissal of the charges by the judge when the prosecution rests its case."

When court convened the next morning, the prosecution surprised us by calling no more witnesses and resting its case. We surmised that they did not put on any of the N.I.S. agents because they would then be exposed to embarrassing cross-examination. Joe Curran and Larry Gudbranson had testified at the Article 32 hearing but—for reasons unknown—neither was called this time.

Jack Blackman made his motion that Judge Cole dismiss the case against me, saying that the only evidence was from "two admitted adulteresses, both willing accomplices, one an admitted perjurer, one clearly dominating the other." "Their charges," he continued, "are scurrilous, incredible, and uncorroborated . . . They are accomplices as a matter of law . . . Since their testimony is uncorroborated, we move for a finding of not guilty. . . ."

Lt. Levy countered with the argument that it was up to the full court, not just the judge, to decide whether or not there had been sufficient corroboration. The judge denied the motion for a direct verdict of acquittal and ordered us to proceed with our defense.

CHAPTER 23

Character witnesses in criminal trials traditionally come on at the end of the defense's case, but Jack Blackmon decided to reverse the procedure and put them on first. Captain Thomas Loomis, who had been my executive officer aboard the *Ticonderoga,* was the first, and his testimony set the tone for the others. Loomis pointed out that our carrier had two tours of duty in the Tonkin Gulf area, that there had been a great many personnel problems aboard the ship and that I had often worked eighteen to twenty hours a day to help solve them while also carrying out other responsibilities. He had written an "outstanding" fitness report on me and said he found Jensen to be "one of the finest examples of moral rectitude on board ship." (Ordinarily one might blush at such encomia, but when you're on trial for, in effect, your life you forget niceties of modesty and welcome every help you can get.)

"How about Chaplain Jensen's reputation for honesty?" Jack asked him.

"I never saw or heard of a single instance that could cast doubt on his veracity."

Jack then asked whether the charges brought against me by the wives of two Navy officers had caused him to change his opinion of me. The answer was, "Definitely not."

Next came Captain Donald Dillard, who had served with me as a fellow chaplain in the 1st Marine Division and was with me later through our advanced program at the chaplain's school in Newport, Rhode Island; Chaplain Richard Boyer; Chaplain Carroll Chambliss, who had to come back from Spain to testify; Chaplain Jim Doyle, who had initiated the ecumenical programs with me aboard the *Ticonderoga*; and Captain Grant Donnelly.

Chaplain Chambliss' testimony was significant because he insisted that morals charges against a chaplain should be handled on an ecclesiastical level, and should never have been the subject of a court-martial. The judge cut him off on the grounds that his opinion wasn't relevant, but I think his testimony had effect on the court. Father Doyle's appearance also had impact—perhaps especially so inasmuch as four out of the six members of the court were Catholic.

Captain Donnelly provided a dramatic touch because he was one of the many defense witnesses whom the prosecution and the judge had turned down. He flew in anyway at his own expense from San Diego, where he served as air squadron commander. He came in the hope that once the judge was advised of the trouble he had gone to in order to testify, he would feel obliged to let him take the stand.

The captain was allowed to testify and proved highly effective. He told the court that, although I was no longer serving with him at the time, he had asked me to come to California to perform the wedding ceremony for his only daughter. He also recalled a time when we had gone on liberty together and he had asked me to have a drink, saying, "Your congregation will never know." My answer, he remembered, was that, as a Baptist minister, I didn't drink and that I would have to answer to my conscience, not my congregation. Chuck Pope remarked to me during a recess, "With all the bouquets you're getting from senior officers, the Navy will have to promote you!" I tried to smile.

Members of our chapel, including Joy Oneth, Jane Center, Margaret Huntsinger, and Isabelle Jaquette testified to the regard in which I was held as pastor and chaplain, to the fact that I was circumspect in private counseling sessions, and to Lora Gudbranson's aggressive behavior—including her relationships with men. Margaret became emotional, began to cry when Lt. Levy asked her if she had a financial stake in my defense. She had been active in my defense fund but, of course, she had absolutely nothing personal to gain. She said it broke her heart that the Jensens had been forced to use up every penny of their savings.

Isabelle repeated what she had said in her affidavit for the Article 32 hearing about Lora and Mary Ann. She described Lora's aggressive behavior toward me this way: "She wouldn't give anyone else much of a chance to say anything to the chaplain. After church we were never able to talk to the chaplain about the sermons because Mrs. Gudbranson was always there. It reached the point where the chaplain would have to leave and go to his office."

She also described her upset at Mary Ann's "flippant" attitude toward the chaplain and affirmed her Article 32 statement about Mary Ann's complaint that I was lax about returning her phone calls and messages—which refuted Mary Ann's sworn statements that I persisted in initiating phone calls to her and that she had tried to avoid my calls. Isabelle also testified that she had seen Mary Ann rummaging through the papers on my desk before a scheduled meeting, which supported our contention that Mary Ann was able to pick up the love-note draft that Mike Wennersten had dictated.

Chaplain Hubbard gave testimony to affirm his affidavit. He told how anxious I was to have Mary Ann Curran and her husband get back together and described my expression of pleasure when they did in fact reconcile. "Chaplain Jensen told me at one point that what they [the Currans] needed was a religious experience because that would help them stay together," he said. He described Mary Ann as a "deeply troubled person [with] pent-up guilt."

Hubbard didn't know much about Lora Gudbranson, but Joe Simpson did. As in the Article 32, he described Lora's disdain for religion, her attitude toward free love, and her open approach to him. He had been so explicit and thorough in his testimony at the Article 32 hearing that Lt. Schraver, the assistant prosecutor, had not tried to cross-examine him and Lt. Levy now made only a brief and ineffective attempt.

Joe Simpson and Paul Gerlock repeated their Article 32 testimony about my weakened condition caused by overwork and strain, that

I had passed out several times and received cardiac tests in the infirmary and been repeatedly urged to get away from the base for some rest and relaxation. They countered again Mary Ann's claim that I kept rushing off to her apartment in Jacksonville during lunch-hour pointing out that I ate lunch with them at the base virtually every day. They also said that my physical condition and heavy schedule of night programs made claims that I played the role of nighttime as well as daytime Don Juan "downright ludicrous."

Lt. Levy tried to discredit Paul Gerlock by reminding the court he had left the priesthood to marry; Paul pointed out that he remained an active practitioner of the Catholic faith and, in fact, his wife had converted to Catholicism. Paul also described my nondrinking as well as my annoyance when I had found liquor bottles strewn about the chapel grounds. He said my nondrinking applied to private as well as public occasions, countering the lies Lora and Mary Ann had previously told about my drinking.

Dale Carroll and Mike Adams, enlisted men who worked at the chapel and who had given affidavits before, testified to the substance of those affidavits: that I had an open door policy at my chapel office, that anyone could walk in at any time, that I left folders, papers, and greeting cards on my desk that anyone could take, that activity at the chapel during evenings certainly argued against my using my office for illicit activities.

Mrs. Dana Nickel said I was at the Methodist Hospital on May 18 when Lora claimed I was in a motel room with her. Chaplain Mudd brought my work schedule for that day to the witness stand, but the prosecutor objected to his using it and the judge upheld him. Mrs. Nickel was effective in telling how she had called me back to the hospital in the late afternoon to comfort the emergency patient. She was precise in her facts and her description of the circumstances. She also volunteered some personal observations which aided my defense.

Mrs. Hale from the Baptist Book Store and Mrs. Jump from the Gator Lodge countered Lora's story that I had a second motel rendezvous with her on July 8th. Although their information bore directly on the heart of the case, Lt. Levy had insisted that their testimony be entered on the record only through depositions. The judge originally had sustained him but in this instance Jack's strong argument caused a change. Jack's position was that the actual appearance of two witnesses whose honesty and impartiality could not be questioned would have much more impact on the court than their words in a statement. Mrs. Hale was uneasy about testifying in a case of this kind, but her account was precise and the prosecutor could not confuse her. She had records to show that she had taken the phone order for my chapel books on July 9th, not July 8th, and she was certain that I had come into the store alone on July 8th, contradicting Lora's story that she called in the order for me from a motel room on July 8th.

Mrs. Jump was a superb witness—articulate, intelligent, and knowledgeable about all aspects of the motel business. She, too, was as precise in person as she had been in preparing her Article 32 affidavit. She had no doubt that I had parked my car in front of her motel that day, that I was in uniform, and that I came alone. Lora's account had me parking way off to the side, wearing a civilian sport shirt she claimed to have bought, and entering the motel with her.

Mrs. Jump also proved effective in explaining that a clerk in her motel or others would frequently write "2" on the registration receipt even if only one person occupied the room. That might happen if the advance registration had been for two—as in my case when Kathleen was supposed to join me but then had to cancel it, or if the only room available was for a double-occupancy price. Mrs. Jump had mentioned all this in her affidavit, of course, but she was much more convincing in person, as Jack had predicted. Lt. Levy's failure to upset her testimony deflated his argument that the number "2" written by a clerk on a registration card or receipt meant *ipso facto* that a couple had come to the motel. Nobody had ever seen me with either Mary Ann or Lora.

The testimony of four women showed that Lora's account of adultery in my home on the weekend nights of July 16th and 17th was fantasy. Betty McKean testified that on the evening of July 16th, I passed her house, saw Frank and herself packing their trailer for the vacation trip they would begin the next morning, stopped to help, visited in their home for a while and, according to Betty, hardly behaved like a man with an appointment to keep. I didn't go home until between 9:30 and 10 P.M., she said. Fay Chase, whose home was directly south of ours, testified about the lights being on in her house that night. Lucille Turner, who was then living across from me, gave her testimony about sitting in her front yard with her husband that night and chatting with me after I left the McKeans'.

She put the time at about 10 o'clock. Jeannine Coleman gave her account of the party that took place in her home the same night, with people going in and out. Jeannine added that the lights were on in the back bedroom of my house and that the curtains were wide open—an indiscreet adulterer indeed!

Lora had said she had met me that same night at 9 P.M., had gone from her house right up to the front door of my house, described the Chase house and the other houses as dark, said nothing at all about the big party going on at the Colemans', and described how I had kept my house dark and made sure that the curtains were drawn.

Both Jeannine and Martha Carcaba, who flew in from California, also expanded on their Article 32 affidavits and testified about seeing my car parked at my house every night except for the night of August 21st. Both Jeannine and Martha now testified about promising Kathleen they'd check on our dog each night and take him in before bedtime if I weren't home. They explained this was why they made a special point of checking whether I was indeed there or not. Their testimony covered a period when Mary Ann claimed she had relations with me on six different nights, both in motels and her apartment.

Lt. Levy then showed these witnesses the motel receipts, stating that I was registered at the Gator Lodge on August 15th and 16th and demanded to know how I could have been home the same nights. Neither Jeannine nor Martha was upset by this—each insisted *I was* home those nights. They were right, of course, since I had come back to Cecil Field at about 10 P.M. on August 15th and even earlier the next night. It wasn't, as Levy tried to imply, a claim on our part of being in two places at the same time. It was being in different places at different times—and for reasons clearly stated and backed up by witnesses. Lt. Levy was not one to be put off by factual evidence.

Mary Ann's credibility was already dropping as a result of her admission of perjury at the Article 32 hearing and her tale of two affairs beginning on August 9, 1970. We planned to finish the process by showing exactly how I spent that entire day. Kathleen would account for a good part of it, but first we brought on Helen Brown to account for the hours taken up by her father's death.

Lt. Levy seemed irritated at the way Mary Ann's testimony about this important day was being contradicted by Helen Brown. At one point he snapped, "Are you *sure* that was the day your father died?" Helen answered, "Don't you suppose I remember the day my father died?"

It should be pointed out that these ladies testified with full knowledge of the command's position and the potential threat to their husbands' careers as a result of what they were doing. I cannot sufficiently express my debt and gratitude to them and their husbands.

Dr. Clay Wickham was another witness who'd provided me with a strong affidavit for the Article 32 hearing, but who proved an even stronger witness in person. His obvious professionalism, his clear presentation, and his explanation of the chigger infection that affected me so intensely during July, 1971 provided a high point in the court-martial proceedings. The painful infection continued to bother me for at least two more weeks, he added; he had examined me at the end of two weeks and although there had been healing, the skin was still irritated and pockmarked with welts. The acts Lora Gudbranson had claimed for me on the nights of July 8, 16, and 17—esthetic considerations aside—were obvious impossibilities. (Kathleen would later testify that she slept in another room during this period because any physical contact caused me so much pain.)

The out-of-town newspapermen made it clear that they had come to Florida expecting the Navy to present damning evidence against a "swinging chaplain." As the weakness of the charges was developed, their stories reflected a feeling of disbelief that a Navy command had brought this kind of case to public court-martial. The ridicule of the Navy that Jack Blackmon had warned about soon became a fact. Radio and TV personalities made the Navy the target of such jokes as: "The Navy is going to court-martial every sailor who commits adultery. This means that the entire fleet will be reduced to one sailboat manned by the last survivor of the Spanish-American war." Not so funny, in more ways than one. Ditto for the one about Navy wives—and Navy chaplains.

I learned from Joe Durham that doubt about the case was growing in the law center. Young Navy lawyers on Waite's staff were astonished by Mary Ann Curran's admission of perjury and by the number and effectiveness of defense witnesses. They had accepted the assertions of their superiors that they had a "mass of evidence against the chaplain." Some of these lawyers refused to believe that the pertinent facts being brought out at the court-martial had been previously known to some members of the prosecution for months.

They assumed we'd found new witnesses until Joe showed them the transcript of the Article 32 hearing, which proved that Lucille Turner was the only person who hadn't given testimony or affidavits for the Article 32.

Levy and Schraver began to look worried (Kathleen commented that it was "time somebody else besides us had something to worry about").

Mike Wennersten's appearance on the witness stand gave small comfort to Lora and the prosecution team. Shortly after the Article 32 hearing ended, Mike had been honorably discharged from the Navy and had taken a job as a drapery installer. We learned through Joe Durham's grapevine that the prosecution had discounted him, figuring he wouldn't risk showing up and publicly exposing his past association with marijuana. They underestimated him. He not only appeared but now repeated in person crucial testimony and withstood the prosecution's efforts to demean him.

The drafts of other letters Mike had prepared outside our counseling sessions were now introduced in evidence, and Mike showed how the phrasing he'd used in these drafts duplicated or closely followed the phrases and comments of the love note Mary Ann claimed to have received from me.

Jack asked Mike if he had married his fiancée following the months of counseling he had with me and he said that he had. "Did you feel you were helped by the counseling?" Jack wanted to know.

"Yes, sir, very definitely."

"What is your present situation?"

"I'm very happily married, and gainfully employed."

"Then Chaplain Jensen's counseling was helpful and beneficial to you?"

"Very definitely."

Levy's cross-examination predictably hit on Wennersten's experiences with marijuana. Mike admitted he had used it during the time he was having his personal problems. He also gave an emphatic "no, sir" when Levy demanded to know if he were "high on marijuana" when he was being counseled by me or writing notes away from the counseling sessions.

Mike's testimony had a further meaning, indicating as it did an element of gratuitous malice in Mary Ann. She may have been dominated by Lora Gudbranson before and in bringing charges against me, the charges of motel liaisons may have been made to cover up affairs with others, but when she appropriated the note Mike had dictated and tried to pass it off as a love letter sent by me, she was performing, it seemed to me, an especially cruel act—not just against me for the various possible motives I've tried to develop earlier in this account, but especially against Mike, whom she had no reason, real or imagined, to hurt.

I especially resented Lt. Levy's tough questioning of Mike when I thought of all the personal and economic problems he'd suffered before making a good adjustment, and compared them with the comfortable circumstances the young prosecutor had enjoyed. I knew that if Mike were to lose his job because of his public exposure, I would have to share the responsibility. Mike came across very well. When Levy pressed him on why he was having some difficulty reading one passage, he said, "I'm quite nervous." His forthright quality won him sympathy, I thought. (After his appearance at the court-martial, a Georgia businessman offered Mike a better job than the one he had, because he was so impressed with the qualities that impelled him to speak out in my defense.)

Witnesses such as Mike Wennersten, Captain Donnelley, Lucile Turner, Mrs. Jump, and Mrs. Hale had proved much more effective in personal testimony than when limited to dry depositions. We now made another attempt to get permission for the experts in psychology also to appear in person. Jack again told the judge that the hardest thing for the jury to understand was why a woman would make a public charge about her own adultery if the charge were not true. We therefore had the moral and legal right to put on witnesses who could explain this. The judge again held that this wasn't a matter for experts to settle but one to be decided by commonsense knowledge. We were allowed to put into the record the statements these people had made for the Article 32 hearing, but we were not allowed to identify the authors of the statements as "experts," and we could make only scant reference to their experience and qualifications in the fields of psychology and counseling.

The prosecution was by no means finished with its special tactics. On the night before Kathleen was to testify, we received a call from Jack Blackmon that Lt. Levy had passed the word to my lawyers that our house phone had been tapped and that they claimed to have details of Kathleen's conversations that could damage her character and mine too. The word from Lt. Levy was that Kathleen would be publicly confronted with these supposed damaging and embarrassing admissions if she did indeed take the stand.

I felt it was a new low—even for men frightened they'd gone too far and who apparently felt pushed to do almost anything to salvage their position. They knew how bad it would look if my wife refused to be a defense witness, that it would seem she didn't believe in me and gave credence to what Mary Ann and Lora had said. Kathleen was even angrier than I was. She knew she'd never said anything on the phone or off that could possibly reflect on her morals or character—or mine either. "They must think I'm so frail I would just collapse at being threatened like this," she said. "Well, they're not going to keep me from testifying and they can play back every word I've ever said on a telephone, no matter how personal."

When I reported Kathleen's reaction to Jack, he said, "I knew she'd feel that way and I was sure she had never said anything that could hurt either one of you, but I felt obliged to bring this warning to you."

During the Article 32 the N.I.S. agents had been asked if they'd used electronic eavesdropping in my case and they swore they had not. They had not obtained any court orders to tap our phone, so if they had indeed planted a surreptitious tap it would clearly have been illegal. Obviously the prosecution was not going to admit to such illegal surveillance when Kathleen testified; apparently the strategy—in the event she couldn't be discouraged from testifying—was to confront her with the "damaging" things she had supposedly revealed on the phone without specifically saying she had been tapped.

In the innocence of pre-Watergate, it was difficult to believe that a government agency would deliberately commit a criminal act, and so we assumed the prosecution had invented the story of the telephone tap to scare off Kathleen. (We were never to learn whether there was or was not ever such a device in place.)

CHAPTER 24

When Kathleen entered the courtroom the next morning to testify, my studied calm broke down. The pain, the awful humiliation she'd suffered from the false accusations and command tactics were suddenly all on the surface for me. As they say, I definitely lost my cool.

Not so Kathleen. Lt. Levy's expression as Kathleen came into the courtroom was one of less than pleasure, and I wondered whether this suggested annoyance over the failure of reported efforts to keep her from testifying. She looked calm, self-assured as she took the stand. Perhaps this was upsetting to him, too. The pressure under which she'd been living for the past seven and a half months had been great, but she had told my lawyers the day before: "I'm not going to break down when I testify. I'm going there to tell the truth. I'll leave the rest to the Lord."

Jack Blackmon and Chuck Pope had arranged for Kathleen and me to testify last. Character witnesses went first to establish my good record in the Navy community, then witnesses were called who could refute Lora's and Mary Ann's conspiracy of lies. These witnesses, in a sense, were setting up the testimony for Kathleen and myself, inasmuch as the court was much more likely to believe us at this stage than if we had come on first.

On direct testimony Kathleen traced our relationship with the two women—a relationship that had begun in a spirit of friendship and ended in these accusations. She described how I had brought the Currans home for dinner after my last counseling session with them, my efforts to keep their marriage together, Mary Ann's appreciation when an apparent reconciliation was managed. She pointed out that the Currans had given us a silver cake knife as an anniversary gift "in appreciation of what Chaplain Jensen had done to help keep our marriage together" and had also given me a ruby tie pin on my birthday for the same reason.

She also talked about the close personal association that had developed between herself and Mary Ann, fostered in part by the fact that their growing up years had been somewhat similar—Kathleen troubled by the divorce of her parents, Mary Ann bitter at the way her father "ran around on her mother." Mary Ann had expressed admiration for the close-knit nature of our family.

"She told me that when she was alone she would sit in a dark room and cry," Kathleen testified. "She was very frightened about being alone—whether in the daytime or in the evening. One time when she visited us when her husband was away I told her that there was no need for her to be alone, that she could stay in the little spare room we used as a guest room. She stayed over other times, too —once she spent three consecutive nights."

"Did you ever have any suspicion or belief that anything might have been going on between Mrs. Curran and your husband?" Jack asked her.

"Absolutely not," Kathleen answered.

She said she had been troubled by two aspects of Mary Ann's personality. She had noticed at various parties that when Mary Ann drank to excess her entire personality seemed to change; a viciousness surfaced. She had noticed this when she happened to come into the chapel when Mary Ann and her friend had accidentally burned one of the carpets and they had thought the chaplain's wife had come to spy on them and had suddenly turned on her in an outbreak of anger. She also became disturbed when Mary Ann began making sarcastic remarks about "good old Chaplain Jensen," and comparing me to her father. She felt Mary Ann hated her father and found it difficult to understand why she was linking the two of us. Kathleen had noticed this on her own—I had not told her how Mary Ann equated me with her father in our conversations at the chapel during counseling. Despite these considerations, Kathleen said she still tried to think of Mary Ann as a good friend until the charges were brought against me.

Although we were not permitted to call Drs. Shetterley and Murphy for first-hand testimony, Kathleen was able to bring their names into the trial record by repeating their advice to "get Andy off the base to rest from time to time before he collapses completely." Dr. Shetterley had told her that a "motel room, even for a few hours' time, would be helpful to Andy, because your house is too near the chapel and people on the base are continually taking advantage of him by calling him [about their problems]."

"Andy had spent two years on the *Ticonderoga* . . . two very difficult, demanding years, and he hadn't been physically the same since," she testified. "He put himself one hundred percent into his job and wasn't able to take long vacations. He had fainting spells . . . was worn out. He'd had surgery for his skin-cancer condition. He had an asthmatic condition . . . twice, on a Sunday, he had very bad attacks after chapel . . . it was very frightening because he was gasping for breath. Some people who had personal problems saw him after the service and he was worried about them, which helped bring on his asthmatic attacks. He's worse in the summer because he has bad allergies in addition to the asthma and it would affect his eyes and his whole system."

She said Lora and Mary Ann both knew about my going to motels—both had actually made the same suggestions the doctors had, Lora as a friend, Mary Ann as a nurse. Mary Ann had even specified, "If you don't have time to get away for a weekend together, then just take an afternoon . . . get away for three or four hours." She had offered to babysit for the children at these times, if she were free. Lora had been just as specific in her advice: "You should try to get away even for just an afternoon, go to a motel and relax. The important thing is to get away from the base and the pressure." (Later, of course, they were to make these respites they had recommended the basis of their accusations.)

As mentioned, Kathleen had gone over all the dates in question at the court-martial and had checked them against the diaries and the activities calendars Kathleen had kept. These records and notations helped jog her memory about the details of those days. She was already certain of all the motel dates and was able to specify that she was either with me at those times or knew when I had gone alone. She handled all the family finances and paid all the bills and so knew of every payment to a motel.

Also as mentioned, Mary Ann had picked my birthday—January 12th—as one of our dates. But Kathleen was able to point out that she had prepared a birthday dinner for me that day (in 1971), and among the guests were none other than Mary Ann and her husband. Kathleen had called me at the Methodist Hospital at about 3:30 that day to urge me to come home early because the children were anxious to give me their present. I made it home at about 5, well before the Currans and our other guests arrived. It was on this night that Mary Ann and her husband had presented me with the ruby tie pin.

Mary Ann had picked a Friday afternoon date in February—when the Cub Scout pack Kathleen was den mother for met at the chapel and Kathleen was with them. She had seen me in my office that Friday, then had gone home with me so we could get ready for a special pizza party at the officers' club. The Currans were again on the scene, and Kathleen even remembered that Mary Ann was wearing white leather boots, which she took off when she started dancing.

Mary Ann's Valentine's Day date was countered by Kathleen pointing out that on that Thursday we had our luncheon at the chapel for men who came for Bible study with me and she had participated in this program, as she did in many other chapel programs, and had come to the chapel to set up the lunch. She was able to refute another Mary Ann date—a Monday afternoon—because she and Drew had gone for his piano lesson, then had come back to the chapel to pick me up. Another alleged date occurred when her mother had come down to visit and I had taken the day off to go for a drive with them. Still another was, she remembered, when we were preparing the chapel for Halloween festivities.

Kathleen had an especially vivid recollection of August 9, 1970, the day Mary Ann had said she began her two affairs. Kathleen described the middle-of-the-night call informing us of the death of Helen Brown's father and specifically cited my whereabouts for the rest of that day. As for the motel date, March 16, 1971, when Kathleen's plans to meet me at the Howard Johnson's motel had been shelved because of Drew's illness, Mary Ann had been in our house with Kathleen helping to take care of Drew until about 4:30. I came home about 5. Mary Ann knew Kathleen's plan to meet me at the motel had been cancelled, having heard her discussing it with me on the phone.

Finally, the alleged confidence to Mary Ann during Kathleen's so-called psychosomatic illness:

"On a Saturday night, in February 1971, I became very weak and felt ringing sensations in my ears and pressure under my heart. My husband took me to the dispensary. We thought I was having a mild heart attack, but the doctor at the dispensary told us it was hyperventilation—something caused by a great deal of anxiety and nervous strain. He gave me an injection that calmed me down. I stayed in bed the next morning, but I began to feel the pressure and weakness again and called my husband at the chapel. He came home and brought Mr. and Mrs. Curran with him. They took me to the dispensary again. Then my husband had to go back to the chapel, and Mrs. Curran remained with me for a few hours."

"Did you have any suspicion of anything going on between your husband and Mrs. Gudbranson or Mrs. Curran?"

"No, none at all."

"Did you tell Mrs. Curran that you were ill because you knew your husband was having an affair with Mrs. Gudbranson?"

"No, that is definitely not true."

"Would you explain the reasons for the nervous anxiety that helped cause your condition?"

"I had been very upset because my closest friend of thirty-two years was dying of cancer. Another good friend had recently died of the same disease."

Kathleen also forced herself to say she was starting menopause at this time and felt some of the pressure which I felt, because "the chaplain's home was open to anybody, day or night."

Concerning Lora, Kathleen said she had been friendly with Lora but tried not to be too close, because Lora's attitudes and behavior frequently disturbed her, among them Lora's views favoring free love and homosexuality between consenting adults. Kathleen was asked: "Did you ever have any feelings that there was any kind of affair going on [between Lora and myself]?"

"No."

Kathleen supplied more details about the chigger bite infection which near-immobilized me during that crucial month of July. "Was your husband able to have sexual relations during this period?" Jack asked her.

"No, he could not."

Mike Wennersten had exposed Mary Ann's misrepresentation of his "love notes." Now Kathleen filled in the rest of the picture as she identified all the other cards and memoranda the prosecution had introduced as love-note exhibits. She explained she had kept them in a box on the desk in the spare room, where Mary Ann slept when she stayed over. She identified the birthday cards and get-well cards the children and I had given her, and testified that one card, signed "from a special someone" had been intended for an elderly friend in New Jersey whom she could identify.

"Had you missed these cards, and had you looked for them before this investigation started?" Jack asked.

"I had no reason to look for them," she answered. It was only after the charges were made and the so-called corroboratory evidence of love notes was introduced that she had gone through that box and found that the cards were missing.

Lt. Levy really tore into her on cross-examination, apparently hoping to harass her into admitting lies, or at least contradictions. His tactics did upset Kathleen and occasionally angered her, but he could not shake her on the essentials of her testimony:

"Is it true you have views against drinking?" he asked.

"Yes, I do."

"You really never do any drinking in your home?"

"No, never. The only drink we would have in our home would be sacramental wine."

"When you met your husband, did he drink?"

"No, he never did drink, and neither did his parents."

"You and your husband seem to have few vices."

"That's right."

"No vices?"

"No." [Doubtless, in my case, a wifely exaggeration, but under the circumstances surely understandable and perhaps necessary.]

"No drinking at all?"

"No."

"Saturday nights at home?"

"Yes."

"Sundays with the family?"

"Yes."

"And this has been going on for how long?"

"For seventeen years—ever since we've been married."

"Ever see *Playboy* magazine in your home?"

"Only when Mrs. Gudbranson would bring it over to ask my husband to read it. She would bring it in a brown envelope."

"Do you recall finding colored keys in your husband's possession?"

"No, never."

"You're under oath, remember."

"I know I'm under oath. I said no."

Levy turned to the court members with a look of exasperation, as if to say, Who ever heard of such a family in this day and age? Kathleen later said to me she had no idea whatsoever what the "colored keys" meant, which was understandable, since the allusion was to keys perhaps used for apartments where some of the wife-swapping was going on.

Even picking up on Kathleen's testimony about menopause, Levy tried to deduce that a resultant curtailment of sexual relations at home had somehow impelled me to seek sex elsewhere. Kathleen wouldn't oblige him.

"During this emotional period in your life, your sex relations with your husband deteriorated, did they not?"

"No, they did not."

"They decreased?"

"No, they did not."

"You said your husband had been under great strain, and showed a great deal of fatigue because of all the time he put in at the chapel?"

"That's right."

"He could have gotten tired somewhere else, though, couldn't he?"

"No, he could not."

"How do you know—you weren't with him all the time."

"I was not with him at all times but I know he was tired from working so hard."

"Wasn't the real reason Mary Ann Curran compared Chaplain Jensen with her father that he carried on the same kind of behavior as her father?"

"No, that's not so."

When court resumed the next morning, Levy tried a switch in tactics with Kathleen:

> Q: To a great extent, it's almost as if you're on trial in the sense that the impact of it could have such a great effect on your family. Is that correct?
>
> A: Well, it's been upsetting to my family.
>
> Q: In fact, you said you had a great deal of pride in being a chaplain's wife—and all that you're proud of is at stake here.
>
> A: It is not the fact that I'm a chaplain's wife that I'm proud of. It's the fact that I'm able to serve the God that I love as the chaplain's wife.
>
> Q: But your ability to serve in that manner is at stake, is it not? You have a stake in everything your husband has worked for over the past sixteen years.
>
> A: I have a stake not in what he has worked for, but in the

fact that they're trying to tear down something we have lived for and believed in.

Q: You won't permit anyone to tear that down?

A: It's not that I won't permit it . . . I don't feel that Christ in heaven will permit it because we are His children.

There was an "Amen" from the rear of the courtroom from Kathleen's mother. Lt. Levy flushed while the judge reached for his gavel.

Q: Is Christ a forgiving entity in your mind?

A: Yes, He is.

Q: So therefore if you would protect your husband in this case to the point of fabricating stories, you would be forgiven?

A: I would not fabricate to protect my husband.

Q: It's not the question I asked. I want an answer.

Jack jumped up to object, but the Judge overruled him.

Q: Do you feel you would be forgiven by your God if you did all you could to help your husband, even if you said things that were not true?

A: Yes, I feel I would be forgiven, but I have no reason to lie for my husband.

Having reached a dead end on this tack, Levy went back to the testimony on motel dates. During the times when I was supposed to be alone at a motel, how could Kathleen know for sure that I *was* alone?

A: I know he was alone because I know my husband.

Q: I'm trying to get facts here, not opinion.

A: I'm giving you facts.

The judge sustained Levy's argument that this was opinion, not fact. Levy continued in this vein. Kathleen agreed that at some times when I was called back to the chapel she could not say positively that I had indeed gone back there. I didn't, after all, call and check in, but of course there were others who worked at the chapel or came in to see me who could verify that I was there when I said I was.

Levy persisted in the argument that "the chaplain could have been elsewhere" in an effort to salvage Mary Ann's account of that all-important day of August 9, 1970. He had Kathleen again recount the timetable of that day and jumped on her testimony that there were two hours in the afternoon when I had stayed home to take a nap. Then during those two hours, he insisted, I could have gone secretly to Mary Ann's apartment. But how could I have gotten there, Kathleen asked, since she had taken the car to the base pool?

"How would Chaplain Jensen come to the pool on other Sundays when he would join you late in the afternoon?" Levy wanted to know. "He would use the childrens' bicycle, or walk," Kathleen answered. "So you did have other transportation at home—a bicycle!"

Her apartment was over eleven miles from the Cecil Field base. To make Levy's theory come true I would have had to pedal the bike twenty-two miles to get to and from Mary Ann's apartment in two hours and get back to my bed. Mary Ann had testified there had been four acts of sexual intercourse with me that afternoon!

Lt. Levy finally tried to imply that Kathleen was standing by me because of the financial income of a Navy commander and for the retirement benefits I would eventually receive. Kathleen told him I had come into the Navy because I thought it the best way for me to contribute to my country and fulfill my obligations to my faith.

Levy later approached Kathleen outside of court and apologized for being hard on her. "I was just doing my job," he said. Possibly he also had a presentiment that he had failed?

CHAPTER 25

When Jack Blackmon called my name to take the stand as the final witness in my own defense, one could sense the heavy atmosphere of suspense in the small courtroom. I was conscious that many of my parishioners were in the room and that I had to control myself, to preserve my dignity as their minister and chaplain. I felt I was controlled in appearance, but inside I was enraged at what Kathleen had been put through on the stand.

For the record I had to deny date-by-date each of the alleged sexual encounters charged against me, and a good part of my testimony on direct examination was taken up with this. As a result I covered much of the same ground that had been covered by Kathleen and by other defense witnesses, but I was also able to supply additional details.

I could, for example, provide fresh evidence of one of Mary Ann's misstatements. She had claimed a reason she remembered a motel date with me on August 21, 1970, was that she had accompanied me that day to the K-Mart, where I had bought new tires for our family car. Following her testimony Kathleen and I came up with the bill of sale that showed—as I'd suspected—I had purchased the tires on August 14. Mary Ann also had the store wrong—it was J. M. Fields, not the K-Mart. Mary Ann knew we frequently shopped at K-Mart, which probably was why she used it in her story. Levy and his assistant Schrader looked rather nonplussed when I testified about the purchase and Jack placed the bill of sale and a charge slip from the Fields store into the record.

Jack also cited the motel receipt the prosecution had introduced for that date. Mary Ann's testimony was that we checked into the motel between 5 and 7 that evening. I knew I had actually gone to the motel that night at a later hour because of a wedding rehearsal; this was backed up by the receipt that showed I checked in at 9:11 P.M.

Levy had argued in his cross-examination of Kathleen that she could not be sure I had actually gone to the chapel when I received calls after-hours to deal with special problems or urgent requests to counsel a parishioner. I was able to testify in detail as to what I did at the chapel and who was there with me. I pointed out the urgency Drs. Murphy and Shetterley conveyed when they advised me to get away from the base from time to time to rest.

Our briefs charging command influence and prejudice in my case had been rejected out-of-hand by the judge at the last-ditch Article 39-A hearing. Now Jack was anxious for the members of the court to hear about this through my testimony. In response to his questioning I described how the charges were filed against me at a time when I was not there to answer them and how demands were made that I stay away from the base and resign, thereby submitting to the charges before any investigation was even held. When Jack asked me to describe the condition of my office when I got back, the prosecutor objected and the judge cut off this line of questioning.

Jack argued that he wanted me to tell the court how my office was "totally searched and totally rearranged" while I was being kept out and how I was searched "coming and going" when I was finally permitted to stop there briefly. Judge Cole was adamant, though, in refusing to allow any more of this testimony.

I did go through the entire history of my association with Mary Ann and Lora, describing how their attitudes toward me changed to the extreme that they both made threats against me. I summarized the efforts I'd made in trying to bring Mary Ann Curran and her husband back together and how Mary Ann's moods shifted from manic to depressive and on occasion from a near winsome air of friendliness to virulent anger. When Jack asked me to explain why I had referred her to a professional marriage counselor in the civilian community, I said I felt her problems were so deep-seated she needed help from somebody with an extensive background in clinical psychology. "She told me she was transferring her affections from the man she had an affair with in Texas to a man she had met in Jacksonville," I said. "In addition, she had revealed to me certain lesbian tendencies—"

Lt. Levy was again on his feet, shouting an objection to any further testimony about "lesbianism." The judge sustained him. My lawyers and I felt—however unattractive—that it was necessary to get Mary Ann's lesbian feelings and tendencies into the record to indicate she was more concerned about this than anything else, and that she might well do and/or say almost anything to keep this information from getting out. Her threats against me became particularly vicious whenever she got the idea into her head that I was going to betray her secret sexual affairs. Since the judge refused to allow us to subpoena the woman with whom Mary Ann had stayed at certain motels, we felt the only way we could have this come out would be through my testimony. Levy did not challenge me in cross-examination on the statement about "lesbian tendencies" that I was able to make, nor did he bring Mary Ann Curran back in rebuttal to dispute what I had said.

I was permitted to recount the details Mary Ann had given me about her affair with Dr. Blanc, about the way bachelor pilots visited her singly or in groups when her husband was on duty and about her friendships with salesmen who called at the nursing home where she worked. I testified that when I felt her behavior was becoming disturbed I strongly urged psychiatric treatment for her and that this provoked her into her threat to "destroy you and your family."

My testimony on Lora Gudbranson amplified what Joe Simpson and Kathleen had already reported about her opposition to religion and the clergy and her support of free love. "She was antichurch and anticlergy . . . She was like a fanatic trying to pull you over to her point of view in favor of free love. . . . I was not ready to be pulled to that point of view. I don't think I ever will be."

I testified about Lora's reaction to the enforced departure of Joe Simpson and Paul Gerlock from Cecil Field, how she seemed to take delight in seeing clergymen destroyed and undermined by rumors. "She felt that with me she could destroy still another chaplain . . ."

I also described how Lora came to my office shortly before Kathleen was due to leave in July, 1971, and approached me. "Was this the first time you were ever propositioned?" Jack asked me. "I've never had anyone be so forceful," I answered.

"What was your reaction?"

"I tried to go off into a different subject. . . . But she got red, very red, very angry, very hostile. Her feeling of hostility increased when she called me at home after my wife left and she saw that my attitude hadn't changed and that she was in a position of having been rejected."

Before I took the stand Jack, Chuck Pope, and Joe Durham decided it was important for me to bring out the information I had about Lora Gudbransons' participation in the wife-swapping activities. As mentioned earlier, I had never wanted to expose publicly the existence of this activity, but only to work against it quietly through channels. I'd not intended to mention specific names in reporting to higher authorities, but Lora had refused to accept this. She still worried I would name names and had threatened to "ruin" me.

I was still reluctant to hurt the Navy's general reputation with such public testimony, but it was important that I show this additional motivation on Lora's part for her accusation against me.

I needn't have worried about what did go against the grain: I never got a chance to say a word. Jack posed the question: "Did you receive some startling information about Mrs. Gudbranson in your counseling sessions?" I started to answer, "I received information about certain activities—" but Levy rose to object and, once again, the judge sustained him. There is little question Lt. Levy knew what we intended to bring out—Lora undoubtedly had forewarned him, and there also had been rumors about it both inside and outside the courtroom.

The judge's ruling infuriated Chuck Pope and during the recess that followed he insisted that the wife-swapping story be revealed to the public. "It's damned important that this gets out in some way so that the public will understand one of the reasons they're trying to crucify Andy," he said.

Jack, however, preferred that we get the message out through the official trial record, and he did convince Judge Cole to allow him to insert into the record an "offer of proof."

"The defense makes this offer of proof in supplement to the previous offer of proof relating to Lora Gudbranson's connection with a "wife-swapping" or "swinger" group. The defense states that if the accused were allowed to testify under oath to the following matters that he would testify substantially as follows:

"That around the time that Lora Gudbranson made the proposition to him to engage in sexual relations, as testified to by the accused in court, she also told him that she had been informed that he knew her connection with a "wife-swapping" or "swinger" group and she had been told that he, the accused, had been asked to bring the matter to official attention; that she threatened to 'ruin' the accused if he did mention the matter to any public authorities."

Strangely—at least to a layman—although the statement went into the record and so was made available to reporters, Judge Cole decreed it not be seen by members of the court. So the only legal purpose it served was that it would be incorporated into the transcript on appeal should I be convicted. Furthermore, the judge told the press, "I wouldn't put any credence in that whatsoever." He made his comment without, to our knowledge, even trying to learn what specifics I could offer about the existence of the wife-swapping group. Neither the prosecution nor the Gudbransons, however, issued any statement on their own denying the wife-swapping charge when it was reported in the media.

I'm sure the spectators in our crowded little courtroom expected Levy's cross-examination of me to be especially dramatic. It turned out to be something less. By this time I knew more about this case than anyone else. I was ready. Lt. Levy must have sensed this after the first few answers; he didn't try to build a cohesive case through his questioning but rather jumped from one subject to another. He was also less abrasive than I'd expected, possibly because he was concerned that he had alienated the court by his treatment of Kathleen.

He pressed me some on the salary I was getting and the amount of retirement benefits I could anticipate if I were allowed to remain in the Navy, repeating the ineffective tactic he'd tried with Kathleen. I gave him the same answer Kathleen had, and also stressed that I wanted vindication through this court-martial so I could continue my work.

He asked me—as he had Kathleen—why I would go to motels for rest when I had a home on the base and the officers quarters for relaxation. I repeated what had gone into the record earlier—that I had to get completely off the base for short periods for relief from the pressures I was under. He tried a few more questions. I answered quickly. He then murmured, "No more questions."

The two chaplains who'd lined up with my accusers—Hoyt Swann and Lew Allred—were called to rebut our defense testimony about the motivation of Lora and Mary Ann. The judge permitted both chaplains to bring notes with them to the witness stand, although defense witnesses had not been permitted to do so. Levy's questioning of Swann was designed to contradict my testimony that I tried to avoid Lora Gudbranson after her attempt to involve me. Swann said the three of us had been at chapel brunch and that my attitude toward Lora was very friendly. On cross-examination, though, he proved forgetful of dates and circumstances, regardless of his notes. Cross-examination also served to establish that Swann had witnessed the charges made by Lora and Mary Ann and succeeded to my job after I was ordered off the base.

Allred was a rebuttal witness whose testimony hurt me, at least psychologically. He of course had no first-hand knowledge of my involvement with either Lora or Mary Ann—which doubtless was why he was not called in the presentation of the prosecution's case. When he began to repeat his Article 32 statement about Mary Ann identifying me—at his prompting—as a partner in adultery, Jack asked that the testimony be stricken on grounds it was not rebuttal material. But the judge overruled him and permitted Allred to go on to say that Mary Ann had asked only for my transfer, not my destruction.

As Jack Blackmon pointed out, Allred was giving the court hearsay, not hard evidence, and Mary Ann had already been exposed as a perjurer who might be assumed to tell any kind of story. I thought with some bitterness that Allred apparently felt nothing about what he had tried to do to me. In fact, he apparently was still trying to prove he had done the right thing.

In the chaplaincy, as in other callings, clothes (including the cloth) surely don't make the man. That, at least, he had proved.

CHAPTER 26

Summations began on the morning of Good Friday. The air was unusually raw and chill, and black rain clouds shrouded the Florida sun.

We felt the testimony of our defense witnesses had discredited my two accusers so effectively that Lt. Levy would have to come up with something new and startling in summing up the case against me. Instead he said the case against Andrew Jensen had to stand or fall on the testimony of Mrs. Curran and Mrs. Gudbranson. He insisted their testimony had "proved" that they had had sexual relations with me and rehashed their courtroom stories without, of course, mentioning they had given different versions of their alleged affairs with me before arriving at a final version at the court-martial. To prove they were telling the truth, he offered only the old negative argument:

"Why would they come forward if their charges were baseless? They had nothing to gain and everything to lose. They put tremendous burdens on themselves and their families, becoming the subject of public scorn and gossip. This is too high a price to pay for anything but the truth."

Levy also made assertions about me which I at least hoped would backfire. He said it wasn't necessary for me to have gone through the ordeal of court-martial because I had been given the option of resigning (and thereby oblige the command's interest in getting rid of the "square chaplain" with the reputation of rocking the boat and, by its lights, threatening to blow the whistle). Levy also stressed that Mary Ann's alleged affair with me began at the time that Joe Simpson's relationship with the petty officer's wife was being probed, concluding that I had discovered Joe was having such fun carrying on with "another woman" that I decided I should partake of the same. It seemed to me the court would find it obvious that the situation involving Joe was convincing reason for me *not* to get so involved even if I were so inclined. With the N.I.S. making it plain it would go to nearly any lengths to make a case against Joe, I would have had to be a fool to get into a situation that would allow them to hang two chaplains instead of one.

To sustain his description of Mary Ann Curran as a "truthful person," Levy glossed over her confession of perjury, saying only that she failed to disclose her affair with the "unnamed man" because she didn't want her husband to know and that even if her statements about some other man (the one in Beeville) had been inconsistent, she had not been inconsistent in her testimony about Chaplain Jensen.

"She is a woman who has held positions of trust both here and in Texas," Levy said. "She is young and attractive, a professional woman who found herself in an affair in Texas, experienced fears over the affair and put her faith and trust in Chaplain Jensen. It is no excuse to argue that Mrs. Curran's weakness existed before she met Chaplain Jensen. His job was to minister to that weakness, rather than turn that weakness to personal advantage." Neither Mary Ann nor Lora wished to be vindictive toward the accused, he went on. It was only after Commander Gudbranson went to the executive officer and after Mrs. Curran spoke to Chaplain Allred about the possibility of transfer that they signed the charges.

He attempted to dismiss our defense with these comments:

My character witnesses from the Navy could hardly remember me.

The women who were members of the chapel were "overly helpful" to me and would not believe charges against their chaplain no matter how strong they were.

How could Mrs. Jump remember who I was, where I had parked my car, and whether or not there was anybody with me if she saw so many people in uniform who came to her motel? (He apparently could think of nothing to challenge the testimony of Mrs. Hale from the Baptist Book Store so he simply ignored her.)

Former Chaplains Gerlock and Simpson had both left Cecil Field under cloud, and Mike Wennersten was just a "marijuana-smoking, LSD-taking, unsuitable dischargee." Clearly not credible witnesses.

My infection had cleared up before the July dates testified by Mrs. Gudbranson to be our rendezvous dates. Dr. Wickham had testified to examining me on July 2nd and two weeks thereafter, but Levy decided he had seen me only on June 28th and July 2nd.

If I needed rest and to get away from pressure, why didn't I buy a second car? (He had only to check my pay rate to answer that one.)

Anticipating that the judge would be obliged in his charge to instruct the court that Lora and Mary Ann were "accomplice witnesses," he insisted that accomplices aren't necessarily unreliable: ". . . The testimony of an accomplice is unreliable only in direct relation to the likelihood of the accomplice being prosecuted himself. In this case, the rationale does not apply strongly because the Navy can't prosecute or punish civilians (and the two women are civilians). Also, it is a matter of common knowledge that adultery is rarely, if ever, prosecuted in civilian courts." (Not to mention military.)

I could hardly believe my ears when Levy went on to say that it wasn't even necessary for the government to show corroboration in this case, that the court could convict me solely on the basis of the testimony of the two accomplices if they felt that testimony to be reliable. Levy began to quote part of Article 153 of the Uniform Code of Military Justice to try to prove his point, but he seemed to mislead the court by failing to read the entire portion on accomplices. Jack saw the look on my face and said, *sotto voce,* "Don't worry, the judge will have to give the court the straight dope on accomplice witnesses in his charge. There just can't be a conviction on the basis of the testimony of accomplices alone."

Levy claimed the government did have corroboration even if—in his view—it wasn't really necessary for the purposes of conviction. The corroboration was represented as being the so-called love notes and the motel receipts, but he made no attempt to show a direct link between this so-called evidence and the commission of the crime of adultery. And, of course, we had presented defense tesitmony to show that the notes were not intended for Mary Ann and had apparently been stolen. The motel receipts could not be called corroboration either—they showed that *I* was at the motels, but they did not show that Lora or Mary Ann were there with me.

When Jack's turn came he started slowly, like a pitcher going through his warm-up. He told me before court opened that his summation would be a long one because "I've got the facts on my side and I want to be sure to spell them all out so there isn't a scintilla of doubt left in the mind of any member of the court." Besides, he added, "that's what you're paying me for." His summation became more and more impassioned as he went along and ended up a five-hour tour de force. Though some people criticized him later for taking so long, I noticed the court members maintaining intent interest throughout.

He began by saying that "One of the most amazing things the prosecution has said is that the accusations must be true or the women wouldn't have come forward. The defense says the accusations must be false or the defendant wouldn't subject himself and his family to the ordeal of the past eight months since the investigation began. Who but a man of God could have survived these last eight months without losing his mind or blowing his brains out? The charges must be false, else how would his friends and neighbors be willing to come forward in such an investigation? Do they not have a lot to lose by incurring the wrath of the Navy command? . . .

"An important defense in a charge of a sexual nature is to listen to those people who know the defendant best. People came from great distance at their own expense to speak on behalf of this defendant's character, even while knowing the nature of the accusations against him. A person of good character is hardly likely to commit this kind of offense. Just like good character cannot be made in a day, it cannot be crumbled into black dust in one second . . ."

The women who had charged me, he asserted, were "sick, scheming, conspiring . . . One of them—Lora Gudbranson—is a pathological liar, while Mrs. Curran is a very sick, confused, disturbed young woman . . . an admitted perjurer and adulteress." The had conceived a vendetta against me, he went on, and had compelling reasons in their own minds to want to destroy me. If Mrs. Curran was at first hesitant about how much damage she wanted to inflict, she nevertheless went along with the conspiracy under Mrs. Gudbranson's strong direction. And far from being a "trusted professional person," she was a woman who "constantly moves, constantly changes jobs, and gets into involvements with her employers or with people connected with her work."

The fact that the Navy couldn't prosecute them for their offenses gave them the heady feeling of being free to concoct any sort of plot. The fact that the Navy command wanted to oblige them added to their sense of power: they were treated with favor by the command, their husbands were given promotions and preferential treatment, all arms of the command were placed at their disposal for eight months. They could cover up other affairs and misconduct and, if admonished in any way, could blame everything on a dirty old chaplain who'd misled them. As the psychologists had pointed out, they could also be variously motivated by the "neurotic kick" of sabotaging a clergyman, being able to advertise their availability and confirm their desirability, or just the desire to get out from under boredom and unhappiness in their own marriages.

With a recall that astounded me for its grasp of every pertinent detail associated with the case, Jack recapped its history from the beginning. His southwestern drawl took on a sharp note of indignation as he described the way evidence indicated the command had mistreated me—he told me to "stay the hell away from Cecil Field and Jacksonville," demanded I resign before getting a chance to defend myself, barred me from the chapel while agents took papers and other potential evidence from my office. Though Lora and Mary Ann gave conflicting versions as to how they came to accuse me and although they were to keep changing their accounts, the command, he pointed out, consistently accepted what they said, sent agents scouring through motels for records to help adjust their testimony, conducted a catch-all investigation of me and a specific campaign of harrassment.

Mary Ann, he said, had delivered a "broadside" of accusations at the Article 32 hearing, but, when it was realized this wouldn't stand up at a trial, her tactics changed. "Instead of a broadside, she now picks specific dates and uses a birthday or some other event as a reason for picking dates. She goes to check on when her husband had duty so she won't be caught in her choice of dates. But she gives us no specifics, and almost no details. Every time we do get a detail, it turns out to be false. The defense says that in each of these occurrences, if you can't believe her in part, if she misrepresents the circumstances, then you can't give credence to the rest of her testimony. If a person lies about one thing, they are apt to lie about other things. If Mrs. Curran had somebody with her when her husband had duty, that's her husband's problem, but it has not been established that this 'somebody' was Commander Jensen."

Jack pointed out that I had been obliged to "reconstruct" my life for the days that were relevant to this court-martial—and that I had been able to do this with the help of my calendars and records, through the many special activities I had going at different times and with the help of others involved in those activities. In each instance, he argued, I had provided a reasoned explanation of what I had been doing. He then went over the testimony of every one of the days, reserving special attention and disbelief for August 9, 1970, and for the day Mary Ann claimed to have had relations with me in the chapel.

As for Mary Ann's account of a date with me in November following the night of the dining-in:

"She had seen her lover—that unnamed man—playing her for the fool so she decides she's going back to her husband. She calls Commander Jensen to tell him the news and when she finds he's at the dining-in social, she tells his wife to let him know about it. She knows Commander Jensen has worked very hard to hold her marriage together and she's sure he'll be pleased to know about the reconciliation with her husband. Well, after all that, and on the day she's going back with her husband, she would have you believe that all Commander Jensen has to do is come to the apartment and talk her into going to bed with him . . . Now, how does Jensen account for his time this day? Well, he's got the devotional luncheon. Mrs. Jensen is there at the chapel, among others. He's got other activities that afternoon. . . . Mrs. Curran's story is just plain ridiculous."

And the alleged occasion in the chapel:

"She picks a Friday date, February 12th, a day that used to be celebrated as Lincoln's birthday and she says she remembers it because it was the Friday before Valentine's Day and she went to the chapel to accept a present of a box of candy. And she tells us they had an act of sexual intercourse there. . . . I want you to think about this picture. It is the worst kind of charge to make about a man of the cloth when you suggest an act of [illicit] sex in the church edifice. So let's look at the facts:

"First, nobody connected with the chapel knew about this or anything like this going on. We brought in every chaplain who had overlapping duty, we brought in the clean-up people, and the ladies active in chapel programs who were there. The Boy Scouts were there, plus the den mother. Mrs. Jensen was there with her Cub Scout group, and was in and out of her husband's office. The navigator group was there, plus the normal come-and-go of people. Mrs. Whitbeck, the secretary, was there. And Mrs. Curran would have you believe she went into the chaplain's office with all these people around and had an act of intercourse with him!"

Jack stressed, as had Chuck in the Article 32, that on a Navy base there are always whispers, gossip, and pointed fingers if such behavior is going on. Here there was nothing:

"Chaplain Jensen was a very well-known man at this base. His car was known, and when people see him coming and going, with his uniform and the cross, they remember him. Mrs. Curran is a striking young woman—she looks even younger than her age, like a girl. She talks of all these comings and goings to see her at the apartment complex, and so it seems very strange that nobody would have noticed this. It is very strange, indeed, that not the slightest whisper of gossip or scandal was heard."

Jack wound up his summation by again reminding the members of the court of the "inconsistencies, the improbabilities, the incredible statements" that had come out of the mouths of my accusers and pointed out the circumstances that showed they had fixed on the motel dates in their testimony only after the N.I.S. agents had showed the receipts attesting to the dates I was there. He then looked directly at the court members:

"How would you like to be in Chaplain Jensen's place? How would you like to be brought up here just because somebody took it upon himself or herself to accuse you in this manner? Is the evidence you heard from these two women the kind you would expect anybody to give credence to if you were on trial? Are these the kind of witnesses you would want to see in court against you? Wouldn't you fight charges that are false? A cowardly man would have taken the easy way out and resigned, but Chaplain Jensen felt someone had to take on the tremendous burden of defending the Cecil Field Chapel.

"The man whose crucifixion is observed this very day in the Christian Church once said, 'Do unto others as you would have them do unto you.' If you reflect on that and if you act under the guidance of a greater power, while weighing the evidence *in the light of your own experiences in life*, I am sure you will find it your duty and your pleasure to acquit this man. Chaplain Jensen now submits himself to your judgment."

Levy came back with a short rebuttal, starting with a complaint about the defense counsel taking so long. He said he didn't intend to rehash the whole case but wanted the court to know the government didn't have to prove its case with mathematical certainty—only beyond a reasonable doubt. He tried to deflate Jack's specifics by saying that the charges alleged that the accused had engaged in misconduct "on or about certain dates." Thus, he argued, even if the women had been wrong on some specific dates, they could still be believed because of the qualifying words "on or about." He asked that the court give me no special consideration as a chaplain—I was to be judged just like any other officer (not mentioning that no other officer had ever been court-martialed on the principal charge of adultery).

Levy was obviously stung by Jack's assertion that the two women finally zeroed in on specific motel dates only after the government agents had obtained motel receipts and showed them. He didn't offer any evidence to indicate it hadn't worked that way and he hadn't put any of the N.I.S. agents on the stand, apparently out of fear that exposure of their behavior on cross-examination would hurt his case. Instead, he tried ridicule: "If you think the two women were able to give their testimony against Chaplain Jensen because the government showed receipts to them in advance, then you should acquit Chaplain Jensen and court-martial Levy and Schraver," he told the court. A comment came from the rear of the courtroom: "I'm for that."

There was still the judge's charge to the court. In view of the judge's attitude toward me in the early stages of the trial, I worried he would carry it over into his instructions on the law. Still, the prosecution and defense lawyers had had a private session in the judge's chambers prior to his delivering his charge, and Jack came out of it convinced we would get a fair shake. "I went over the whole legal question of accomplice testimony with him and he assured me he would be very explicit on this when he instructed the jury and would see to it that there were no misinterpretations," he told me. Jack said the judge no longer seemed, as some had said, like a "hanging judge"—perhaps he'd heard the criticisms about his running something like a kangaroo court and taken it to heart. Or perhaps what *we* considered the weakness of the prosecution case had become so apparent to him that he no longer could overlook it.

In any event, when the judge delivered his charge following a recess for dinner it came out this way: "Any references made by counsel on the law is not to be accepted by you members of the court. It's *my* responsibility to instruct you on the law."

He then covered *all* of the material in the Uniform Code of Military Justice that pertained to accomplice testimony and prefaced it by saying that Mrs. Curran and Mrs. Gudbranson were clearly accomplices as a matter of law: "There are cases in which the court would not be warranted in accepting certain testimony as being sufficient to constitute a determination of guilt . . . a conviction cannot be based upon uncorroborated testimony given by an alleged victim in a trial for a sexual offense or upon uncorroborated testimony given by an accomplice in a trial for any offense, if in either case the testimony is self-contradictory, uncertain, or improbable. Even if apparently corroborated and apparently credible, testimony of an accomplice which is adverse to the accused is of questionable integrity and is to be considered with great caution."

He went on to say that some testimony of Lora and Mary Ann had to be considered "uncertain," citing Mrs. Curran's admission of perjury about the affair with the "unnamed man" as well as such inconsistencies that had come out at the trial as her testimony that she had been given the note signed "Andy" at the Holiday Inn when she previously said she had received it from me in my office: her testimony that she had told her husband about a relationship with me in April, 1971, where previously she had put the date in March; her inconsistent testimony about an affair in Texas. As for Mrs. Gudbranson, there was the conflict in her testimony about her supposed meeting with me at the Gator Lodge in July, 1971, whereas she had previously prepared a written statement fixing the date in June. We had, as mentioned, been prevented from getting many other and more substantial inconsistencies into the court-martial record. However, it was not the judge's role to argue either side's case—his citations were minimal and intended only to illustrate the guidelines of the laws of evidence for the court.

In discussing corroboration, the judge said that evidence tending to show corroboration must be examined to determine if it is substantial. "If not, there is no corroboration. The fact that Mrs. Curran and Mrs. Gudbranson each testified to more than one act of intercourse is not to be considered as corroboration. Mrs. Curran's testimony cannot be considered as corroboration of Mrs. Gudbranson's testimony and Mrs. Gudbranson's testimony cannot be considered as corroboration of Mrs. Curran's testimony. . . . Also, the defense has introduced evidence that the accused could not have committed some of the acts because he was at other places. This is known as 'alibi' testimony. If you accept the alibi testimony, then in law it is to be considered a complete defense."

Now followed the period of agonizing suspense that every defendant in a military court-martial or a criminal trial must endure while the jury of his peers considers what should be done with him. The court members began their deliberations at 7 P.M. I went out to have coffee with my lawyers. Kathleen stayed with her mother and a few of her friends. She couldn't bear sitting with the lawyers and me rehashing the trial while the verdict was in doubt. She had held up well during her own ordeal on the stand, but with her job done she had let down the floodgates for her pent-up emotions. She had come into the courtroom early in the day but she couldn't tolerate Levy's attitude and what he had to say and so she had gone back to the witness room. She would be ready, though, to stand by me when the verdict was announced, be it for good or for bad.

The members of the court had only been out for twenty minutes when we got a call to come back to the courtroom. The sudden summons seemed ominous, but it turned out to be only a touch of bureaucratic irony. One of the court members had to go to the lavatory, and the court-martial procedure decreed that in order to oblige him the court had to be reconvened with all parties present and then dismissed for a brief recess!

The deliberations resumed, and so did the waiting.

Navy people and civilians came up to talk to me. So did reporters. A few of the local reporters apologized for earlier stories, saying that their editors had wanted to please the command. They told me that the opposition was acting uptight—Swann, for example, had been questioned by a newspaperman after his appearance as a rebuttal witness and had torn the notebook from his questioner's hand. All newspapermen had been ordered to stay away from Cecil Field, but one had managed to get in to see Shute, the executive officer, who gave a no-comment to every question, then had the newsman escorted off the field. Lt. Bob Ford, Cecil Field's legal officer, had apparently been dispatched to the courthouse to get the result. Some said he looked apprehensive. I'm sure I did too.

Jack Blackmon complimented Chuck Pope for his excellent legal research. Jack and Chuck had their differences over strategy, but they were one when it came to a concern about what happened to me and to the Navy. Both lawyers were also Navy loyalists concerned with how this court-martial would influence the public's opinion of Navy justice. They agreed that on the basis of all the facts and the testimony in the case, no *impartial* court could adjudge me guilty beyond a reasonable doubt. But would the command at this naval installation, which had gone to such extremes first to induce me to resign and then to discredit me by trial, be able to dictate the verdict of a court of Navy officers?

After the deliberations had gone on for over an hour, Jack turned to me. "Andy, it looks good." He explained that the time consumed meant that they were seriously looking over the record of testimony for the twenty-two dates on which adultery had been charged. "And if they are studying it on the merits, it means acquittal," he said, implying that a quick verdict in a court-martial usually means a decision of "guilty."

But then came disturbing news. Levy and his assistant prosecutor, Schrader, who had been shooting pool during the waiting time, passed the word that they would hold a press conference following the verdict. I felt they wouldn't be planning to hold court for the press if they weren't very confident the verdict would go their way. We also were told that the Gudbransons had a party going in their quarters with friends in attendance. Larry Gudbranson, still much in favor with the command, had been recommended for a prestigious post with the supply division of the Navy up north, and he and his wife would soon be leaving Cecil Field. The party struck me as their way of dancing on my grave before they left.

"Don't think that way," my lawyers told me in an effort at reassurance. Levy might be acting on his own, out of sheer bravado signifying nothing. And the Gudbransons might be thinking court-martials usually end in convictions so we can start celebrating right now. It didn't prove they knew what this court was going to do. . . .

The call came at 9:16 P.M., after the members of the court had been out just after two hours. As I went back into the courthouse with my lawyers I thought of all the courtroom dramas I'd seen in the movies and on TV when the defendant is asked to rise and listen to the verdict, a wax figure with glazed eyes.

I was no different as I listened too but I hardly heard the ritual in which Judge Cole requested of Captain William Hall, the medical service officer who was the senior member of the court, the rendering of the verdict. A moment of silence, then the words

"NOT GUILTY."

There was a whoop of joy in my ear from Chuck Pope standing next to me, and momentarily I turned on him in anger because I knew there were two specifications in the charges against me and I felt the verdict had not yet been announced on the second specification. But then there was an outburst of cheers and shouting as the judge announced the adjournment of the court, and I finally realized that Captain Hall had bound both specifications into one in announcing the verdict. Kathleen leaned over the railing behind me to kiss me, wetting my face with her tears—finally tears of happiness. The newspaper reporters, radio and TV men milled around asking for comment. I mumbled about the thanks I owed to those who had stood by me—words that sounded like clichés and yet the sincerest words I had ever expressed in my life. I remember one reporter asking me, "Where are you going to unwind?" And I answered, "To the malt shop, I guess—in keeping with my image!"

There was a wonderfully heartwarming reaction to the verdict that night, and most especially at the home of Petty Officer and Mrs. Willey, where Drew and David were staying that night. The Willeys were the first to receive our call. David had fallen asleep but Drew was standing by waiting for word. "If you could just see Drew's face when he got the news from you and then watched the TV news show!" Mrs. Willey told us. Kathleen and I indeed *could* see it.

What of the others? Hoyt Swann was at the chapel with the Young People's group, and his face reportedly turned pale when he heard the verdict. He hurried to the telephone and was overheard calling the duty chaplain at N.A.S., Jacksonville, asking for John Danielson's phone number. (I felt the next call he would make would undoubtedly go to Lew Allred.)

At the Gudbranson party Larry Gudbranson was reported to have gone into a fit of anger and had to be given sedation. The party broke up, and Lora Gudbranson finished packing. The Gudbransons were seen leaving Cecil Field that same night in their station wagon, with Lora driving and Larry full-length in the back seat.

The prosecution never held its press conference. While people were milling about in the courtroom, Lt. Levy slipped out quietly. Later he and his superior, Waite, appeared at the officers' club and created something of a scene when they encountered one of the members of the court. Several who were there said they felt that Waite violated the ethics of his office as Staff Judge Advocate by berating the court member for the acquittal verdict. My path happened to cross Waite's a few times during the following weeks and each time he turned his face away. What were the consequences of his role in staging this disastrous court-martial? For one thing, he was promoted to captain . . .

The command was at least consistent. But something far more important had happened. On a personal level, my life, my career as minister and chaplain had been, at least officially, restored to me. On a broader level, six members of a Navy court had stood up to pressures applied by some contemporary Romans and thereby preserved their honor and the honor of the Naval service. They had proved that old notions like "justice," "truth," and "conscience" still had meaning in a government and nation which too often laughed at them.

EPILOGUE

I learned that no man escapes unaffected from a trial even when fair-minded men recognize he has been falsely accused and finally acquit him of all charges. The agonies my family and I suffered during the eight months I was the object of conspiracy and bureaucratic harassment did not end with the Easter Week not-guilty verdict. Costs incurred in the preparation of a defense weigh equally on the innocent and the guilty. The costs in this case included money I had set aside for my sons' education. Costs in physical and emotional damage were even higher, never to be completely offset or recouped.

The military system I had taught my boys to respect and trust now brings chilling fears of uncertainty to them. Although Kathleen and I have reminded them that it was only comparatively few members of this system who were directly responsible for my ordeal, they were well aware that nobody in positions of leadership in the military did anything to stop the injustice. To them, the system appears to be one in which a few people can destroy lives while others in high positions either encourage them or, like the monkeys who see no evil or hear no evil, look the other way.

Navy tradition, and indeed Navy law, says that when a man is acquitted in a court-martial he must be granted full rights, privileges, and all considerations given to men of equal rank who have never been charged. He is not to be discriminated against in any manner. The rule is too often honored only by lip service.

In my case the pledge that I was to be recommended for accelerated promotion should have been honored once I was cleared by the Navy court. There was no accelerated promotion—no promotion at all. When my name came up for promotion in the regular turn, I was passed over. When Congressman Sisk made inquiries, he was told my role as a defendant in a court-martial had nothing to do with this decision.

Indicators of what was—or rather was not—to come began when Admiral Geis called me into his office after the court-martial to make remarks about my Baptist denomination interfering in Navy business. After my acquittal my denomination asked that I be given my promotion in line with the original recommendation; the admiral said that this would not help my chances but rather would hurt them. I left the meeting with the feeling that the decision had been made against the promotion and that the admiral was using my denomination as an excuse.

An incident that occurred while I was attending Princeton Theological Seminary after I was passed over for promotion is revealing. I was having lunch with friends when we were introduced to a young man who began talking about the Navy chaplaincy. He said he recently had heard a Navy chaplain discuss a situation that had come up while the chaplain was serving on the selection board that passes on promotions for chaplains. I tried to keep a straight face as the young man told us that this particular selection board had turned down the promotion for "that chaplain who was involved in that adultery trial in Jacksonville, Florida."

The young man obviously had not caught my name when we were introduced or had not remembered my name from the stories about the court-martial. I pressed him on whether this chaplain on the selection board had explained the reason for the board's turn-down.

"Why, it was because the chaplain was caught committing adultery," the young man answered. He said he'd read about the case in the papers but had forgotten just how it turned out. He inferred from remarks the chaplain on the selection board had made that the chaplain in question had been found guilty but had been treated leniently and allowed to remain in the service.

The young man obviously saw the strained expression that had come over my face and stopped abruptly. I then told him who I was, that I had been acquitted, not convicted—that if I *had* been convicted I couldn't possibly have remained in the service. I'd probably be in the brig instead.

The attitude of that selection-board chaplain reflected the stated thinking of people who had reason to know better—people in position of command who had seemed determined to convict and begrudged the not-guilty verdict.

The attitude of those who for their own selfish reasons joined the plot against me was best summed by Captain T. T. Coleman, the C.O. at Cecil Field, who had behaved as if he wanted to protect my accusers and their husbands, had made pretrial statements about my guilt, had tried to lock me up in a hospital with an armed guard —all on the basis of unsubstantiated charges. When Kathleen and I saw him after the court-martial he made no mention of these matters, no mention of the evidence we had been able to present to prove my innocence. In effect, his attitude was, they didn't have enough evidence to convict me in court. He suggested that adultery was not really the issue in my case and criticized Kathleen and myself for not having offered statements for the Article 32. But, of course, our offer of statements was contained in the Article 32, which convinced us he hadn't adequately read the Article 32 transcript before recommending a court-martial.

The families at Cecil Field who had supported me felt that official vindication would have returned me immediately to my post and that, indeed, I would have been in the chapel pulpit on Easter Sunday. Admiral Geis, Captain Coleman, and the Chief of Chaplains all took the position that since my assistant had been promoted to senior chaplain, the post was no longer open to me and I would have to be transferred. I was not allowed inside the chapel except to pick up my professional equipment that someone had pulled out of desk drawers and closets and packed in boxes.

The chief did congratulate me on my acquittal and said he was delighted that one of his chaplains had been cleared of charges against him. In view of what happened, I admit to a certain skepticism about his sincerity. He proposed to send me back to a base where I once served as a lieutenant—a gesture he understood would be interpreted as a demotion and reflection on me. I pointed this out, and through the help of my denomination I was assigned instead to an advanced course at the Princeton Theological Seminary and then to my present post on the chaplain's staff at the U.S. Naval Hospital in Philadelphia.

When a Naval vessel is steered off-course and rams onto the rocks, the Navy will act to discipline and punish those responsible for such negligence. There was no discipline or punishment for those who tried to steer Naval justice off-course and who wasted an exorbitant amount of government funds in an unwarranted court-martial. As noted, quite the contrary ocurred when virtually everyone who took part in the action against me was promoted or advanced—including those who concealed that a principal accuser in my case had admitted to perjury.

I realize it's naïve to expect it, but the Navy lawyer who had the guts to go all-out in my defense *should* have been rewarded for his devotion to justice. Instead, Chuck Pope was passed over for promotion, given the silent treatment at the law center, and provoked by his superiors to the point where he blew his top and further complicated his career.

One likes to feel that an experience such as mine and my family's has some broader impact for good. I think, in part and even if indirectly, this has been true. Articles 133 and 134 of the Uniform Code of Military Justice were both declared unconstitutional in the federal courts following my court-martial. (One Article was ruled unconstitutional at the appeals level, the other in a federal district court case.) We had argued the unconstitutionality of both Articles during my proceedings and although the actual rulings were made on the basis of other cases, I strongly believe that the attention given to my case at least helped give focus to the unfair way these Articles were being used to gain convictions. Article 133—"Conduct Unbecoming an Officer and a Gentleman"—and Article 134—"Conduct Prejudicial to the Service"—habitually were used as catch-alls against defendants whose alleged violations didn't breach ordinary military regulations. In fact some military personnel have been tried and convicted for something they didn't even know was an offense—and which at other bases or at other times would not have been regarded as illegal or even improper.

My denomination's support tended to weaken. At first the denomination insisted it would endorse no more chaplains to the Navy unless the government repaid me for the costs of my defense, gave me my promotion in accordance with the original recommendation, and provided a guarantee that chaplains charged in the future with morals offenses would have their cases referred to their denominations rather than be tried in military courts. Apparently pressures finally caused denominational officials to compromise. The guarantees never came; a verbal assurance from the Assistant Secretary of the Navy that the recommended procedure regarding morals offenses would be followed was accepted instead of a firm guarantee.

Many chaplains have told me that the Assistant Secretary's verbal assurance at least represented an important step forward. Still, without a strong guarantee that such cases involving chaplains be referred to the proper ecclesiastical denomination rather than be handled under military strictures, there is nothing legally to prevent military commanders seeking to get rid of uncomfortably outspoken chaplains from using accusations such as were made against me.

My denomination made compromises, but I will always appreciate the support its officials gave me when the going was especially rough. They showed real guts, and I understand that they felt they had to compromise in the end because their originally strong stand never seemed to get the backing of the General Commission on Chaplains in the Armed Forces, which has always been close to the military hierarchy.

The General Commission, founded in 1917, is a liaison on chaplaincy matters between the civilian churches, on the one hand, and the armed forces and the Veterans Administration, on the other. It has representation from over forty different denominations and unofficial representatives from the Roman Catholic, Jewish, and Southern Baptist organizations that attend its meetings. All the representatives of the denominations have jobs dependent on the goodwill of the chief of chaplains in the military services and the military officials of the services. Since the Chaplains Corps in the armed services is the only one with a waiting list of applicants anxious to get into the service, and since the denominational representatives often have surplus ministers they hope the Corps will absorb, there tends to be a benign approach to the wishes of the heads of the services. There is also an unsympathetic feeling toward anybody who would rock the boat. When my denomination first took the position it would not endorse any more chaplains as long as I was being deprived of my rights, certain denominational representatives immediately expressed resentment—their position being that they didn't want, in effect, to stop doing business as usual.

An official of the General Commission served the Navy command in relaying the allegations by my two accusers to my denomination. He did not relay any of the statements that refuted these allegations nor did he relay any of the evidence gathered by the defense. He was also heard to repeat the remarkable statement by Chaplain John Danielson that Mary Ann and Lora were actually "two lovely housewives."

Many of the denominational representatives are retired senior officers from the Chaplains Corps who receive retirement pay as well as pay from their denomination. This too probably is an inducement for these representatives to reflect the wishes of the chiefs of services. The Southern Baptist official, for example, is a retired chief of chaplains who draws a rear admiral's retirement pay.

A committee appointed by the General Commission to investigate the position taken by my denomination met about six weeks after the end of the court-martial. The committee heard from the chief of chaplains and a Navy legal officer while Jack Blackmon represented my denomination. Jack's report on mistreatment was, he reported, heard with little interest. Chaplain Herman Benner, who represented my denomination at my court-martial, should have been one of the first to be heard by the committee, but he was not allowed to make any report. Instead the committee received second- and third-hand reports representing the chief of chaplains as a great pastor and the procedures in my case as legal and proper. One denominational representative said later, "They heard what they wanted to hear."

The committee took no specific remedial action and, as mentioned, settled for a promise that morals charges against chaplains in the future would first be referred to their denominations. Just prior to this meeting the chief of chaplains of the armed services took denominational representatives on a tour of bases in Florida and Alabama at taxpayer expense. When the question of my promotion came up, several representatives said they hoped I wouldn't be promoted, especially over their personnel. They got their wish. *The Chaplain*, official publication of the General Commission, printed an article announcing that I had been passed over for promotion. I imagine this was the first and only time that such intelligence rated a news item.

A not irrelevant aspect of the relationship between several of the religious denominations and the Chaplains Corps of the various services was demonstrated by the position these denominations took on the Vietnam war. They denounced the war as "immoral, indecent, and unconstitutional" among other things—but they rarely expressed criticism of their own ministers who were serving as chaplains and were firm in their support of the war. No matter what the principle, because of their indebtedness it seems the denominations won't seriously offend the military services.

I think there is growing feeling that the present system of ecclesiastical-military relations needs reform. It seems self-evident, not to mention the studies that have been made, that so long as the present system is maintained, denominations endorsing ministers to the services will remain subservient to the wishes of the military command and/or will make unfortunate compromises on matters of principle. More important, chaplains wishing to remain and advance in the service will be inclined to make paramount pleasing military C.O.'s who write their fitness reports and so determine their futures. The interests of the rank-and-file whom the chaplain is supposed to serve in the first instance often tend to take a secondary position.

Of course there are chaplains who have done outstanding work in the service and who have been encouraged by enlightened C.O.'s to put the interests of the men above all other interests. But it would be naïve and inaccurate to deny that many chaplains receive fitness reports that help secure them promotions primarily because the C.O.'s value them as social, drinking, or golfing companions.

A considered alternative is the establishment of a Civilian Chaplains Corps. This corps would serve the members of the armed forces as chaplains now do, but in a civilian capacity. Civilians presently perform various functions for the military in all parts of the world. There are even civilian technical representatives aboard Navy ships.

Members of such a Civilian Chaplain Corps would not be uniformed except in appropriate overseas areas. They would not have to indulge the whims of C.O.'s or senior officers to preserve their position and get promotions. They would, however, be subject to such regulations as other civilians on military bases are required to follow. They would be ministers in fact, as well as name, and would perform only those duties that relate to the ministry. Too many chaplains in the armed forces now spend much or all of their time on administrative functions; some have not functioned in a ministerial capacity for years.

Members of a civilian clergy would be responsible directly to their denominations and their consciences. They would not be under the command of a uniformed chief of chaplains with the rank of admiral or general who has himself been obliged to consider the interests of the military command foremost to achieve, maintain, and improve *his* position. It also has been pointed out that numerous able, well-trained clergymen who want to minister to military personnel do not do so because there is a *military* chaplaincy. If these clergymen were allowed to extend their on-the-scene ministerial duties to the bases both in the U.S. and abroad, it would be a real service to military-civilian community relations, to say nothing of saving tax dollars.

One argument made against the use by the military of a civilian clergy or a civilian chaplains corps is that military chaplains are better able to understand the problems of military men and that military men can better identify with a clergyman in military uniform. I have found no basis for this argument and have heard strong arguments from enlisted men to the contrary.

Another argument strongly backed by senior line officers and many chaplains is that the military chaplaincy should be continued because of tradition. What would the Navy be without its Chaplains Corps, they ask you. And they remind you that the Corps is nearly two hundred years old. It is true that the Chaplains Corps in both the Navy and the Army is rich in tradition and has a proud history. But times and attitudes have changed and we should take these changes into account and do what seems appropriate for the members of the armed services in the modern era.

Beyond the question of the chaplaincy is the larger one of the administration of justice in the United States Navy—indeed, in the armed forces. I was accused of adultery by unsupported statements accepted by a military command that gave the choice of resigning or a court-martial before beginning investigation of the charges. The husband of one accuser threatened to kill me and was never disciplined. Lora and Mary Ann never provided corroboration to make a case. They were allowed to concoct new stories to fit evidence. When their stories were shown to be improbable and confused, the command seemed to ignore the facts. Papers and records were stolen from me, friendly witnesses were threatened and frightened off. A pattern of prejudgment of guilt was pervasive. I was barred from my chapel. False statements were brought in by the N.I.S.; favorable evidence was not brought forth. Evidence provided by the defense obliged one accuser to admit to perjury (and never be prosecuted for it). The admission of perjury was either withheld from the admiral who convened the court-martial, or he convened it with the knowledge that a witness who'd committed perjury would be used to testify against one of his personnel. The admission of perjury was not reported to the defense until the court-martial was well under way. If the staff judge advocate and the prosecutor withheld the information from the admiral who convened the court-martial, it would seem an investigation of their conduct by military authorities is overdue. An investigation by the appropriate bar association might also be in order. If an admiral was responsible for withholding such information, an investigation might be indicated on that level.

Perhaps saddest to me is that the chief of chaplains apparently encouraged the signing of allegations and, in any event, approved a line investigation that he must have known in itself could destroy a minister's reputation and career. Like the immediate command he may have believed I would resign—I had already seen how his office had used allegations against chaplains to persuade them to resign quietly—thereby disposing of "troublemakers."

After my acquittal Congressman Sisk wrote the Inspector General of the Navy asking for an investigation of the handling of my case. The response: no investigation necessary; the fact of acquittal meant the system had worked fairly and properly. Unsaid was that acquittal was possible because I was fortunate enough to amass overwhelming evidence in proof of innocence. The officers who served as members of the court were men of honor, but there is a reasonable question as to how they would have voted if I had not been able to find irrefutable witnesses and documentation. I knew I would need to destroy the prosecution's case to have a chance of winning. It goes—or it should go—against the grain of American justice to force the defendant and not the prosecution to prove his case.

If my experiences were unique there would be no need for reform of the military court-martial system. But the fairness of the system has been questioned for years and particularly by responsible attorneys. The approximate ninety-five percent rate of convictions raises questions about the prejudice inherent in the system. Since acquittal I have received hundreds of letters from men in the service—primarily enlisted men—who have reported being victimized and unfairly convicted in courts-martial which were never publicized as mine was.

It's true that I've heard from Jack Blackmon—who has become a judge in Texas—that there have been more acquittals in courts-martial since the attention given to my case and that some commanders are at least being more careful about insuring fairness to military defendants. This is surely good news, but the system seemingly is still in need of reform—a need highlighted by a study made by U.S. Senator Birch Bayh, who concluded that command influence was the biggest obstacle to the administration of justice in the military, thereby confirming the widespread practice of what I'd experienced at Cecil Field.

Some lawyers believe that the establishment of a *civilian* judge advocate general corps to process cases in the military would be a likely reform. A bill has already been introduced in Congress to make such reforms. Just as a civilian chaplaincy has been proposed to replace the present militarized chaplaincy, a civilian legal system might well replace the present one of military control. A commanding officer would request an Article 32 investigation, but the attorneys for the prosecution and defense would be civilians and the hearing officer who would decide whether or not a court-martial was warranted would also be a civilian. The C.O. could not use the power of his rank and position to let a military investigation officer know that he wanted the case to go to court-martial, which would discourage an overzealous C.O. or his superior from instigating for whatever reason a court-martial unjustified on the merits. The defense attorney would not be a junior member of the military dependent for promotion on higher officers seeking court-martial and perhaps conviction. As a civilian, he would not feel safer in losing his case. The judge in courts-martial would also be a civilian and civilian rules of procedure would be followed. No longer would the defense have to go through the humiliating procedure of asking a miltiary prosecutor for permission to put on witnesses for the defense and to give away his case in advance by explaining what each witness would be expected to say. Also, the civilian JAG Corps would take on only cases involving charges clearly military in nature. Those cases involving charges of a civilian nature would have to be referred to the nonmilitary, civilian courts. I was charged with a nonmilitary connected offense and the charges were made by two civilians. My case, as mentioned before, should have been heard only in civilian court (which I'm reasonably sure would have thrown it out quickly).

To improve Navy justice in the future, some believe on the basis of my experience that it's necessary to review and change the role of the N.I.S. Its agents may be good and necessary for basic security functions around Naval bases, but it is suggested they should go no further than that. I think I've shown how the N.I.S. acted improperly in my case, how they said from the start that their job was to make a case for the prosecution, how they harassed and threatened prospective witnesses, hid favorable evidence, spread gossip and innuendo, accepted false affidavits and in general were practitioners—or forerunners—of Watergate. The allegations against me that were supposed to be kept confidential were circulated, I'm confident, by the N.I.S. which had no discernible official right to have them. To check on my handwriting, they sent some of my handwriting samples to the handwriting-analysis lab at Fort Gordon. On the request for the handwriting check they listed the charge against me as "forgery." Later they said this was a "clerical error," but they never changed it. This false statement that I was charged with forgery remains on file and may well follow me around for years.

Some Navy officials have suggested that my experience with the N.I.S. was an exception. I'm afraid, though, that I've heard about too many other cases involving similar N.I.S. tactics to accept this. But if not the N.I.S., then who should conduct investigations when charges are made? Jack Blackmon has suggested the F.B.I. It is true that at times during recent years accusations have been made that this nonpolitical agency has become politicized. However, under director Clarence Kelly—a professional with good qualifications—it seems to be regaining its former reputation as the most reputable federal investigative agency available to us.

I said earlier in this narrative I hope I am not guilty of a holier-than-thou attitude, but one can be reasonably humble in such matters and still look with less than equanimity at the moral and ethical tone and conduct around Navy bases that obviously reflect a broader problem for our society. "Square" I may be, especially if it means persisting in the belief that the so-called life style of such as my accusers, as I knew it, hardly indicates it to be the way to a happy life, and that Judeo-Christian values retain their validity. The great challenge for organizations such as the Chaplains Corps is, it seems to me, to reaffirm at least their faith in these values by their actions rather than by lip service too often at odds with actions.

I've always loved the Navy and strongly supported its mission at home and abroad. What happened to me in the name of the Navy was carried out by individual men, not the institution itself. I feel, in fact, that these men debased the standards and traditions that are part of the Navy's history but are too often ignored. I want the Navy to remain a strong, vital part of American life, but to be that it must also be a Navy demonstrably committed to honor and justice. The men who control its destiny need to open closed minds and take a positive attitude toward instituting reforms. Those of us who look for change hope it will be reflected in a more independent relationship of the denominations to the military services.

I am heartened—and hope others will be, too—by this clear lesson of my experience—that so-called little people who ordinarily are thought to be powerless do have a chance to go up against and win out against the power of bureaucracy when it is turned against them. It takes—I immodestly if realistically suggest—guts and stamina, and it requires an enormous amount of help from others with similar determination to win out against the odds. It *can* be done. I believe our best hope for elevating honor and justice in the Navy and all the military services and in our society generally lies in getting others among the so-called powerless to stand up to injustice wherever, whenever it is practiced instead of assuming the struggle is doomed to failure and subsiding in the presumed inevitability of defeat before the fight.

If the outcome of the ordeal my family and I went through has encouraged some others to overcome their feeling of powerlessness in an impersonal society, and impressed on them the advantage in standing up and battling for their rights, then something of value will indeed have come out of the first court-martial of its kind in American history.